Trade and Contemporary Society along the Silk Road

This book provides an ethno-historical study of the trade system in Ladakh (India), a busy entrepôt for Silk Route trade between Central and South Asia. Previously a part of global networks, Ladakh became an isolated border area as national boundaries were defined and enforced in the mid-twentieth century. As trade with Central Asia ended, social life in Ladakh was irrevocably altered.

The author's research combines anthropological, historical, and archaeological methods of investigation, using data from primary documents, ethnographic interviews and participation–observation fieldwork. The result is a cultural history of South and Central Asia, detailing the social lives of historical Ladakhi traders and identifying their community as a cosmopolitan social group. The relationship between the historical narratives and the modern ethnographic context illustrates how social issues in modern communities are related to those of the past. It is demonstrated that this relationship depends on both memories: narratives about the past constructed within present social contexts, and legacies: ways in which the past continues to shape present social interactions.

This book will be of particular interest to anthropologists, historians and specialists in South and Central Asian studies, as well as those interested in historical archaeology, science, sociology, political science and economics.

Jacqueline H. Fewkes is an Assistant Professor at the Harriet L. Wilkes Honors College, Florida Atlantic University. Her research interests are in the anthropological study of cultural change, historical transnational networks, and globalization. She has recently begun a new project in the Maldives.

Routledge Contemporary Asia Series

Trade and Contemporary Society along the Silk Road
An ethno-history of Ladakh

Jacqueline H. Fewkes

Routledge
Taylor & Francis Group

LONDON AND NEW YORK

First published 2009 by Routledge
2 Park Square, Milton Park, Abingdon, Oxon, OX14 4RN

Simultaneously published in the USA and Canada
by Routledge
711 Third Avenue, New York, NY 10017

Routledge is an imprint of the Taylor & Francis Group, an informa business

First issued in paperback 2011

© 2009 Jacqueline H. Fewkes

Typeset in 10/12pt Times NR MT by Graphicraft Limited, Hong Kong

British Library Cataloguing in Publication Data
A catalogue record for this book is available from the British Library

Library of Congress Cataloging in Publication Data
Trade and contemporary society along the silk road : an ethno-history of Ladakh / Jacqueline Fewkes.
    p. cm. — (Routledge contemporary Asia series ; 8)
    Includes bibliographical references and index.
    1. Ethnology—India—Ladakh Region. 2. Ethnohistory—India—Ladakh Region. 3. Ladakhi (South Asian people)—History. 4. Ladakhi (South Asian people)—Commerce. 5. Ladakhi (South Asian people)—Economic conditions. 6. Commerce—India—Ladakh Region—History. 7. Trade routes—India—Ladakh Region—History. 8. Ladakh Region (India)—History. 9. Ladakh (India)—Economic conditions. I. Title.
    GN635.I4F49 2008
    305.800954—dc22
    2008021898

ISBN 10: 0-415-77555-8 (hbk)
ISBN 10: 0-415-69315-2 (pbk)
ISBN 10: 0-203-27369-9 (ebk)

ISBN 13: 978-0-415-77555-7 (hbk)
ISBN 13: 978-0-415-69315-8 (pbk)
ISBN 13: 978-0-203-27369-2 (ebk)

This book is dedicated to my parents, Mary Anne and Robert Fewkes, with thanks for all their love and support.

Contents

viii *Contents*

PART III
The modern context 145

Plates, Figures, Maps and Tables

Preface

The concept that the modern world is a global arena where people, ideas, and beliefs flow freely across borders is incomplete. While many regions of the world are indeed experiencing the much-touted effects of globalization, other areas have become increasingly isolated with the formation of state borders. Cosmopolitanism, popularly associated with the "modernity" of globalization, is even a part of the past in some communities. This book addresses the contrast between common impressions of the modern experience and the actual experiences of a local community isolated by modern processes, through the relationship between past and present in Ladakhi social life. This is an ethno-historical study of an early twentieth-century trade system in Ladakh (India), a busy entrepôt for Silk Route trade between Central and South Asia. Previously a part of global networks, in the mid-twentieth century Ladakh became an isolated border area as national boundaries were defined and enforced. As trade with Central Asia ended, social life in Ladakh was irrevocably altered; however, these historical events have a continuing role in defining what it means to be "Ladakhi" today.

This project began in 1997, while I was staying in a house in the center of Leh town, in a small neighborhood called *Chu-tay Rang-tak* (Watermill). With an interest in both historical trade and social life in present day Ladakh, I was fascinated by conversations with Leh residents about their memories of the past. One day Mohammed Deen Khan, the owner of the house, was telling me about the role his grandfather played in trade between South and Central Asia, when he suddenly mentioned, "You know, I have his business papers, would you like to see them?"

The research project was born from this sentence. Business papers stored in the Khan house for several decades included thousands of pages of detailed documentation of trade with Central Asia from and through Ladakh. These documents were the personal and business papers of two Arghun caravan route officials in Leh, Bahauddin Khan and his son Shamsuddin Khan.

These papers had languished in various parts of the owner's house, had been boxed, re-boxed, and sometimes were in threat of being consigned to the rubbish fire pile. But they had survived because Bahauddin's grandson had felt that these letters, accounts, and other materials were valuable representatives of Ladakh's past.

Reading these papers, which I have named the Khan Archives, gives us direct access to the primary sources concerning regional trade transactions in early twentieth-century Ladakh. Combined with other sources of information, such as oral histories, interviews, and cultural material, the transactions of the past reveal the rich history of trade in Ladakh and their legacy in the present.

The archival documents contain a varied body of information about the material culture of the trading networks, the trade goods. As I will discuss later in this book, the variety of trade goods in these documents refute common perceptions of trade in the area being comprised mainly of *silk* and *pashmina* (cashmere). Using the documents to trace the movements of goods we can observe trade in carpets, cloth, synthetic dyes, manufactured pharmaceuticals, drugs, weaponry, household items, jewelry, and clothing. Many transaction accounts raise questions about the interests and ideologies behind this trade system. Why were the German dyes on the market so popular? What do orders from Ladakh for American-made Gillette blades from a British dry goods purveyor in Calcutta, found in papers from the 1920s, inform us about a Ladakhi elite and their economic status in this system? In spite of the novelty of this line of questioning I found the document information partially incomplete without ethnographic work, as these goods only tell half of the story about trade in early twentieth-century Ladakh. Thus a larger project began, in which I combined historical research in the archives, with ethnographic research in contemporary north Indian communities. The result is detailed in this book, which I hope will convey a sense of the relationships between social networks in Ladakh's regional trading history and contemporary identity issues in this present-day border community.

Acknowledgements

I would like to thank all of the people of Leh, Kargil, Amritsar, and Hoshiarpur who gave generously of their time and for sharing with me their viewpoints. The traders and their descendents have enriched our lives by sharing their family history for this book.

To the family of Khan Manzil I owe particular thanks for inspiring this book and taking me into their home – this includes especially Mohammed Deen Khan, Fozia Khan, "Nani" Diskit, "Kaga" Hussein, Shabina Khan and Shahbaz Khan. Thank you to the many individuals who helped to translate documents from the Khan Archives, including Munshi Baqir, Rukina Bhatt, and particularly Amma Nulha Tak, who worked with me for long hours translating most of the documents. Thank you to Arshaad Hussein for help in interviewing. A general thanks to Nissa Azmat, Tsering Drolma, Sarah Goodall, "Sony" Sonam, Tashi Cho, Neelu, and Adelina Jaan for their friendship and assistance while living in Ladakh. I would also like to thank all of the members of the following organizations in Ladakh who assisted me in this project, including Save the Children Fund, Leh; Ladakh Ecological Development Project, Leh; and Kargil Development Project, Kargil.

To my family members in both the USA and India I would like to say thank you for all the years of support during this project. My parents, Robert and Mary Anne Fewkes, constantly encouraged me to reach my goals with their advice and practical assistance. My siblings, Robert Fewkes and Rebecca Fewkes, and their spouses, Renee Sekel and John Farrow, have helped by smoothing the path for my fieldwork in many varied ways. My sister Rebecca deserves extra thanks for proof-reading many of these chapters for me. My father-in-law, Ramazan Khan, has been very supportive of my work and provided much kind encouragement over the years. My sisters-in-law – Attiya Khan, Rubina Khan and Rafiya Anjum – were always gracious hosts and warm friends during my time in Ladakh. My grandmother, Anne Wienges, has always asked about the progress of this book and my aunt and uncle, Noreen Wienges and Malachy Wienges, have provided me with assistance during my research as well. And of course, special thanks to all my nieces and nephews whose amusing messages and antics provided much needed comic relief: Aaman, Adil, Arju, Ayaan, Henry, Maggie, Miranda, and Tanu.

Innumerable mentors and peers have provided me with assistance on details in this book, as well as given general collegial support. Thank you to all of my past and present fellow academics at Johns Hopkins University, University of Pennsylvania and Florida Atlantic University. Special thanks for help on particular aspects of this book go to Espelencia Baptiste, Laura Barrett, Rachel Corr, Chris Ely, Praveena Gullapalli, Terje Hoim, Yu Jiang, Holly Loth, Amy McLaughlin, Bill O'Brien, Uzma Rizvi, Tim Steigenga, and Miguel Vasquez. I am always grateful for the guidance of my Ph.D. advisor Brian Spooner, who helped me navigate through graduate school successfully and has continued to provide timely advice. I would also like to thank the following individuals for the roles they have played as faculty mentors at different stages of my education – Sidney Mintz, Michel-Rolph Trouillot, Elizabeth Sheehan, Brackette Williams, Erik Mueggler, Gillian Feeley-Harnik, Peggy Sanday, Greg Urban, and Gregory Possehl.

I would like to say thank you to the anonymous reviewers of the initial manuscript for this book, whose comments have helped me in revision, and to all of the people with Routledge who have worked on this book, especially Dorothea Schaefter, Associate Editor Asian Studies Division, editorial assistants Tom Bates and Suzanne Chilestone, and copy editor Sarah Reeve.

Last, but certainly not least, I owe a great deal to Abdul Nasir Khan for his constant assistance at every stage of this project. From research to the writing he was by my side at every point, offering help and advice. Thank you.

Introduction
Global memories, local accounts

During the late nineteenth and early twentieth centuries, the north Indian region of Ladakh was neither a primary production center nor key market. Yet Ladakh played an important role in historical Central and South Asian regional trade during this time period, as a trading entrepô that connected multiple geographic areas. Ladakh was a dynamic center of global flows where local participation was based on roads and transactions rather than fixed production or consumption points. This regional role was irrevocably altered, however, when India closed the northern borders in the mid-twentieth century.

Today, Ladakh is often simultaneously discussed as a remote, "tribal" area and a key national border of India. Before conducting this research, I had assumed conflicting accounts of regional identity stemmed from such contestations of separate local and national interests in the region. This view employed Benedict Anderson's (1983) classic concept of "imagining a community", often used by anthropologists to explain the ways that local communities are a part of national community imaginings, and privileged the concept of observable separate local and non-local social interests. This dichotomy contrasted the social concerns of a local area with those of national concerns in nation building processes. There are a number of studies on South Asia that support this view within a well-established scholarly dialogue about the nature of nation building programs in India (see for example Brass 1994, van der Veer 1994, and Brown 1994), and understanding local social relationships and cultural groups as the building blocks of national culture is relevant in the case of India. As a diverse young nation with an established policy for the political categorization of ethnic groups in the forms of Scheduled Caste and Tribe statuses, India has utilized social signifiers such as religion, caste, and ethnicity to structure the ways in which segments of the population interact with national interests. Ladakhi identity politics have also been framed within such processes, and this formulation of Ladakhi identity is thus often emphasized in present day studies of modern political identity in Ladakh (see for example Jina 1999 or Kaul and Kaul 1992). Focusing on social networks rather than local and national spheres, however, my study reveals the central role of identity groups formed through historical regional interactions in debates about Ladakhi identity.

One such identity group formed through trade interactions is the Arghun community, a sub-section of the Ladakhi population. A search for the basis of identity in this community defies many common concepts of social and cultural groups. While the anthropological conceptualization of an ethnic group has expanded the disciplinary understanding of how groups of people share common interests both within and beyond fixed geographic locales, ethnic identity is an incomplete conceptual category for the purposes of this discussion. Traditional views of ethnic groups do not fully define the cultural worlds of the groups of Arghun traders in question, in spite of the fact that anthropologists have analyzed the ways that ethnicity can be situational, even providing a social basis for trading networks in response to modernization processes in markets (Cohen 1969). Even broadly conceived ethnic groups, such as the elite London businessmen of Cohen's study in "Urban Ethnicity" are described as having taken on ethnic forms with particular social identifiers, such as distinct clothing, language, norms and customs (1974a). Such descriptive criteria are not wholly applicable to multiple groups of traders who traveled through Ladakh, and thus give rise to further questions about how people are bound together in social groups.

Martijn van Beek has also identified this problem in defining modern Ladakhi identity in general in the article "The Art of Representation", where he notes, "Ladakhiness does not exist as a stable or uniform set of characteristics, forms, idioms, or practice. . . ." (van Beek 2003:286). My primary argument in this book is that to understand the complexity of modern Ladakhi social life, including defining the Arghun community in particular and Ladakhi-ness in general, we must examine the relationship between memories and legacies of historical trade.

Methods and sources: The documents

As described in the preface, this project began as an examination of documents in the Khan Archives.[1] I soon found, however, that many Ladakhi households contain a wealth of archival material about the past. Thus while the Khan Archives form the majority of document sources for this research there are also contributions from other families, including the papers of Ahmed Khan, an ancestor of the Khacho family of Kargil. Ahmed Khan collected letters of references from travelers including key colonial history figures such as Francis Younghusband, John Biddulph, and J.C. Hutchison. Assembled, the archival evidence consisted of approximately one thousand pages of documents including personal memos, personal and business letters, registered letter envelopes, money order receipts, export permits, telegrams, account books, and telegram receipts.[2] These documents include correspondence with a number of areas linked to Leh and Kargil, with addresses on envelopes, telegrams and receipts from areas in present day China, England, India, and Pakistan. A majority of the correspondence was between towns in North India and Leh, particularly with Hoshiarpur (Punjab), Amritsar (Punjab), and Srinagar (Jammu and Kashmir). The documents also represent trading networks that extend much farther than these areas as letters, receipts, memos, and account books refer to goods and traders coming from areas in present day Afghanistan, Uzbekistan, Germany, Japan, and the United States.

A majority of all the documents from these archives date from between 1900–48 in the Gregorian calendar. When viewing and reading these documents particular attention must be paid to the dates. Many early twentieth-century papers were marked with years such as 1982 or 1352, causing considerable confusion if the reader is not aware of the different calendars that were in use in North India in the early part of the twentieth century. The two calendars most often in use in addition to the Gregorian calendar were the Vikram Samvat and Hijri calendars, two of the many calendars used in South Asia. In the Vikrami calendar the year 2061 corresponds to the Gregorian year 2004–05 CE,[3] while in the Hijri calendar the Gregorian year 2005 CE translates to Hijri 1425–26 AH.[4] Many of the historical North Indian documents used the former dating system. Older generations of Ladakhis remember the Vikrami calendar as the calendar most commonly used in pre-partition Ladakh; however the presence of British officers and a telegraph office in Leh made the Gregorian calendar also of common use. Telegram stamps show that the Kashmir State Telegraph office used both dating systems, as seen in Figure 0.1.

Publications of the Maharaja of Jammu and Kashmir's government from 1920–40, such as law books and census reports, confirm this dual system; many are marked with the Vikram Samvat dates in the titles of the books and charts, yet have a Gregorian publication date (e.g. Jammu and Kashmir 1941). British colonial publications in colonial

Figure 0.1 Telegraph office date stamp. The Vikrami month Phagun is symbolized by the abbreviation "GN".

North India had similar notations to show other calendars, as evident
in a 1913 publication that lists the Vikrami dates for officers working
in Delhi and the Punjab (Jacob 1913). Stamps from the British colonial Punjab simply used Gregorian dates during this time period.
While traders in early twentieth-century Chinese Central Asia also sometimes used the Vikram Samvat calendar when writing correspondence,
perhaps due to the volume of trade with Northern India, most of the
time they used the Hijri dating system.

Translation of these documents was a group project due to the variety of languages and specialized jargon. A majority of the archival papers
were written in Urdu; some documents were also partially or wholly
in Bodyig,[5] English, Uighur, and Persian. Most of the descendents of
Central Asian traders in Leh can fluently read and write Urdu; however the Urdu of these documents was difficult for modern readers
as it was written in what some informants called "*patawari*" type
writing, a traditional style of Urdu. Thus individuals who were highly
literate in Urdu had trouble reading these papers. In one interview
an older man explained that he felt this was due to changes in the
education and use of Urdu in modern Ladakh. When asked if he felt

there was a difference between the Urdu used then and now, he quickly answered:

> So many differences. Very different . . . in pronunciation also different. Even the writing of sentences is different. Now if *arzinaviz* write . . . now petition writers write . . . how it was clear in the old times, [one could] quickly understand. Now it's like a business; there is "*hota*" and there is "*hoti*", we can understand nothing of what is written. It is like the army's talking. We can see, look at the old cards of Bahauddin, how clearly [they] wrote in a few words. Now we can't write like that.

This man made a few particular points about Urdu language use in Ladakh. The references to *"hota"* and *"hoti"* is meant to show how modern users of Urdu in Ladakh often know so little of the language that they fail to differentiate between the masculine and feminine forms. When the informant says that modern Ladakhi Urdu speakers speak Urdu like the army, he is saying that they speak it as a second language, or perhaps a foreign tongue. This common perception is due to the large number of military personnel stationed in Ladakh who are not native Urdu speakers or have different accents. The same man then went on to explain how, in his opinion, these changes had occurred:

> Changes came into Urdu because now in education all the knowledge comes from every place. At that time there was not this much, very limited, was limited. There was Farsi, there was Urdu, or some other . . . Hindi was very limited. Now there is all the knowledge. So it is . . . now [schools] are giving stress on English and Hindi. So [Urdu] remains [behind].
> *People were using only Urdu?*
> Everywhere, in court Urdu was used in all the departments, Urdu was used everywhere. Judges gave judgments in Urdu, everything was in Urdu. There was Urdu and at that time Farsi also, and they were good.
> There are letters from other countries which are also in Urdu . . .
> *They were also using Urdu there?*
> Mostly was Urdu . . . at that time the environment was of Urdu in old times. In India the environment was Urdu and everything was done in Urdu. All the officers that came here, the *Wazir-i-wazarat* [minister of the state] was coming, [those officers] higher than him were coming, their decisions were in Urdu, otherwise they could write in English.

Although the informant would like to blame the decline of Urdu standards on the modern use of English, he acknowledges towards the end of this section that English was also being used in official settings in pre-partition Ladakh. The popularity of other languages in education and the modern use of English in business and government settings are often referred to by Ladakhi individuals as proof that education in Urdu had declined since the establishment of an independent India. The motivation for this discursive pattern will become clearer later in this book, through analysis of trade legacies in present day Ladakhi social life.

Another common problem for modern readers of these trade documents is with the vocabulary of trade; specific words, such as the names of goods, are not familiar to contemporary readers. While examining these terms with individuals who had been involved in historical trade, we found that many were either words from another language or brand names. In an effort to efficiently communicate large amounts of details, often on a small receipt and sometimes through costly telegrams, the traders also used codes. Here they would refer to numbers associated with numbered letters or receipts. For example, examining one letter a Ladakhi descendent of the trader read, " 'After the salaam it should be known . . . that one letter dated 17–1–35, 1706' . . . I think that is the letter number, 'is received . . .'."

The rest of this letter makes little sense, as the writer is answering unquoted questions. Piecing together sequential correspondence and cross-referencing numbered letters were the only ways to make sense of these types of references.

Translating the documents thus became a process of searching in Ladakh, literally from house to house at times, for individuals who had the ability, knowledge, and willingness to read these documents. In this process I was aided by Abdul Nasir Khan, who worked as my research assistant for over two years on this project. Our ideal document reader was one who had some type of training in Urdu before partition, had used Urdu in government contexts, and had participated in trade to a certain degree so that they were familiar with trade jargon.

There were a few people in Leh with these abilities, including Mohammed Amma-Nulha Tak of Leh, an ex-*patawari* who could read classical Urdu and explain the trade words used during those times. He was born in approximately 1928 and attended school up to the eighth standard in Leh Government Middle School. After school, he briefly became a teacher and then a policeman, before settling into a successful career as a *patawari*. He attributes his abilities in the Urdu language to his teachers such as Baba Pir Sahib, Master Sultan, and Old Leh Akhon, as well as his time as a *patawari* when he was responsible for writing legal petitions and applications for the land revenue office. He worked for thirty years as a *patawari* before retiring. After retirement Mr. Amma-Nulha Tak has kept busy working as a storekeeper in a government co-operative shop. When contemplating the value of this translation work, his message to readers who want to learn from these documents was:

> I found in these [documents] that before I was born this [trade] was there. One letter was more than a hundred years old. Now in this time there are only sixty, seventy year-old [people]. From these [documents] it is known what was in those times. How it was. How the trade was being done. How it was working, while people were informing each other how they were doing. If something happened, what they did. Things . . . [and] how they were. This is known from [the papers]. From this we can know properly what the old people were doing.

Methods and sources: Ethnographic interviews, family histories, and surveys

In addition to general participant-observation work in Ladakh, my ethnographic research in Ladakh utilized formal interviewing, genealogical research, and survey data collection techniques. The formal interviews were designed to better understand the social networks that facilitated the movement of goods in Ladakh's trade with Central Asia. After reading the historical documents, I would note the names and addresses of individuals involved with trade in the early twentieth century. Sometimes addresses were enough to follow to find and interview the descendents of the traders, as many families in Ladakh have lived in their houses for multiple generations. Other times, when the address was incomplete or there was no address, this meant reading the names of the individuals from the documents to other past traders, who were able to identify descendents of those traders. I began this work with Nasir Khan in Leh, and as more documents were translated we began to travel for interviews throughout Ladakh, and then to areas in the Punjab such as Amritsar and Hoshiarpur. Many of the chapters in this book begin with brief accounts of these ethnographic encounters. Unfortunately I was not able to follow any of the connections between Ladakh and Calcutta, or those with international destinations such as China, Turkey, or Pakistan; tracing of these trade networks was limited solely to North India. Due to current political conditions, I was not able to follow addresses to Srinagar, however, I was able to speak with a few of the documented Kashmiri traders' descendents who are now located in Kargil.

Travel yielded its own surprises and new perspectives on this project. As described in the beginning of Chapter Six, upon arriving in Amritsar I discovered that all of the Muslim traders who had lived in that city before the 1940s and traded with Ladakh had immigrated to Pakistan during the partition of India. Amritsar was the first, and only, place where I was not able to find most contacts from the documents. I found the discontinuity with the past a disturbing reminder of the upheaval of the Partition era as I walked along large, bustling *bazaars* of Amritsar that contained few traces of the old businesses, although building architecture hinted of another era. The missing traders of Amritsar were a startling reminder of the disproportionate experiences of Partition between Ladakh and the Punjab.

Interviews with traders and their descendents yielded many types of data. I would always bring the historical document that brought me to the address, so that the informant could read it for themselves. For some elderly men and women this was an unexpected and emotional reminder of a very different time in their lives, and all of the families were fascinated by novel views of their ancestors' businesses. Nostalgia about the past often then led effortlessly into reflection on the social relations that supported the historical trade system.

In addition, I was able to chart genealogies of trade families to understand relationships between people involved in the system. Kinship charts were invaluable tools to untangle complex narrations of the past, and understand how views of trade differed between generations of the trader's descendents. Family histories are a way of following strands, or markers through time. I am not trying to rebuild the past through these narratives, but rather understand how the past is interpreted today. Collecting enough of these stories, and comparing them with other types of data, I started to understand the popular ideas surrounding trade networks. Interviewing multiple generations in families has helped me to follow stories about trade through time, threads of the complete story of trading networks in Ladakh.

In the spring of 2001 I decided to conduct a comprehensive survey of Leh town. I was curious how many families in Ladakh actually had participated in inter-regional trade networks in the past, and wanted the chance to ask more open-ended questions about perceptions of history and social relations to Leh residents. After more than a year of interviewing traders in Leh town I was well aware that many traders' descendents were often clustered in specific neighborhoods of Leh. I did not know, however, if there were other clusters in other neighborhoods.

The difficulty of obtaining a proper sample of the population was compounded by the fact that the last Census of India conducted in the state of Jammu and Kashmir had been in 1981; the 1991 Census of India was not conducted in Jammu and Kashmir due to political unrest. The 2001 census had started in the fall of 2000; however threats against census takers in Srinagar, general threats to boycott the census in Jammu and Kashmir, and the difficulty of organizing a comprehensive census in remote areas meant that even preliminary results were not yet available in spring 2001. So there were no recently published population figures on which to base my sample. I received help in this matter from the Chief Medical Officer of Leh, whose office kindly provided a copy of population data for Leh organized by household and neighborhood. Based on these figures, I calculated the number of households that would need to be surveyed in each neighborhood to equal five percent of the total population. The breakdown by neighborhood was to ensure that diverse communities and economic classes were included. With a team of researchers[6] I conducted the survey in Leh in April 2001, and later in May used the same survey[7] to provide supplemental data in Kargil. The survey results, included in later sections of this book, clearly display variation in attitudes and experiences between sub-sections of the Ladakhi population.

Methods and sources: Material culture

In December 2000 I found myself in Kargil working with hundreds of trade artifacts, cataloging the items and trying to establish the context of excavation for these goods. This surprising addition to my fieldwork was made possible by the descendents of a Kargili trader, Munshi Abdul Aziz Bhat, who lived from 1866–1948. That month I had traveled to Kargil to talk with Munshi Habibullah, one of Aziz Bhat's older sons. I carried a letter written by Munshi Aziz Bhat in 1934, about goods that he had sent from Kargil to Bahauddin Khan in Leh. Munshi Habibullah, although his health was not good at the time, kindly agreed to speak with me. We spoke about trade in Kargil, and he explained that in 1923 his father had constructed the Aziz Bhat *serai*, a trading facility for Kargil. As Munshi Abdul Aziz Bhat became older, the *serai* fell into disuse. His sons were less interested in trade as regional networks began to unravel, and the trading company of Munshi Aziz Bhat and Sons closed. The *serai*, having fallen into disarray, was closed officially in 1950–51, and in the ensuing years of disuse large portions of the roof collapsed under heavy snow. In 1994 construction began on the front portion of the old *serai* ruins to dismantle the structure and make room for new shops. At this time one of Munshi Aziz Bhat's younger sons found a number of old crates in the *serai*. He brought these to his extended family and opened them to find, as his nephew Gulzaar Hussain Munshi called it, "a whole treasure of ancient trade, antique and artifacts in front of us." During our interview Munshi Habibullah instructed his sons to show the goods that had been taken from the *serai*. His sons, Gulzaar Hussain Munshi and Ajaz Hussain Munshi, arranged the trade goods from the boxes on a series of tables for me and my research assistant to view. The collection contained an amazing array of trade goods and provided a great deal of insight into Ladakh's early twentieth-century trade.[8] The photographs and packaging details from these goods are used throughout this book to supplement data from the archival records and provide readers with a material culture centered view of trade networks in Ladakh.

Organization of this book

In this book I have attempted to bring together these diverse sources of information to create a view of Ladakh's present that is not only informed by the past, but shows the relationship between the past and the present through memories and legacies of trade. In the introduction I will be discussing the sources for this material and the methods used to gather data about both the past and the present in Ladakh.

In Chapters 1 and 2 of this volume, in Part I, I outline a general historical trajectory of relevant social, economic, and political processes in both Ladakh and its surrounding regions. This section will orient readers both spatially and chronologically, and sets a tone for the book's ethno-historical model that addresses Ladakhi discourse about local and regional communities through time. Chapter 1 provides readers with an introduction to Ladakh and common perceptions of the region, while Chapter 2 draws reader's attention outwards. In this latter chapter I examine Ladakh's history as a trading entrepô between South and Central Asia and provide readers with background information about the geographical history of Ladakh in relation to the historical British, Russian, and Chinese empires. Building on the work of other anthropologists who have contributed to the ethno-historical model (see for example Geertz 1980, Comaroff and Comaroff 1992, and Comaroff 1985), this is an opportunity to add depth to our understanding of cultural settings, a diachronic view of culture in motion. Ethno-historical anthropological work provides an understanding of culture in terms of trends and changes, reaching beyond the common definition of a cultural area as a particular geographic location or even the classic anthropological view of social life as bounded by "tribe, village or category of people" (Cohn 1980:220). This general ethno-historical component of the study will demonstrate that social life is not easily bound by either geography or chronology.

In Part II of this volume I then examine the ways in which historical trade through Ladakh was related to particular social networks. To identify cosmopolitan social groups, in Chapter 3 I describe the variety of types of interest groups involved in trade through Ladakh between Central and South Asia. In this chapter I provide a detailed look at how social scientists can define the historical trading communities of Ladakh in social and cultural terms, in relation to the concepts of kinship, religious, and/or ethnic groups. Here I draw upon the work of Abner Cohen, who discusses how ethnic, religious and kin network roles are used to facilitate and provide order in trans-regional trade systems. His attention to the symbolic and political dimensions of human experience (Cohen 1974a and 1974b) helps to explain the ways in which community formation processes can be a vehicle for economic interests, as the symbolic elements of identity organize and express political relations. My focus on kinship groups is particularly important to understand the cosmopolitan social group as simultaneously both local and non-local. The role of kinship is contrasted with both religious and ethnic identity as the former is commonly employed by public discourse about identity politics in India, and the latter by anthropologists discussing non-state-based social groups in the modern world. After establishing the existence of these groups within the historical trading networks of Ladakh, the next segment of this argument addresses why these cosmopolitan groups were a necessary feature in the historical trading networks of the region. In Chapter 4 my discussion of the economic features of the historical trade networks in late nineteenth- and early twentieth-century Ladakh will demonstrate that social networks, partially in the form of hierarchical social groups, were economic strategies for profit within the confines of the existing political and geographic features of the system. While this segment of the argument may seem to make the cosmopolitan social group a phenomena particular to Ladakh, the role of cosmopolitans in economic systems should display some of the features of this system that are employed beyond the culture area. With material in Chapter 5 I will then address how this community formed a cosmopolitan elite, through an examination of the role of commercial goods in creating consumer networks in Ladakh. I argue here that trade goods helped to reinforce an idea of an "elite" by offering material connections to other commercial and cultural systems that were only available to a limited section of trade participants, and discuss three specific commodities of the trade system, cotton piece goods, synthetic dyes, and *charas* (*cannabis* resin). Examining the extent to which commodities play a role in the maintenance of the social aspects of Ladakhi trading networks offers cultural insight into the symbolic dimensions of the trade system. The disruption and cessation of this historical trade system in Ladakh is then described in the final chapter on historical Ladakh, Chapter 6 "The Demise of Trade". In this chapter I will begin to address the second component of my main argument, that the formation of modern political borders not only severs trade connections but also social structures. The specific features of border formation are important at this point; this chapter presents the argument that the closing of the borders around a state represents only one facet of the border formation experience of a region, as most frontier zones experience political boundary formation over time in numerous ways. This study will illustrate how the role of regional trade networks changes within historical contexts of trade relations, political systems, and global interests, attempting to formulate an understanding of social organization across historical and geographic locations. This is relevant for conceptualizing the social experience of many frontier zones in the modern world.

Finally, in Part III of this volume I will address the modern ethnographic context of Ladakh, and offer a view of the ways in which the existence of a cosmopolitan elite identity group in Ladakh has complicated discourse about social identity in the region. In Chapter 7, I demonstrate how the legacy of Ladakh's trading cosmopolitan elite is a central part of Ladakhi identity struggles today, through a case study of public art and discourse on the future of a modern Ladakh. In the conclusion I will reflect upon the relationship between the past and present in the Ladakhi reconciliation of notions of a cosmopolitan past and the bordered present, through the intersubjectivity of memories and legacies. My arguments concerning the intersubjectivity of memory and legacy is in agreement with, and explanation for, the claim by Edward Gewertz and Deborah Schieffelin that ethnohistories "must fundamentally take into account the people's own sense of how events are constituted, and their ways of culturally constructing the past" (Gewertz and Schieffelin 1985:3).

My aim in this book is to understand and represent the relationship between the past and present in as ethnographically detailed terms as those with which anthropologists understand the present. That is, to create an ethno-historical work grounded in a specific locale and peopled by individuals with experiences rather than historical outcomes. To this end, many of the chapters begin with accounts from my ethnographic fieldwork of meeting with people and hearing their first-personal narratives about the trading past. While I recognize many individual contributors by name in this book, in these ethnographic accounts personal and place names, as well as other identifying information, have been changed or omitted to respect the privacy of those interviewed and maintain the confidentiality of our exchanges. These ethnographic sections are included to help show how varying and sometimes seemingly contradictory notions of Ladakh and Ladakhi identity reside within a dialogue about memories and legacies of the past. The memories of the past are historical narrative strands in community discourse, while the legacies are the ways in which those communities continue to experience the effects of historical social, political and economic processes in the context of the modern world.

Part I
Settings

1 Beyond the roof of the world

Hemmed in by mountains on every side, the area of Ladakh is often
geographically defined in relation to its surroundings. Near the valley
of Kashmir, the region is on the western edge of the Tibetan plateau,
situated between the Himalayan mountain range to the south and the
Karakoram[1] Range to the north. In synchronic geo-political terms it
includes two political districts in the state of Jammu and Kashmir, Leh[2]
and Kargil; these are also the names of the two main towns in Ladakh,
each an urban center of their respective district. Ladakh comprises close
to 70 percent of the geographic territory of Jammu and Kashmir, yet
its current population, notoriously small by Indian national standards,
is less than 3 percent of the state's population. This sparse population
makes Ladakh the least populated region in the nation of India, with
a regional population of only 232,864 (Census of India 2001). Yet, at
times there can be at least twice this many people in Ladakh. Walking
through Leh's main bazaar today are many individuals who have come
from other parts of India for work, including transient laborers, shop-
keepers with seasonal shops, and army personnel. A large number of
traders from other areas within the state of Jammu and Kashmir come
to Ladakh during the summer months to run shops and restaurants
during the busy tourist season, which attracts thousands of domestic
and international tourists.

Many of these tourists come to Ladakh in response to descriptions
in tourist advertisements such as this one:

> See towering mountains reach up to a clear blue sky. Hear the rhyth-
> mic chant of Buddhist monks in an ancient monastery where time
> stands still. See the rushing waters of an icy river surge down from
> a glacial height. Ladakh – the Land of Passes and the Roof of the
> World awaits you.
>
> (Indianvisit.com Pvt. Ltd. 2006)

Although shallow, this view of Ladakh offers a key to a more complex and holistic view of the region. Contrary to the claim that "time stands still" here, designations such as "the Roof of the World" are notions of Ladakh that have been constructed over time in response to political, social, and economic trends in the region.

Consider for example two tourists' views of Ladakh from opposite ends of the twentieth century. Early twentieth-century visitors to Ladakh frequently wrote of its main city, Leh, as a cosmopolitan hub for activities, technologies, and people from around the world. Eleanor Holgate Lattimore explained in 1935 that her traveling party had looked forward to arriving in Ladakh after a long journey through Central Asia,

> for we knew that in Leh we would find the beginnings of civilization and a traveled road. And so it proved, for while we are still half a month from Kashmir and India, Leh's *dak* bungalow [government rest house], post office and telegraph office spell the beginning. . . . There are even tourists here, a German novelist, an artist, and a Harvard student.
>
> (Lattimore 1935:307)

Her version of Ladakh is quite unlike that of tourist Andrew Harvey nearly fifty years later; while Lattimore saw Ladakh as the beginning of civilization, Harvey saw the end. He answered the complaints of a disappointed tourist:

> it is true that there is only one main street with an ugly inefficient post office, an ugly Cultural Academy, and two rows of ugly tumbledown over-expensive under-stocked shops; and there is no graceful order to the streets or houses, that run into each other haphazardly. Yet Leh does have charm. There is nothing whatever to do. That is Leh's charm.
>
> (Harvey 1983:28–29)

Both tourist narratives focus on the material veneers of Ladakh in the twentieth century. Viewing the marketplace, Ladakh in 1935 is an outpost of "civilization" along Central Asian trading routes, while in 1983 it is a dull backwater of the Indian tourist circuit. The convenient facilities of the past seem to have vanished in Harvey's account, although the travelers remain. The differences between these accounts are reconciled only through an understanding of what has changed in Ladakhi politics, economics, and society between 1935 and 1983.

Ladakh has many nicknames, such as "the Moonland," "Little Tibet," "The Last Shangri-la," and "Roof of the World"; invocation of any these names evinces a particular set of assumptions about and interest in the region. While we cannot understand Ladakh solely through the lens of these nicknames, upon examination each phrase, and its associated myths, reflects different facets of discussion about the region of Ladakh as well as economic, political, and social issues faced by the Ladakhi people. Therefore in this chapter I will use these nicknames as an orientation point from which to introduce readers to significant social trends in contemporary and historical Ladakh.

The Moonland and the Land of Passes

Use of Ladakh's nickname "the Moonland" conjures a mental image of remote, rugged terrain with an otherworldly beauty, devoid of humans and human artifacts. The Moonland nickname is used more specifically in reference to an area of extreme geological formations located along the Leh–Kargil highway road near Lamayuru Monastery. The monastery is part of many tour itineraries for visitors to Ladakh, and the area is also in viewing distance from the highway used

Figure 1.1 The "Moonland" terrain is lighter than the high mountains above and settled valley below. Photograph by Abdul Nasir Khan.

by all land traffic on the road up from Srinagar; thus this high profile bit of land has become an icon for the rugged terrain of Ladakh.

This particular part of the landscape is, according to geologists, comprised of sedimentary limestone that dates back to a time when the Paleo-Tethys Ocean covered the area, before South Asia and the Asian continent "collided" (Upadhyay et al. 2005:982). Geological analysis has indicated that there are strata in the Kohistan–Ladakh region that were neither a part of the sub-continental plate of South Asia or the continental plate of Asia, a curious metaphor for social studies of the region since many twentieth-century social scientists consider the mountain ranges surrounding Ladakh a definitive cultural boundary between Asia and South Asia (see for example Hambly 1966:1–2). Even seasoned geographers/geologists are struck by this unique terrain. There is evidence for uncharacteristically sudden movements of glaciers in the chain of mountains surrounding Ladakh (Mason 1935, and Stellrecht et al. 1998), and a surprising variety of geological sources present in material analyses of the mountain structures (Zeitler, Sutter, et al. 1989). In spite of the other-worldly nature of the land that the "Moonland" nickname implies, however, the terrain of Ladakh is certainly of terrestrial source.

While the Moonland name for Ladakh over-emphasizes regional geography to present the region, and its inhabitants by extension, as other-worldly, geography does play a role in shaping social life in Ladakh. The surrounding mountains block most of the sub-continental monsoon rains from reaching Ladakh's inhabited valleys, which have some of the lowest recorded amounts of rainfall in South Asia. Limited precipitation makes Ladakh arid, and enables its inhabitants to construct large multi-story buildings from mud bricks that would quickly crumble in more humid environments. While uninhabited areas of Ladakh resemble a high altitude desert, carefully constructed irrigation using glacial streams and water from the Zanskar and Indus rivers have enabled inhabitants to create lush green inhabited areas and fostered agricultural production of grains such as barley and vegetables such as carrots, cabbage, and more recently, potatoes. Approximately 84 percent of Ladakhi inhabitants live in rural areas engaged in such agricultural practices (Census of India 2001), although this number is shrinking as twenty years ago 91 percent lived in rural communities (Census of India 1981). Yet, as less than 1 percent of land in Ladakh is classified as urban area, agricultural practices continue to play a role in Ladakhi economies and in shaping Ladakhi culture. Residents use the unique high altitude flora as medicinal plants (Kaul 1997), and socio-political relations in villages are partially structured in relation to irrigation. A number of regional ecology studies based in Ladakh have provided a view of the relationship between environmental conditions and cultural practices in the region that emphasize ecological issues faced by populations in many parts of the world such as the impact of the intensification of agricultural practices and waste from tourism industries (see for example Sagwal 1991 and East and Luger 1998). Such studies that link Ladakh's socio-geographic issues to global trends easily contradict claims made in the following newspaper passage that reflect the geographic exoticism that results from conceptualizing Ladakh as a moonland. The author writes:

> Ladakh is a land like no other; mystic, pristine and remote. Belted by snow-capped peaks, rugged mountainscapes sculpted by time, wind and glacial ice. These natural barriers have constantly and powerfully guarded the beauty of Ladakh (Jayetilleke 2005).

The latter claims, of a guarded Ladakh, depend upon a notion of Ladakh's extreme moonland geography invoked in explanations of regional isolation. Yet the high mountain peaks were not barriers for human movement, and there is a long history of movement between Ladakh and neighboring regions precisely due to this extreme geography.

Of all the English language nicknames for Ladakh, "The Land of Passes" or "Land of High Passes" is the most appropriate; the nickname is actually a direct translation of the word *Ladags* itself, as *la* or *lakha* means "pass" and *dags* means "land." The naming of the region after the many passes that provide ways through in the surrounding mountains refers to the importance of conceptualizing the Ladakhi region as a busy conduit for movement of people between regions, rather than an isolated mountain region. Much of this movement has historically been concerned with trade between South and Central Asia, as will be detailed in the next chapter.

"The Roof of the World"

"The Roof of the World" is a phrase commonly used to allude to Ladakh in particular, and as a nickname for the Himalayan region in general – although the phrase originated in reference to the Pamir region of Central Asia. This phrase appears a great deal in late nineteenth-century geographic literature, and was thus used by the President of the Royal Geographical Society in London in an 1877 assembly address. Here he referred to "the lofty plateau and passes of the Pamir, poetically termed by the Persians, with a touch of Oriental imagery, the 'Roof of the World' " (Trotter 1877:284). Later British authors seem to contend that this usage implied that the term Pamir literally meant "the Roof of the World." G.N. Curzon wrote in 1896 that he thoroughly disagreed with this claim, as well as others, about the origins of the word:

> The various suggestions may be classified according as the word is supposed to be of Sanskrit, of Turki, or of Persian origin . . . [According to some authors] the word Pamir is said to be a contraction of *Bam-i-Dunya*, or "Roof of the World," another local appellation for the same region, which was mentioned to Wood in 1838. This, I think, is frankly fantastic. Others have suggested *Bam-yar*, or "Roof of the Earth" (*bam* being a Persian and *yar* a Turki word), which is perhaps worse. Finally comes a series of derivatives of the Persian word *pai*, signifying "foot," and some word of kindred sound to *mir*. Of these the least fanciful, and, if a Persian origin be accepted, to my mind the most likely, is the combination *pai* and *mir*, the latter, . . . being a word of not uncommon Central Asian use for "mountain", as, e.g. Tirich Mir, the famous mountain in the north of Chitral . . .
>
> (Curzon 1896:30)

Curzon pointed out that the seventh-century Chinese traveler Hsuan Tsang[3] used the name Pamir for these mountains, and thus the term could predate Arabic use in the region. A different author claims that "the name may come from the ancient Iranian *paimar*, meaning 'the foot of Mithra' (aka Mithras, the sun god)" (Horsman 2006:283).

Yet even if Pamir predates Arabic use in the area, "roof of the world" may still be related to an Arabic name for the region. In the 982 CE Arabic language geographic work *Hudūd al-'Ālam* ("The Regions of the World") an anonymous author called the groups of mountains from India up into Central Asia "*Kamar-i Zamīn*," "the Belt of the Earth" and a later author, Ibn Hauqal, wrote of mountains as "the spine of the earth (*'ala zahr al-ard*)" (Minorsky 1937:263–264). One author implies that the phrase "roof of the world" later replaced "belt of the earth" in published Arabic works (Ward 1983:137). Many people refer to Ladakh, as well as Tibet, Bhutan, Nepal, Tajikistan, Kirgizstan, Afghanistan, and Sinkiang Province in China as "the Roof of the World" in this sense of the term.

Late nineteenth- and early twentieth-century British authors, geographers and explorers commonly used the phrase while exploring and writing extensively about Central Asian geography (e.g. *Across the Roof of the World* Etherton 1911). During this time of political struggle for empire, English and Russian agents focused on the area, trying to form alliances, control trade routes, map new areas, and assert their political power through advantageous treaties with local powers. This intense activity was a part of the "Great Game," a political power struggle between European powers for empire in Asia (see for example Drege and Buhrer 1989, Myer and Brysac 1999, and Hopkirk 1980). Thus some of the highest profile books on the Great Game in Central Asia in English and Russian languages invoke this nickname, such as *Trespassers on the Roof of the World* (Hopkirk 1995) and *Encounter on the "Roof of the World"* (Postnikov 2001).

While these works imply that "The Roof of the World" is simply an epic site of this European struggle in the nineteenth and early twentieth century, a survey of historical literature on the region indicates that European travel through the region during this time period was far more commonplace. The "Roof of the World" was both a political arena, and a tourist destination. European and American adventurers published travelogues and hunting expedition descriptions based in Ladakh during this time period (e.g. Adair and Godfrey 1899, Brinckman 1862, Knight 1905, and Vigne 1844). These texts, however, are linked to the political context of colonialism. There was no separation between political and tourism infrastructure in the region, as detailed in Major General De Bourbel's book, *Routes in Jammu and Kashmir Arranged Topographically with Descriptions of Routes, Distances by Stages, and Information as to Supplies and Transport* (1897). Sites such as telegraph offices and government rest houses were used by casual tourists and British officers enroute to new postings.

Recent books have used the politicized sense of this nickname to frame discussion of more recent political intrigue in the region, e.g. *Spy on the Roof of the World* (Wignall 2000), which is part of a literature on Ladakh that focuses on post-independence Indo-Chinese and Indo-Pakistani political rivalry in the region (see for example Birdwood 1952, Fisher et al. 1963, Johri 1969, and Lamb 1968 and 1973). The strong military presence in contemporary Ladakh is thus part of a new political arena on the roof of the world. Even during peacetime a large percentage of the Indian army is stationed in Ladakh, such as the estimated 30–40,000 army personnel in Ladakh in 1998 (Angeles and Tarbotton 2001:101). Even larger numbers of troops are posted there during periods of heightened border tension with Pakistan. The military presence within Ladakh today is a sensitive issue, rarely studied due to Indian national security concerns.

One author has noted that there is social tension concerning the presence of the Indian army population in Ladakh, which can outnumber

Ladakhi civilians five-to-one during the summer months (Powell 1992:157). While the social disruption associated with the relocation of large groups of people is sometimes evident in Ladakh, we should not assume a complete separation between the interests of a "native" population and the Indian army. Ladakhis are an integral part of the Indian army; the Ladakhi unit "The Ladakh Scouts" has played key roles in armed conflicts in the region, and Ladakhi men have served in all sections of the Indian military. The presence of the army is also part of the contemporary Ladakhi economy. One author has estimated that, in addition to those in military service, one in every three Ladakhi men have paid employment related to the military, either as sub-contractors, service providers, or suppliers of good (Angeles 2001). Many residents of Leh, as the relatives of veterans and/or army personnel, are eligible to purchase household items and staple dry goods at substantial discounts from local army canteen stores. When there are winter market shortages of food such as fresh vegetables or eggs, Ladakhi households are eager to buy their food at the canteens as well.

Military concerns on the roof of the world also serve to bring Ladakh into nationalist discourse in India. The military role during the 1999 Kargil War made Ladakh a central theme of the January 26 Republic Day celebrations in New Delhi, featured in speeches as medals were distributed, in a Delhi city tableau where people climbed mountains to fight, in many parade floats, and as school bands played the "Kargil Song" on nationally televised programs. Thus in the past few decades the expansive military arena associated with "the Roof of the World" has transformed in the Indian national consciousness into a political realm of fixed national boundaries located in Ladakh and other border areas.

Little Tibet

Prior to its conceptualization as a zone of military confrontation, Ladakh was viewed by European travelers as a part of, or significant in relation to, Buddhist religious communities in the neighboring state of Tibet. While Ladakhi politics have been historically linked with Tibet, as will be discussed in the next chapter, seventeenth and eighteenth century European travelers visiting Ladakh on their way to Lhasa were more interested in Ladakhi-Tibetan religious links. The interest in Ladakh as a site of Tibetan Buddhist practice has continued to the present, even becoming more pronounced in the late twentieth century. Since the Chinese occupation of Tibet modern travelers interested in Buddhism view Ladakh as an alternative destination. The Ladakhi tourism industry literature sometimes emphasizes the practice of Tibetan Buddhism as a distinguishing feature of Ladakhi culture to increase sales, and such characterizations extend into literature beyond that aimed primarily at the tourist market. One magazine author writes of Ladakh:

> The Ladakhi people are principally of Tibetan origin, and the area welcomed refugees following China's 1950 invasion of Tibet. "Little Tibet," as Ladakh is sometimes referred to, represents one of the last remaining enclaves of Mahayana Buddhism, its principal religion, now suppressed by the Chinese in its native Tibet. In fact, many people believe that *Ladakh is a more accurate representation of Tibet before the Chinese invasion than Tibet itself.*[4]
>
> (Bestaggini 1998)

This idea of Ladakh as "Little Tibet" depends on the perception that Tibet was, in the past, constituted as a community by Buddhist practice alone. From this point of view changes to Buddhist practices therefore constitute a challenge to the "Tibetan-ness" of Tibet. Thus the maintenance of Buddhist monasteries and other social institutions in Ladakh confer validity on the notion of Ladakh as Little Tibet. But Tibetan social life and practice is far more complex; Tibet is, and was in the past, more religiously diverse than popularly thought. For example, Tibet's little known Muslim population played an important role in economic networks and political life of the region, as explored in Wahid Radhu's article in the book *Islam in Tibet* (1997).

Notions of "Little Tibet" are dependent on the fact that the monasteries of Ladakh allow scholars of Buddhism a glimpse of monastic life that has been uninterrupted by Chinese political rule, and many consider these to be the last retainers of monastic religious traditions, historical Buddhist art (Genoud 1982, Pal 1983, and Khosa 1984) and Tibetan manuscripts (Jina 1998). The monasteries of Ladakh, however, cannot be considered accurate models of study for their historical Tibetan counterparts. Monastery organization is linked to local economic and political structures through historical practices such as monastic land holding and the political power held by religious leaders. Since Indian independence Ladakhi monasteries have created their own methods for organizing territory (Singh 1977) and leasing land (Asboe 1951:191, 227), and several heads of Ladakhi monasteries have become elected officials in the Indian national government. There are therefore fundamental differences between the historical Tibetan monasteries and Ladakh monasteries situated in the modern Indian economy and political structures. If ignored in studies of monastic life these differences may obscure real understanding of Buddhist practice. Literature on lay Buddhist social practices in Ladakhi communities, such as death rituals and the politics of location (Aggarwal 2001), the role of village oracles and possession rituals (Day 1989), village architectural practices (Murdoch 1981), harvest festivals (Joldan 1985), folklore practices (Mehta 1975), gender roles (Aggarwal 1995), and kinship structures (Vohra 1989 and Phylactou 1989) also emphasize the uniqueness of Ladakhi Buddhist practice. Recently lay Buddhist organizations in Ladakh, including the Ladakh Buddhist Association, have become key participants in the Ladakhi public sphere, with active political wings. There are a number of magazine articles and newspaper reviews of lay Buddhist organizations' social and political programs in Ladakh (see Bertelsen 1997), yet few anthropological studies have focused on the subject as a whole. The Ladakh Buddhist Association (LBA) offers a number of social welfare programs, and has created new concepts of Buddhist social agendas through linkages with programs developed in partnership with international development agencies such as the International Trust for Nature Conservation, Heifer International, and Save the Children (UK).[5] Thus Buddhist social life in Ladakh cannot be simply evaluated as a sign of Tibetan-ness, but must be understood as unique and studied holistically within modern Ladakh.

Although the "Little Tibet" characterization of Ladakh in scholarly and popular literature seems to indicate Ladakh is populated by an ethnically Tibetan and religiously Buddhist community, the region is in fact peopled by communities that express a variety of ethnic identities and practice many different religions. While known for its Buddhist community, the population of Ladakh actually reflects the heterogeneity of modern Indian religious life. A majority of the population of Ladakh is either Buddhist or Muslim, and there are also small Christian, Sikh, and Hindu communities of Ladakh. The two districts of Ladakh also have distinct religious identities; while the Leh district is about 15 percent Muslim, with an 81 percent majority of Buddhist residents, the Kargil district has a 77 percent Muslim majority and a 19 percent Buddhist minority (Census of India 1981).

The Muslim community of Ladakh must also be studied within its own cultural context to understand Islam in Ladakh today; the Ladakhi Muslim community is linked to the global Muslim community through religious belief and practices while maintaining their own cultural identity. Ladakhi Muslim scholars have translated the Quran into Ladakhi, and Islamic holidays are sometimes celebrated in

Muslim households with cooking of local foods such as *khura* (fried dough) and *gyathuk* (noodles). The relationship between Islamic practice and Ladakhi culture is readily apparent at rituals such as weddings. At Ladakhi Muslim weddings it is customarily required that hosts give women, who come to the house earlier than the men, a variety of typically Ladakhi food items including juice from *phating* (high quality apricots) and *khambir* (homemade bread). During the wedding celebration *khatags* (ceremonial white scarves) are presented to the bride and groom, a Ladakhi custom similar to that of Tibet. The guests are often attired in traditional Ladakhi clothes; men will wear the *gos/goncha*, a robe that is belted around the waist, and women the *mogos* or *gos-sulma*, a Ladakhi women's robe with gathered waist. This integration is symbolically materialized in the main Sunni mosque in Leh, Jamia Masjid, an archetypal landmark situated below the Leh palace at the end of the town's central bazaar. As explained in the next chapter there is a long history of Muslims in Ladakh, and intermarriage between Muslims from other areas and individuals in Ladakh has played a role in the creation of a cosmopolitan Muslim community.

In contrast to the aforementioned studies of Buddhism in Ladakh, there is less scholarship on other religious communities in the region. The Muslim communities of Ladakh have been studied in the context of general religious histories of Ladakh (Jina 2001), and there are a number of reference books about this community, which focus on the history of Islam in Ladakh (Sheikh 1995) and give a general description of the community in Ladakh (Sheikh 2000). Other studies of the Muslim community in Ladakh have looked at Buddhist–Muslim relations in Ladakhi villages (Raether 2000 and Aggarwal 2001), and the social networks of Muslim families in Tibet that are related to some Ladakhi Muslim families (Pallis 1997).

Van Beek claims that there is an "emergent Muslim orthodoxy" that he attributes to "the growing number of older men who went on the *Haj*, a practice made possible by growing affluence and improved communication" (van Beek 1998a:313). As in other Muslim communities around the world, the traveling on *Haj* to Mecca is an important rite for Ladakhis, which helps to solidify the community. There is a ritualistic expression of these community bonds in the Leh market, when the community associations organize processions through the main bazaar to see the *Hajis* off to the airport. The travelers' family members may join them on the trip through town, while everyone in the main streets watches the procession. The movement of buses is accompanied by cheering crowds, encouraged by youths who ride on top or on the side of the buses.

While these journeys are thus significant for the community as a whole, they have not changed everyday religious practice and behavior in the Ladakhi Muslim community. The scholarly study of Islam by Ladakhi Muslims has played a more significant role in creating new awareness about Islamic thought as Ladakhi scholars have studied at national institutions such as Darul Uloom Nadwatul Ulema School in Lucknow, Uttar Pradesh, and Madrasa-tul-Banat in Malegaon, Maharashtra (Sheikh 2000). One of the important outcomes of the increase in *Haj*, however, has been an increase in awareness of what it means to be a Muslim in relation to the rest of the perceived Muslim world, an awareness that is certainly also fostered through growing international dialogue concerning the Kashmir conflict and media attention on Islamic communities. Thus the Ladakhi Muslim community sometimes engaged in reflexive dialogue about the relationship between global and local Islamic identity issues. This dialogue will become particularly important later in this book, when considering the post-border world of cosmopolitan traders in Ladakh.

Lay organizations also play a significant role in patterning social interactions in the Ladakhi Muslim community. The Sunni association, Anjuman Moin-ul-Islam, and Shia organization, Anjuman Islamia, function as social welfare organizations. Anjuman Moin-ul-Islam supports a local school, offers aid to needy families, and provides counseling to members. As discussed in the final chapter of this book, the Ladakhi Sunni and Shia Muslim communities work together on some religious issues, offering a case study of religious sect interaction that accentuates the specific political roots of Sunni–Shia conflict in other parts of the world.

The small Christian community in Ladakh also contributes to the unique blend of social relations that constitutes Ladakhi daily life. Moravian missionaries arrived in Leh at the end of the nineteenth century, when the Reverends A.H. Heyde and Pagell opened missions in Leh and Keylong (Himachel Pradesh, India). These preachers had come to India in 1853 with the original intention of opening a mission in Mongolia, but did not get permission to pass through Russia (Ahluwalia 1988). They then established a Christian community in Ladakh, which numbered approximately one hundred in the 1870s (Snellgrove 1977:xiii). Moravian mission scholars such as Mr. H.H. Jaeschke, Dr. K. Marx, and Dr. August Hermann Francke made significant contributions to scholarship about Ladakh (see Francke 1914, Jaeschke 1965 and Bray 1985 and 1983), and the mission hospital tended to many in Leh. The Moravian Mission church continues to function in Leh town, with a few Christian families and temporary members from migrant communities (such as those in Leh for seasonal employment). The church also runs a school, the Moravian Mission School in Leh, which is a popular education venue for children from elite Buddhist and Muslim families, as well as those from area Hindu and Sikh families. There was a nineteenth-century Catholic presence in Ladakh as well (Bray 1997), and today the army population has its own Roman Catholic Church and priests who have recently established a new Catholic school in Ladakh.

While the religious grounds for calling Ladakh "Little Tibet" are thus flawed, there is certainly historical evidence of links between the Tibetan political and economic spheres and those of Ladakh, as discussed in the next chapter. To claim that Ladakhi are ethnically Tibetan, however, ignores the heterogeneity of Ladakhi communities. Past studies of social groups in Ladakh have recognized the cultural plurality of the region, although doing so through a categorical approach to ethnicity (Jina 1996, and Sumi and Hassnain 1975). Such studies have divided Ladakhis into varying numbers of ethnic groupings and sub-groupings based on reported origins of the communities and linguistic differences. The constructionist or situational approach to ethnic identity has become more common in recent works that examine how "Ladakhi-ness" as an ethnicity plays a role in modern socio-political discourse in Ladakh, particularly in mobilizing identity groups in response to the popular movements for Scheduled Tribe and Hill Council statuses in the region (Behera 2000a and van Beek 2000a and 2000b). This political movement has been linked to modern social conflict in the region that challenges a final notion of Ladakh as "The Last Shangri-la".

The Last Shangri-La

The first Shangri-la mentioned in English literature was that of James Hilton's 1933 novel *Lost Horizon*, which brought unwilling travelers to an unspecified isolated valley in the Himalayas, where they found a utopian society. Shangri-la was distinguished for being remote, mysterious, isolated, and peaceful. Most popular publications about travel and culture in Ladakh invoke this last alias, as does the author of this *National Geographic* article from 1978 titled "Ladakh – the Last Shangri-la":

> As my jeep rumbled across the narrow bridge over the Indus, I watched the setting sun ignite the rows of high peaks that rim

this last Shangri-la. Source of all life, dwelling place of the gods, the eternal Himalayas shelter and nourish these pious folk.

(Abercrombie 1978:358)

This category of literary description has been prevalent in writing about Ladakh throughout the twentieth century, yielding literature with such provocative titles as *Magic Ladakh: An Intimate Picture of a Land of Topsy-Turvy Customs and Great Natural Beauty* (Gompertz 1928), *Ladakh, the Wonderland* (Kapur 1987), *Ladakh: Between Earth and Sky* (Wahid and Storm 1981), *Ladakh: Land of Possessive Powers and Charm* (Pandit 1997), and *Ladakh: Where Serenity Prevails* (Sharma 1999). Such works represent in more explicit terms the subtle exoticism prevalent in a great deal of literature concerning Ladakh.

Ladakh's Shangri-la literature is partially dependent on the aforementioned concepts of Ladakh as a "Little Tibet," as Tibet is most often called "Shangri-la." Peter Bishop's *The Myth of Shangri-la* (1989) and Donald Lopez's *Prisoners of Shangri-La* (1998), both on Tibet, have outlined the various ways that Euro-American idealizations of Tibetan Buddhism, Buddhist practices, and the Tibetan landscape contribute to these ideas. Lopez claims that some European myths of Tibet as a Shangri-la were developed as "many of Europe's fantasies about India and China, dispelled by colonialism, made their way across the mountains to an idealized Tibet," which had not become a colonized region (1998:6).

Shangri-la literature presents a view of Ladakh that is populated by people who are cut off from modern global, political, and technological change. When taken to the extreme, this view of traditional Ladakh is dangerously flawed, obscuring the history of the area and ignoring the multiple ways in which Ladakh as a region and Ladakhis as a people have been implicated in a number of extra-local systems. This perspective on Ladakh is encouraged, however, because Shangri-la is a powerful motivator for international tourism. Ladakh-based tourist operators and local businesses alike are poised to profit from increased tourism due to the common idealization of Shangri-la in the imaginations of outsiders.

International tourism existed in Ladakh before India's independence. The cool Kashmiri climate was popular with British and other European travelers, and some also ventured to nearby Ladakh on their holidays and shooting expeditions. Tourist guides to Ladakh for Europeans existed as early as 1913 (see Neve 1913, 1918, and 1923), although tourism was not a major source of income to most Ladakhis in the early twentieth century. In post-independence India Ladakh was closed to foreigners due to security concerns. Later Indian national efforts to maintain control in their border areas made an expanded tourism market possible; the 1960s border war with China led to major highway construction projects on the Leh–Srinagar route, which was reconstructed and made passable for modern vehicles from 1962–74 (Kreutzmann 1991). The improvement of routes and later construction of tourist facilities resulted in profound cultural changes in Ladakh in the late 1970s. During this time there was a dramatic increase in the influx of international visitors; while in 1974 there were no recorded international visitors, there were 15,000 by 1982 (Grotzbach 1984). Ladakh came into popularity as a tourist site during the height of unrest in Kashmir in the late 1980s and early 1990s. Kashmiri merchants shifted their tourist oriented shops to Leh, and the state government began to develop a number of tourism related facilities to compensate for tourism losses in the conflict ridden Kashmir valley. Ironically the re-opening of the region meant an increase in perceptions of Ladakh as a closed region, as interested writers emphasized the remoteness, inaccessibility, and isolation of Ladakh. Thus pieces such as the earlier quoted National Geographic article, "Ladakh: The Last Shangri-la" (Abercrombie 1978) began to appear in the late 1970s and early 1980s.

Today, although tourists are much more transient residents in Ladakh than migrant laborers, they occupy a significant space in the public life of Ladakh as a force of social and economic change. Cultural tourism venues also provide an arena for representations of diverse claims of what it means to be Ladakhi, a recent politically motivated debate that has caused social conflict in Ladakh and further complicated the utopian claim of the Shangri-la nickname.

In the late 1980s Ladakh became involved in a struggle for increased regional autonomy. This struggle, although resolved governmentally, continues to resonate in the Ladakhi public sphere. At the heart of this struggle were many diverse opinions of what it meant to be Ladakhi, and how to define a Ladakhi identity within the political realm. The autonomy movement of the late 1980s was largely focused on the state level as Ladakhis were articulating increasing feelings of alienation within the state of Jammu and Kashmir, with concerns over state practices in governmental hiring, funding allocation, and decision making.

During the struggle for autonomy Buddhist–Muslim conflict erupted in Leh as Buddhist social identity was mobilized as a defining feature of Ladakhi-ness in the political arena. Religious groups in Leh were intimately involved with the autonomy movement; the Ladakh Buddhist Association was the main organizing force between most of the events demanding regional autonomy (see discussion in Jina 1994 and Stobdan

1995) and has been credited with much of the political mobilization of the masses. The organization

> launched a violent struggle in October 1989, gave the call to "Free Ladakh from Kashmir" and demanded Union territory [UT] status. This resulted in a tripartite agreement with the LBA, the state and central government representatives, under which Leh was to have an Autonomous Hill Council (AHC). The LBA rescinded its demand for UT status in favor of an AHC and called off the agitation in consideration of the larger national interest.
>
> (Stobdan 1995:8)

The LBA power was further evidenced as the former president of the Ladakhi Buddhist Association, Mr. Thupten Tsewang, later became chief executive of the newly formed Ladakhi Autonomous Hill Council. Part of the political agitation was comprised of a Ladakhi Buddhist boycott of all goods from Kashmir.

In July of 1989, two bombs exploded in the town within one week, one of which was aimed at the Leh mosque; this violence culminated in a confrontation between Buddhist and Muslim youth in the main bazaar (van Beek 1998a:309–310). In this atmosphere of increasing communalization, social relations also became a weapon as hostility was manifested in the form of a "Buddhist social and commercial boycott against Muslims" (Jina 1994:31). The social boycott, although used as political tool for discrete political goals, had more lasting social results. Martijn van Beek wrote:

> A very significant aspect of the agitations was the imposition of a social boycott on the entire Muslim population of Ladakh. The boycott, known as *me len chu len chad pa*, is a "traditional" method of dispute settlement, or rather to enforce compliance within a village community, but had hitherto not been applied to a community as whole.[6] The boycott is a total one, banning all interactions with the boycotted people. The boycott, imposed in August 1989, caused much bitterness among the Muslims, but also cost the LBA the respect and goodwill of many Buddhists, precisely because of its wholesale application and rigorous enforcement. It also needs to be recalled that it is not uncommon to find Muslims and Buddhists in the same family, and in many villages Muslims and Buddhists live side by side.
>
> (van Beek 1998a:323–324)

These boycotts had a certain level of success, since in December 1992, a meeting in Delhi with the central government caused an agreement "in principle to give "Hill Council" status to Leh district on the condition that the Buddhist social and commercial boycott against Muslims was withdrawn" (Jina 1994:31). The political result of these events was the formation of a Coordination Committee for Leh Autonomous Council (CCLC), which is credited with the 1993 victory, when Leh was granted the right to have an Autonomous Hill Council.

While Ladakh's Hill Council is now an established political entity, conferring increased regional powers for local government in Ladakh, this conflict still reverberates in the Ladakhi public sphere. Social relations have irrevocably altered, and Ladakhis still remember today with bitterness the betrayal of seeing a close relative who no longer greeted them, or worse actively engaged in persecution, during the social boycott. While older members of the community were able to understand this as a political issue, many who were teenagers and children during the social boycott were not, and felt such events as personal betrayals. The utopian Shangri-la bears little resemblance to the actual political scene where these young Ladakhis are now of the age to start taking leadership positions.

The debate over what, and who, is fundamentally Ladakhi continues to be at the center of Ladakhi social discourse. This debate did not begin in the 1980s, but rather came to fruition during the time period. To understand the complex stratification of society within Ladakh we must examine more closely the historical networks of regional trade that made possible the formation of a pre-independence cosmopolitan elite in Ladakh, a social standing that was crucially dependent on access to certain types of commodities, and non-local social networks unfettered by national borders.

2 Recognizing the terrain: An historical background

Ethnographic present: The Leh trader's house and local history

At the time his son-in-law had arranged with us, Nasir and I went to the elderly trader's house for an interview. It was less than a five minute walk, as the trader lived in the same part of town that we did. The house was behind the main bazaar, in the part of town where roads are narrow, and houses built closely together. Like the surrounding buildings, it was made of mud brick and concrete, with a flat roof. The second story had windows decorated with wood lattice carvings, on the street a bench was built next to the bottom of stairs, which led up to the main door. Another Ladakhi had once pointed out this house to me as definitively local architecture, and said, "You know why the old houses had benches at the bottom of the stairs? Because when they were built, there was still respect for old people, and families made sure that there was a place to rest at the bottom of the stairs, before they had to walk up."

We walked up the stairs, and knocked. A smiling woman opened the door, greeted us, and ushered us inside. In the alcove we took off our shoes, before walking through the door into the living area. The room was warm, heated by a round wood burning stove with a metal chimney going up to the wood roof. The floors were covered with carpets, and along the wall were low seating areas piled with cushions. The walls were decorated with family pictures and an image of Mecca. There was a small bookcase containing a few books, a vase of plastic flowers, and some porcelain animals. Next to the stove sat an elderly Ladakhi man, dressed in a woolen robe, covered with blankets, and holding a tea cup.

His daughter gestured us to sit, myself next to the stove and Nasir next to the man. "Get them some tea and biscuits," the man's daughter told one of her daughters/younger sisters/cousins, from the group of assorted young adults and children near the door.

Figure 2.1 Local architecture in Leh, 2000.

As the children came in to sit around the room and listen, the daughter began to explain to her father, "You know this boy and his family, and this girl you talked with once last year. Now they have come to ask you some more questions about when you were a trader . . ."

The Leh trader agreed to discuss trade again, and instructed us, "Write it very nicely, otherwise it will be shameful."

We agreed to certainly try, and asked him what Central Asia was like when he lived there. "It was very good," he answered, "very developed. At that time the British government was there. The British councilor was there, and it was very good. When I went in 1936, at that time in Kashgar, the head there was Thomson-Glover. He also knew a little Urdu. After two years I came back. After that when I went again the counsel offices of Pakistan and Hindustan were divided."

"Before that the counsel offices were together?"

"Together. It was a British office . . . those times were British times. In Kashgar there was a very big counsel office, at a very nice place, with flowers and fruit trees. The flag was made in roses. After that when Hindustan and Pakistan became separate countries, the office was divided into two parts." He continued to reminisce for some time, and then suddenly paused and looked up, asking, "Are you writing this down?"

"Yes, I am writing."

"Write it nicely."

"Yes, I will grandfather."

His relative stepped in to offer us some local tea, meaning savory Ladakhi butter tea, a salty soup-like drink. After thanking her for the tea, I considered the tea offer. I had noticed before that people in Ladakh often used the term "local" to describe a good or item, in contrast to the term "Ladakhi," which is often used only to describe people or refer to the language. Thus one can buy local pickle, local wool, local butter and local peas in the marketplace, rather than Ladakhi pickle, etc. Many of the goods described as local are produced in Ladakh. Yet, this concept of the local is also rooted in the relationship between the item, and the purveyors of that item, as once I was even asked to purchase, on a trip to Kargil, "local tea," meaning tea sold in that area, although not grown there. In these verbal transactions, a sense of place associated with the goods is constructed through relationships of distribution and consumption. Local tea, for example, is most often comprised of Amul butter (a national brand of butter produced in Gujarat) and tea leaves from Assam, but conceptualized as local in contrast to "sweet tea" or "milk tea," which is a drink common to other parts of India. The "local-ness" of that cup of tea offered was in its consumption in a particular way. Similarly, saying that the architecture of the Leh trader's home was "local," was not simply judgment of an aesthetic style, but attention to particular expectations and patterns of usage associated with the building.

In such a way the Leh trader might refer to these accounts of the past as local history. This is not because it is a past of concern only to an immediate geographic locale, but rather because the accounts have been constructed in a particular way by and for the people concerned. Local history in this sense is unbounded, as the people who produce, distribute, and consume local history are themselves not limited to only one ethnic, religious, or linguistic group, or even a limited geographic region. Local history is owned by all those who transmit it, hence the Leh trader's concern with seeing it written well, as anything less, he felt, would reflect badly upon them.

Arranging history

The history of Ladakh has been organized and owned by others through various narrative devices in chronologically structured histories that emphasize particular issues and debates. In one chronological history an author has divided Ladakhi history before the formation of India into four periods: a) the Pre-Tibetan, b) Independent Ladakh, c) Under the Influence of the Dogra Regime, and d) British rule (Jina 1994); another makes only two pre-India distinctions in Ladakhi history, that between the monarchical age and the era of colonization, including the Dogra and British regimes (Michaud 1996). These two constructions of the past are a part of discourse about the modern political role of Ladakh, as the Dogra conquest of Ladakh led to the region's annexation into the princely state in 1947 and therefore inclusion in independent India. Whether differentiating Dogra and British claims to political power in Ladakh, or emphasizing their similarities, neither view of the past is incorrect. As Marshall Sahlins notes, "[h]istory is culturally ordered, differently so in different societies, according to meaningful schemes of things" (Sahlins 1985:vii); thus we have multiple versions of the past. This multiplicity is further compounded through authorship from multiple cultural and social viewpoints, with meaningful schemes of the past thus formulated in relation to diverse agendas and interests. Ronald Inden argues in his article "Orientalist Constructions of India" (1986), that histories of India with multiple versions are most often falsely constructed as dichotomous with either facts or theories/explanations. Facts in Indian history are also produced by epistemes, which assume that,

> true knowledge merely represents or mirrors a separate reality which the knower somehow transcends. Adherence to this position has allowed the scholar to claim that his (rarely her) knowledge is natural and objective and not a matter for political debate. It has also operated to produce a hierarchic relationship between knower and known, privileging the knowledge of the scientists and other experts and leaders who make up the former while subjugating the knowledges of the people who comprise the latter.
>
> (Inden 1986:402)

The chronological arrangement of a history is not the truth of how things occurred, but one particular cultural arrangement of knowledge about the past. Thus in this history I will present the past structured in another manner, fitting to the subject of trade – organized around trade routes and markets. This history does not ignore chronology altogether; time is an index without becoming the linear structure of this narrative. This geographically organized history allows us to experience the past through connections and distances, and conveys a general understanding of Ladakh's history up to the twentieth century, which is necessary to understand for later discussion. The lines of the past followed in this narrative are roads that spread out from the Ladakhi trading hub, the town of Leh, within the historical arena of the Silk Route, and multiple political empires. This geographically oriented history should further challenge notions of the Ladakhi region as a traditionally isolated land; the interconnectedness of these historical narratives make it difficult to relegate the history of Ladakh to any one political, economic, or cultural region history. This network-organized history is both the framework for, and part of, the history that all of my Ladakhi informants produced, distributed, and consumed as local history.

The Silk Route

Caravan trade routes in historical Asia betray the porosity of geographic boundaries, as seeming obstacles such as mountains and deserts have acted for centuries as conduits for Silk Road trade. While the Karakorum and Himalayan Mountains may have impeded the southward expansion of the empires of the nomadic steppes of Central Asia (Soucek 2001:2), they did not stop the spread of culture between the regions. Overland trade caravan routes have long been a vital feature of Central Asia, linking east with west, and involving regions such as South Asia.

The long history of trade in Central Asia in the regions surrounding Ladakh is associated with what is today commonly called the "Silk Road"[1] or "Silk Route." The Silk Road routes were traveled by traders from China to Eastern Europe; however few individual traders traveled from one end of the network to the other. Most traders would travel small segments of the routes from their point of origin. The main sections of the Silk Road routes bifurcated into northern and southern routes around the Taklamakan desert to join again at Kashgar, with several branches to bring in the surrounding regions. The term the "Silk Route" is misleading, as many types of goods actually traveled along these roads. Trade between Asia and Europe featured commodities such as perfumes, drugs, spices, precious stones, metals, cotton, dye-stuffs, coffee, tea, and art objects (see for example Haellquist 1991); silk was only the most famous of these early goods.

Trading contact between the neighboring regions of Central Asia and other areas appears in the early archaeological record, with evidence for trading communities from the territory of modern India present in Central Asian cities and Central Asian communities in the region of Hunza near Ladakh as early as the second century (Frye 1998:124–125). Peter Hopkirk refers to Chang Ch'ien, the Chinese traveler who crossed Central Asia on a mission from the Han Emperor Wu-ti, as the "father of the Silk Road" (Hopkirk 1980:17) as he brought intelligence back to China of new kingdoms to the west. Trade in silk grew under the Han Dynasty (202–20) in the first and second centuries, involving local populations in Central Asian as trade middlemen for empires as far west as the Roman empire (Rizvi 1999 and Hopkirk 1980). This trade continued across the region for centuries, with trade between the Chinese Tang Dynasty and Byzantine Empire documented during the seventh to tenth centuries (Major 1995). The continuing growth of this trade is a well documented component of the history of the Eurasian continent (see for example Drege and Buhrer 1989, Franck 1986 and Foltz 1999).

Ancient South Asia also participated in some forms of trade linked to that in Central Asia. These trade linkages provided South Asian empires with access to the valuable resources of Central and East Asia, including silk. In the late Gupta period (approximately the fourth to sixth centuries) of South Asia, Central Asian Hunas[2] invaded the subcontinent. Huna rulers established themselves in Northern India (reaching as far south as present day Madhya Pradesh) in the sixth century. Their presence in the north severely destabilized the Gupta Empire as it undercut the economic base of the Guptas with control of important trade routes that had formerly connected South Asia with Central Asia, China, Tibet, Ladakh and Kashmir (Ahluwalia 1988:48).

The idea of Buddhism followed the trade roads of Central Asia in the early years, and is well represented in the archaeological record, especially in the form of ancient art (see Klimburg-Salter 1982 and Hopkirk 1980 about European collections). During the period of the Kushan Empire (approximately third century) Buddhism began to spread from South Asia into Central and East Asia, "across the Hindu Kush from Gandhara to Bactria, the Tarim Basin, and China" (Hambly 1966:48–49). The origins of Buddhism in the Ladakh region are of some debate. Popular local theory has ascribed the growth of Buddhism in the region to influences from early Indian Buddhism from the pre-Tibetan Buddhist period, although some authors have said that there is little evidence to support this theory (Snellgrove and Skorupski 1977). Ancient religious architecture and art indicate that Buddhism appeared as a monastic institution in Ladakh by the fifth century (Snellgrove and Skorupski 1977:8). The distinction of this presence of early Buddhism, as a monastic institution rather than a religion, is a particularly important one to make, as the religious practice of the more ascetic form of Indian Buddhism may not appear as clearly in the archaeological record. Another ideology traveling the Silk Route, Islam, was most probably introduced to the Ladakh region in the seventh or eighth century. Ladakhi scholar Abdul Ghani Sheikh has written that in the Tangchey area of Ladakh there are boulders with seventh- to eighth-century inscriptions of the Qur'an and the engraved names of Muslim Central Asian army commanders and administrators (Sheikh 2000). Most of the major Islamic influences in the region, however, occurred in settings discussed later in this chapter.

Many paths to the bazaars: Historical trading routes through Ladakh

One of the most vital components of Ladakh's participation in the Silk Route was its geographic location. Leh town in Ladakh, located near key mountain passes, was a trading network "hub," a place that offered traders access to a number of routes. In this section I will describe the geography and paths of some of the most salient routes that went through Ladakh. As shown in the maps below, there were a variety of routes through Ladakh that were used by traders from the area as well as South and Central Asia. For the purposes of simplicity three main networks of routes to Central Asia, South Asia, and Tibet have been categorized as one route each; however, these routes were actually a series of interconnected roads that traders might have chosen depending on the weather, the type of goods they were carrying, and the type of financial backing they had for the expedition. All three main routes were only open for a brief window of time in the summer, when snow had melted in the mountains and the passes were passable for travelers. The routes pictured show some of the main towns to which 47, was connected; these should not be thought of as endpoints, but rather as access points for trade that spread throughout the respective regions.

The Tibetan Route

The Tibetan route connected Leh with the Tibetan city of Lhasa, as well as intermediate points. This route includes the roads that ran from the east of Leh, through the Chang-tang area near Pangong Lake. Traders had to traverse the mountain passes of Chang-la or Taglang-la to reach these areas. In the nineteenth and twentieth centuries this was a common route for local traders as well as traders with government permits from Kashmir. Because of the rough terrain along this route the primary mode of transportation was livestock, usually either *dzo* (a cross breed between a yak and cow), yak, or donkey. While this is not one of the main routes of the traders I will discuss in upcoming chapters, the valued trade along this route conveyed *pashmina* into South Asia. The *pashmina* trade was, and continues to be, an important mainstay of Kashmir's economy, generating income and fueling the local handicrafts industry.

The Tibetan route is of historical importance as it provided connections between Tibet and Ladakh that shaped the history of Ladakh in the tenth century with the formation of political linkages between the two areas. A Tibetan prince, Skidley Nimagon, came to Ladakh with troops and conquered the region to become the king of Kuge and Purang in approximately the year 900 (Leh Nutrition Project 1989:6B).[3] When a war between the *Cho* of Gya and Central Asian regimes broke

Figure 2.2 The Tibetan Route from Leh.

out, Nimagon supported the *Cho* regime and was later given the area below Martselang (today a town to the southeast of Leh) as a reward. Nimagon's eldest son, Lhachen Spalgygon, is considered the first king of Ladakh, and ruled from 930–60. During this time he commissioned many public works including canals and a royal residence.[4] During the tenth century Buddhism ideology also traveled in Ladakh, as the Buddhist scholar Lotsava Rinchen-bZangpo of Western Tibet made his way through Ladakh on the way home from Kashmir (Jina 1994:23).

This exposure to the religion of Buddhism signified some cultural change, although the monastic institutions of Buddhism do not occur until later in the historical record of Ladakh. The first Gelupa monastery, of Tibetan Buddhism, was built in Spituk during the reign of King Grags-pa-'bum in the early fifteenth century (Snellgrove and Skorupski 1977:82). Gyalpo Grags-pa-'bum ruled from the Bagso area and began a dynasty that ultimately united what is recognized as Ladakh today (Snellgrove and Skorupski 1977:82).

Later histories along this route were influenced by this early exposure to Buddhism; in the seventeenth century Tibet's trade in Ladakh was often styled as a form of tribute between Buddhist powers (Rizvi 1999:10), so trade was profoundly affected by the waxing and waning of Tibetan power in the region. The 1684 Treaty of Timisgong, at the end of a war between Ladakh and Tibet, radically restructured this trade system and shifted emphasis to Kashmir.

The South Asian route

The South Asian route plays a central role later in this book, as the highway on which many of the featured traders and trading families traveled. The South Asian route connected Leh through many roads to key trading centers in Srinagar, Jammu, Lahore, Rawalpindi, Manali, and Amritsar; traders had choices depending on the city of their main destination. For example, to travel from Leh to Amritsar a trader had to choose if they wanted to go to the Punjab via Upshi to Hoshiarpur towards the east or via Srinagar to the west. The eastern way to the Punjab meant traveling from Upshi to Rupshu, over Taglang-la, Lunga-lacha-la, and Bara-Lacha-la passes, and then in the Lahul and Kullu valley areas. The market town of Hoshiarpur was a key stop along the way to Amritsar. As noted later Hoshiarpur was actually the trading center for a number of families who participated in Ladakh's trading networks. These roads were rough and the journey using livestock as transport could be painstakingly slow. Thus by the early twentieth century Punjabi traders working with trade in the

Ladakh region found it much more convenient to use the western branch from South Asia to Ladakh. With development of transport facilities in India, by the 1930s traders could send their goods by rail to Rawalpindi, have them transferred to trucks (before the 1930s carts were used) to travel to Srinagar by Muree and the Jhelum valley, and then re-pack the goods for pony transport from Srinagar over Zoji-la pass, to Kargil (Rizvi 1999:27). In Kargil local families from surrounding areas would contribute labor and livestock in the form of ponies, donkeys, or *dzo* to transport the goods to Leh.

The South Asian route is a setting for a cultural and political history of Ladakh between the early thirteenth and fifteenth centuries that affirms the participation of the region in trans-regional spread of Islam. In the fourteenth century a Ladakhi political leader named Richen linked Ladakh to Kashmiri political regimes along this route, as what is variously called king, prince, or chief by different chroniclers of history. Rinchen traveled to Kashmir with aspirations to power, and through political maneuvering was able to occupy the throne of Kashmir by the end of 1320 (Mohi-ud-din-dar 1992:26–27). The Kashmir chronicles, the *Rajatarangini* of Pandit Jonaraja, support this narrative through allusion to a king Rainchan *Bhoti*, which means Tibetan or Ladakhi in Kashmir (Rizvi 1983:43). One scholar of Ladakhi history has criticized the story as a legend, pointing out that

Figure 2.3 The South Asian Route from Leh.

the sole princely Rinchen mentioned in the Ladakhi chronicles was the son of *Gyal* Ngorub, at a projected time period that does not fit with the Kashmir chronology (Petech 1977). There is some basis in the Ladakhi chronicles to support the idea that Rinchen did indeed come from a royal family in Ladakh, as the Rinchen in the Ladakh chronicles is listed as a *Gyalbu* (prince), rather than a *Gyal* (king), although he did produce a son who later became a king of Ladakh (Rizvi 1983:44). This has led to conjecture that Rinchen's relationship to Ngorub was not fully known to the historian responsible for the Ladakhi chronicles, and Rinchen was listed as the son of Ngorub simply to indicate that he was a direct descendent. Inclusion of Rinchen in the history of Ladakh's South Asian route provides a partial explanation for Islamic communities in the region in later times. Rinchen converted to Islam, and became the first Muslim king of Kashmir. Originally a Buddhist, Rinchen was converted to Islam by the teacher Sayyid Sharafu'd-Din, commonly known as Bulbul Shah. Sayyid Sharafu'd-Din, reportedly the first Sufi to visit Kashmir, was "a disciple of Shah Ni'matu'llah Farsi of Suhra wardiya order of Sufis," and "had come to Kashmir during the reign of Suhadeva, from Turkistan" (Mohi-ud-din-dar 1992:26). Upon conversion Rinchen took the name Sadr-ud-din (Kaumudi 1952), and is reported to have converted a large part of Kashmir during his rule of only three years. Sultan Sadr-ud-din is listed as ruling from 1320–23, after which followed "years of chaos and misrule" from 1323–39 (Mohi-ud-din-dar 1992:27–28). Thus the establishment of Islam in Kashmir, and the subsequent movement of Islamic communities into the areas of Kashmir and Ladakh are directly linked to the history of the Ladakhi people themselves. The story of Rinchen provides a way of understanding Ladakh as a participant in the events along routes through multiple regions, rather than supporting a common representation of historical Ladakh as operating in a primarily Tibetan political realm.

The flow of information, ideas, and political power between Kashmir and Ladakh continued throughout the fourteenth century. One of the most famous Islamic teachers who later traveled to Ladakh was Sayyid Ali Hamadani Sufi, who lived from 1314–85. Sayyid Ali Hamadani came to Kashmir in 1372 as the second major Islamic figure to travel to Kashmir after Bulbul Shah (Hamadani 1984:3). Hamdani cites Haider Badakhshi[5] to support the claim that Sayyid Ali Hamadani had traveled to Ladakh during his life (1984:8), an idea generally correlated by the testimonies of Leh Muslims. One aspect of Sayyid Ali Hamadani's work in Kashmir that may have had additional impact on the later development of Islam in Ladakh is his encouragement of handicraft industries; he is also known for having re-established the failing Kashmiri handicrafts work through the transport of several hundred Persian handicraft experts to Kashmir (Hamadani 1984:43). Thus the spread of Islam in the region also laid the foundation for important trade relations between Kashmir and surrounding areas. The demand for fine wool from the Kashmiri shawl industry that grew out of the presence of these Persian artists would become an important impetus for the establishment of Kashmiri Muslim communities in Ladakh at a later date (Michaud 1996:288).

This came to pass in the seventeenth century, when the Mughal Emperor in South Asia lent military aid to Ladakh in a war with the Tibetan empire. At the end of this conflict in 1684, the Treaty of Timisgong conceded to Kashmiri traders the right to free access to the Chang-tang region of Ladakh for the trade of wool and *pashmina* (Rizvi 1999:53–55, 70). At this time a number of Kashmiri Muslims came to Ladakh for work in a variety of positions including smiths to mint coins, and court interpreters/scribes (Sheikh 2000) who wrote in Persian, which had been the language of the court in Kashmir since approximately the twelfth century (Kaumudi 1952). Kashmir's political center shifted with the establishment of Afghan governors, who occupied the territory from 1753–1819 (Kaumudi 1952), and trade with this region carried new cultural influences from Central Asia. The establishment of Afghan authority in the region re-centered Ladakh's South Asian trade networks, making the city of Jammu a key trading center for Central and South Asia (Rizvi 1999:10).

In 1820 Gulab Singh was created ruler of Jammu as a reward for his political support by Maharaja Ranjit Singh of Lahore (Kaumudi 1952); this was the beginning of the Dogra regime and its eventual power over Ladakh. An invasion in 1834[6] led by General Zorawar Singh of the Dogra regime of Jammu ended an era of Ladakhi monarchs with political power, although the royal family continued to have some ceremonial importance. The Dogra regime, as noted earlier, is a political body of current debate. Historical scholars have variously called this political regime one of "Hindu rulers" and "Muslim invaders" in apparently contradictory descriptions if conceptualized as a religiously motivated invasion. Simply put the regime had Hindu leaders; however a majority of the population was actually Muslim. Religious affiliations are only of incidental interest; numerous authors have shown that a desire to participate in Ladakh's trade in *pashmina* with Kashmir was the primary reason that Gulab Singh's forces invaded Ladakh (Lamb 1960, Huttenback 1961 and Rizvi 1999:50). The Muslim populace of the Dogra regime influenced Ladakh; demographic shifts occurred as Muslim settlers came into Ladakh with the momentum of increased international trade. The Dogra interest in Ladakh's coveted *pashmina* trade was actualized and trade representatives were quickly sent to Ladakh after conquest. The Dogra's first few years of power in Ladakh were spent dealing with a series of Ladakhi revolts. While the Dogra had at first left Ladakhi kings some political power and required them to pay a yearly tax, a series of revolutionary conspiracies initiated change in this policy (Jina 1994:24). The Dogra regime forced the Ladakhi royal family out of power, placed representatives in Leh, and restructured the system of tenant farming. Although the political changes still left a great deal of power within the region, the power of local elite in Leh was weakened (Michaud 1996:289).

Nineteenth-century politics of the South Asian routes would continue to influence the politics of Ladakh as British colonial influenced increased in northern India. In an 1845 struggle between British and North Indian Sikh forces, Maharaja Gulab Singh conspired with the British. After the British captured Lahore in 1846, they repaid this debt through the terms of the Treaty of Lahore of March 9, 1846. In this treaty the parties agreed that the British were in control of Lahore and recognized Raja Gulab Singh as an independent sovereign. A later document, the Treaty of Amritsar, granted Maharaja Gulab Singh the territory of Kashmir for the price of 75 *lakh* rupees,[7] including outlying territories such as Ladakh and Skardo (Kaumudi 1952 and Gadru 1973). Of particular importance in this historical narrative is a Dogra and British recognition of the importance of trade with Ladakh; Maharaja Gulab Singh's token payment to British government was a symbolic gift that included "twelve pashmina goats and three pairs of shawls" (Gadru 1973:xvi), representing some of the important commodities that Kashmir would contribute to the British South Asian economy. Although three shawls may seem like a paltry sum these terms represent an ongoing symbolic statement of the relations between trade and politics in the region, as the shawls were to be a yearly tribute (Kaumudi 1952:133). In subsequent years there was little direct British colonization of Ladakh, while indirect rule was maintained through the Maharaja of Jammu and Kashmir (Michaud 1996:289).

When Maharaja Gulab Singh died in 1857, his son Ranbir Singh succeeded him as the Maharaja of Jammu and Kashmir; Ranbir Singh ruled from 1857–85. It was during this time period that the British first stationed an officer in Leh town. The initial posting was in response to trade concerns, which of course played an important political role during this time period. According to a report was published in 1862 by R.H. Davies, then secretary of the Punjab government, trade with Central Asia was harmed by duties levied by the government of Jammu and Kashmir as much as those claimed in Chinese Central Asia (Henderson and Hume 1981:5). Inter-governmental negotiations resulted in a reduction of the transit taxes on goods passing through Kashmir on the South Asian routes. At this time, in 1867, Dr. Cayley was the first British officer to be stationed by the British colonial government in Leh during the summer months.

> The officer at Lèwas instructed to see that no duties were levied in excess of those fixed in tariff; to inquire closely into the nature and extent of the trade between India and Central Asia, and to suggest measures for developing this trade.
>
> (Henderson and Hume 1981:5)

Thus the British officer was a trade official and a political agent to ensure that the Maharaja did not have full control over the trade with Central Asia (Jina 1994:25). Later political issues emphasized the political importance of this posting as both the starting point for the aforementioned expeditions to Chinese Central Asia, and a key British presence in Kashmir through a number of political tempests.

In 1925 Hari Singh, said to have been raised "in western ways," became the Maharaja of Jammu and Kashmir (Kaumudi 1952:25). The new Maharaja established the state Legislative Assembly, and initiated a series of new legislation in Jammu and Kashmir. This included a 1931 proclamation that legally defined the "Hereditary State Subject," so that individuals from other regions could not own land in the state of Jammu and Kashmir. This act tightened government control on traders from other regions, and would give rise to new methods of conducting business in Ladakh.

The British in early twentieth-century colonial South Asia were facing radical and well documented challenges to their political power as the "Quit India" movement grew. British attempts to appease their increasingly vocal Indian critics meant that by 1919, land revenue income had to be diverted to benefit provincial administrations, a significant loss of income to the British economy (Tomlinson 1982). Between 1900 and 1935 British Indian market prices fluctuated widely in response to political pressures on trade and industrial changes (Roy 1995), making South Asia in the early twentieth century a volatile market for producers, investors, and traders. Across India British management declined, while Indian owned local firms began to form more multinational alliances (see for example in Bengal, Goswami 1989). Mahatma Gandhi's *swadeshi* movement in India stimulated local economies by encouraging the purchase of local products, which benefited Indian textile producers, as well as those in other Asian regions. While the British colonial government had operated on a general free trade principal in India before 1914, in order to cover the Empire's deficit incurred in India the colonial government attempted to increase import revenues in India to raise money through customs taxes (Tomlinson 1982). This action provoked further resentment and economic instability in South Asian markets all along the South Asian routes to Ladakh.

The Central Asian (trans-Karakorum) route

The final series of roads from Leh, which play a central role in the upcoming narratives of trading networks in Ladakh, were the trans-Karakorum routes that linked Ladakh to Central Asia. These were the routes used when traders wanted to travel from Leh to towns such as Kashgar, Khotan, Yarkend, Kargilik, and other towns of the Sinkiang region. Travel along the trans-Karakorum route was a perilous journey; on the northern road from Leh traders had to traverse mountain passes at Khardung-la, Saser-la, Karakorum, and Suget, none less than 4500 meters in elevation (Rizvi 1999:13). Historian Janet Rizvi has argued that the difficult Ladakh route for trade with Central Asia was used more frequently in the nineteenth century than the easier Baltistan route via the Mustagh Pass, which had been used in the seventeenth and eighteenth centuries, because there was no viable alternative; the Baltistan route was closed for political reasons in the nineteenth century as Hunza and Chitral were politically unstable, and other routes had too many, sometimes unstable, glaciers (Rizvi 1999:34). Yet, in an 1896 publication, British officer and explorer Sir Francis Younghusband claims that the most common route for trade from Leh to Kashgar was via the Mustagh Pass (Younghusband 1896:172). It is possible that Younghusband was confused by the fact that there is a western branch of the northern route that departs via the same road from Srinagar north to the Baltistan area, but branches off west towards Gilgit to go to Kashgar via Tashkurgan, rather than east through Skardo over the Mustagh pass. Or, it is also possible that a group of traders that he spoke with were part of the small number who still went on the Skardo–Mustagh route. As described later in this book, other factors also played a role in choosing particular segments of the Trans-Karakorum route. The everyday choices made by traders were part of a complex cost-benefit analysis that included the costs of transport and labor, as well as the trading relationships they had in other regions.

Figure 2.4 The Central Asian Route from Leh.

The Central Asian towns of Kashgar, Yarkend, and Khotan are oasis towns wrapped around the edges of the Tarim basin. These cities have a long history of trade and cross-cultural contact as travelers depended on their presence for relief from the difficult desert terrain. Many travelers found the southwestern routes over the mountains to this area easier to traverse than the arid north-eastern. Thus as early as the first century, Ladakh's trading partners in the eastern cities of Khotan, Yarkend, and Kashgar were linked with South Asia through the spread of Buddhist ideology by missionaries from the Mauryan Empire (Frye 1998:161–162). Islamic influences, while circulating in the region earlier, became widespread in this region in the tenth century, and by the end of this century Kashgar had become the capital town of the Karakhanids, who founded an Islamic Central Asian state (Frye 1998:237).

Early Chinese influences can also be seen in the region's history of language use; in as early as the first century the official written languages of Kashgar were Prakrit[8] or Chinese (Frye 1998:248). The official languages of Kashgar had changed to Saka or Sogdian, illustrating Iranian influences in the region, by the seventh century; yet at this time in neighboring Khotan the Chinese language was used for trade (Frye 1998:249). Direct Chinese political control of the region occurred much later, when they captured what became known then as the Sinkiang region in 1758 (Soucek 2001). Sinkiang was incorporated into the Chinese administrative structure in 1844 (Soucek 2001:16), however political instability continued as the region became an arena for Anglo-Russian rivalry.

In the late nineteenth century two of the largest and most prosperous Central Asian trading towns in Chinese Central Asia were Yarkend and Kashgar. Yarkend had become the main commercial town of Chinese Sinkiang where the Indian traders who traveled the Central Asian route through Leh would reside, but Kashgar was considered the key political city. The geography of Kashgar reflected the complexities of this period; there was an old "Muslim" part of town with a large market and mosque, a newer "Chinese town" two and half miles to the south, and a Russian consulate building located just outside the wall of the new town (Skrine and Nightingale 1973:19).

Before the 1860s the British in South Asia were disinterested in trade along the Central Asian routes through Ladakh, considering Chinese Central Asia a restricted market as the Russians had established trading privileges and a factory in Kashgar, and the journey was hazardous enough that profits were not assured (Skrine and Nightingale 1973:10). This changed in the early 1860s, when a general uprising of Muslim Tungans spread revolutionary action throughout Chinese Central Asia. Yakub Beg, a soldier of Kwodja Buzurg Khan, was sent to Kashgar by General Khudoyar Khan Alimkul of Tashkent "to help his co-religionists" (Gadru 1973:329–330). This religiously communal view of their alliance is supported by that fact that Yakub Beg, upon winning power in the region from the Gobi desert to the Tian Shan Mountains, was called "*Atalik*" or "Defender of the faith," and European powers took notice of this formation of a powerful new "Muhamadan State in Central Asia" (Gadru 1973:329–330). Yet this was not a religious movement within the political realm; the supplanted Kwodja Buzurg Khan had also been Muslim. Instead, this struggle was for the establishment of a regional government independent of China. The abrupt power shift in Chinese Central Asia prompted British and Russian governments to scramble for alliances, sending ambassadors and establishing embassies with Yakub Beg's government. British interest was excited by Yakub Beg's refusal to recognize Chinese granted Russian trading rights in the region, which resulted in cessation of Russian trade with China (Skrine and Nightingale 1973:10). Through Ladakh, and the Trans-Karakorum route, the British government in South Asia attempted to formulate a trade agreement with Yakub Beg's government as part of a plan to create a buffer state with Russia. To this end they sent a trade mission with Douglas Forsythe through Leh in 1870 (Rizvi 1999).

Yakub Beg's forces were not strong enough to keep Russian forces from re-entering Kashgar, and he was forced to sign a treaty with the Russians in 1872. Thus when the British Forsyth mission went to request similar trade rights from Yakub Beg's government in 1873, they were rebuffed (Skrine and Nightingale 1973:10–11). This flurry of political activity subsided, however, as the Chinese recaptured Sinkiang and regained control of this part of Central Asia in 1877 (Soucek 2001:16). Yet this region continued to be of significant interest to the British in South Asia. Captain John Biddulph, who had spent a number of years as an officer in Gilgit, concluded in a 1874 report that the Chinese Central Asian region was easily passable through Ladakh and if a Russian army decided to invade, they would control the whole region to threaten North India (see Gadru 1973:xix–xxi as well as Biddulph 1874). Thus although the Karakorum Pass route through Ladakh had been declared a free highway for commercial trade under a treaty from 1870 between officials of British India and Jammu and Kashmir, little money was spent on its maintenance. The Trans-Karakorum routes were deliberately not maintained, and remained difficult to traverse as the British colonial government had planned.

While the trading towns of Ladakh's neighboring eastern regions such as Kashgar, Khotan, and Yarkend would not become part of Sinkiang Province, an autonomous region of the People's Republic of China,[9] until 1955 (Soucek 2001:338), the government of China began asserting further direct control in the region in the beginning of the twentieth century. Import taxes on goods from British South Asia, coming through the Trans-Karakorum routes from Ladakh, were repeatedly raised and lowered in response to Chinese regional interests. By 1900 the volume of trans-Karakorum trade to Chinese Central Asia was noticeably lower; Russian traders had gained an economic advantage since the existing trading infrastructure meant the cost of transporting goods from Russia to Chinese Turkistan was half of that from British India (Skrine and Nightingale 1973).

When the British Commissioner of Ladakh, Ney Elias, visited Yarkend in 1880 with Chinese permission, new agreements were reached about regional trade. The Chinese allowed British trade, but would charge high import taxes on goods sold in the region and transit duties on goods moving through (Skrine and Nightingale 1973:11). A later expedition by Elias in 1885 was also only partially successful, and the British government was concerned that the Chinese government resented the

British attempts to ally with Yakub Beg's government while he was in power (Skrine and Nightingale 1973:11). The Anglo-Russian rivalry of the Great Game had served to intensify trade restrictions in the nineteenth century with trade in Central Asia (Jalalzai 1992 and Warikoo 1989) through Ladakh along the Trans-Karakorum Route. In the last few years of the nineteenth century, the Russians were selling a great deal of goods in the Kashgar region, having developed well maintained roads and a railway for inexpensive transportation. In contrast the traders from British India still had to make their way through some of the world's most difficult terrain (Skrine and Nightingale 1973:25).

Crossroads: Leh, "A very cosmopolitan city"

At the intersection of these major trade routes, Leh's role as a market town was primarily one of a transit stop. Most of the goods that traveled through this town were not sold on Ladakhi markets for, as I will discuss later in this book, the area in itself was not considered an important market. In spite of this the Leh *bazaar* (market area) was a site of intense commercial activity, as items of commerce flowed through, were traded, and taxed.

Most accounts by Europeans in Ladakh during the late nineteenth and early twentieth centuries make a point about the strong impressions on their memory of Ladakh of the Leh *bazaar*. Edward Knight wrote, upon entering the *bazaar* in early spring,

> The passing through this wicket into the bazaar is a sudden burst from the wilds into civilization. The merchants, many of whom are white-robed Hindoos from Kashmir, were sitting cross-kneed among their wares at the entrance of their shops . . . But the bazaar was comparatively deserted at this early season. I was informed that later on, when the passes into Central Asia are open, this place would be full of life, and be exceedingly picturesque and interesting for a stranger to behold.
>
> (Knight 1905:177)

A survey of travelogue literature shows a surprising number of illustrations of the Leh bazaar, perhaps more uniformly acknowledged as an important site than any other single place in the Kingdom of Jammu and Kashmir.

This may be because it was the only focal point in Leh; the sights of Srinagar may have simply provided more varied sights to visitors. As Rizvi points out, in the trading networks of Central Asia the "most

Figure 2.5 Leh Bazaar in a sketch from *The Graphic* newspaper, 1878.

vibrant of the trading stations" were towns between inhabited and uninhabited sections of routes, where traders would rest and refuel before
continuing onward, or the "first sizeable settlement reached by caravans" after inhospitable terrain. In this region such locations included
the towns of Yarkend, Khotan, Kashgar, and Leh (Rizvi 1999:11–12).
Thus, according to Knight again, (this time in the summer and early
fall) in Leh,

> there is such a motley collection of types and various costumes,
> and such a babble of different languages, as it would not be easy
> to find elsewhere. Savage Tartars in sheepskins, and other outlandish
> men, jostle with the elegant Hindoo merchant from the cities
> of Central India, and the turbulent Mussulman Pathan scowls
> at the imperturbable idolaters from the Celestial Empire. Leh in
> September is, indeed, one of the busiest and most crowded of cities,
> and the storekeepers and farmers who have to supply this multi-
> tude must make a very good profit for this time. Leh is therefore
> a very cosmopolitan city, even in the dead season; for there are
> resident merchants and others of various races and creeds. Small
> as is the permanent population, at least four languages are in

common use here – Hindostani, Tibetan, Turki, and Kashmiri – while several others are spoken.

(Knight 1905:177–178)

The social impact of the presence of such international diversity in the small community of Leh will be discussed later; however we can conceptualize the bazaar space as an important cultural contact zone with a variety of forms of cultural expression and social interaction. This type of diverse international *bazaar* scene was not only found in Ladakh, but common in most of the cities linked to Ladakh along the trade routes of Central Asia.

This town was the site of the palace of the Ladakhi King Sengge Namgyal, who ruled during the early seventeenth century, in what is called the Golden Age of Ladakh. His father, Jamyang Namgyal, is also remembered as one of the key historical figures in Ladakh's history, although there are differing versions of his life. David Snellgrove has written that the King Jamyang Namgyal was forced to marry the daughter of the invading ruler of Baltistan, Ali Mir (Snellgrove and Skorupski 1977:86). While this implies that the marriage of Jamyang Namgyal and Gyal Khatoon (Ali Mir's daughter) was a sign of colonization by Balti powers, Ladakhi history accounts have a different version. One Ladakhi text relates that rather than being invaded by Baltistan, the Ladakhis tried to invade Baltistan under the direction of Jamyang Namgyal, who was captured by the enemy. While a prisoner of war in Baltistan he developed a relationship with Gyal Khatoon and was subsequently peacefully released (Leh Nutrition Project 1989:10B). Despite the subtleties of the story both accounts agree that the couple had a son, named Sengge Namgyal. The dates of Sengge Namgyal's rule are a site of further dispute;[10] however most authors agree that this period from the last few decades of the sixteenth century to the first few decades of the seventeenth century was a key time in the monarchical era of Ladakhi history. The Leh palace, which Ladakhi royalty inhabited until their fall from power, was constructed at this time along with many important Buddhist monasteries that still function today, including Hemis, Chemre, and Tashi Gong.

Leh became an important power center of Ladakh and during this time period the Leh based royal aristocracy/nobility comprised approximately three percent of the total population (Michaud 1996:288).

The rule of subsequent Ladakhi kings can best be characterized as a series of conflicts and alliances with foreign powers. During the reign of King Deldan Namgyal, 1620–45, Moghuls attacked from Kashmir and were defeated in Ladakh. In the times of King Delek Namgyal,

Figure 2.6 Nineteenth-century sketch of Leh Palace (Cunningham 1854:314).

1645–75 (Huttenback 1961) the Tibetan army invaded and Ladakhis paid tribute to the Mughal emperor for military aid from the Mughal army in Kashmir under Fidai Khan. The war during the reign of Delek Namgyal actually involved several international political powers of the times, since the Tibetan army was commanded by the fifth Dalai Lama, whose political power was backed by the Mongols and the Mughal army represented the power of rulers in Delhi and Srinagar (Snellgrove and Skorupski 1977:xiii). As part of the political agreement with Mughal Emperor Aurangzeb for protection, King Delek Namgyal became Muslim, although his descendents were Buddhist. Delek Namgyal is attributed with the construction of Jamia Masjid of Leh in 1666–67 (Sheikh 2000), a Sunni Muslim mosque that continues to occupy the site of original construction at the end of the main bazaar road under the Leh palace. The original form of this mosque, now obscured by recent construction, was influenced by the architectural traditions of Central Asia and Tibet. These patterns of international contact and alliances with neighboring Asian countries continued under King Deskyong Namgyal (1720–39), who was married to princess from Mustang (Leh Nutrition Project 1989:16B).

In Ladakh, the final reigning local monarch was Tsepal Tundup Namgyal (1808–30), who constructed Stok palace (Leh Nutrition Project 1989:17B). Political conditions are generally thought to have deteriorated during the rule of this king. Descriptions of the royal family and Leh elites were written by two English employees of the English East India Company, William Moorcroft and George Trebeck, who traveled to Ladakh from 1819–25 (published as Moorcroft and Trebeck 1841). Many of these descriptions were soon outdated, however, with the advent of the Dogra regime in Ladakh and subsequent stationing of a British officer in Leh in 1867. This policy change was the result of a number of political changes taking place in the geopolitical landscape surrounding Ladakh, especially to the east, where the fermenting political issues change in Chinese Turkistan, or Chinese Central Asia[11] was a site for the power struggles of the Great Game.

During the final decades of the nineteenth century the politics of the Great Game managed to continue to radically alter trade interactions between Chinese Central Asia and British South Asia. Ladakh, poised in the middle, continued to be involved with traders from both regions. By 1870 the British government and the Maharaja of Jammu and Kashmir's government had jointly agreed to free trans-Karakorum trade of duties, which increased the importation of *pashmina*[12] from Chinese Central Asia and Western Tibet to the Punjab region (Rizvi 1999:65). While this may have decreased the importance of the Ladakh region as a production center, it increased the importance of the regional trade routes, markets, and traveling infrastructure. The establishment of the British Agency in Leh reportedly quadrupled trade going to British India within four years (Henderson and Hume 1981:144), in spite of the trade restrictions on the Chinese side. Among other goods, fine carpets continued to travel from Chinese Central Asia producing centers through Ladakh to South Asia and ultimately sometimes to European markets. In the Sunni mosque in Leh today one can view a pair of long carpets, spectacular specimens of nineteenth-century carpets transported along the trade route, which were offered by two traders Khwoja Hydershah and Nasar-Ul-Din-Shah and brought on camels from Yarkend in approximately 1861.[13]

Thus by the beginning of the twentieth century seeds of change were sown that would ultimately lead to the end of many trading networks through Ladakh. The strengthening of Chinese power in Chinese Turkistan, weak position of the British trade in Central Asia, and increased resistance to British involvement in the sub-continent signified great changes were about to come. Ladakhis of the late nineteenth and early twentieth centuries were immersed in this cosmopolitan world of diverse social customs, political interests, and economic arenas. This diversity would shape not only an entire society, but families and individuals as well.

Part II
Historical trade

3 The family business
Community, kinship, and identity

Ethnographic present: The Hoshiarpuri traders

Nasir and I walked down a small street, with the address we had gotten from a Hoshiarpuri trader in Leh. Neither of us had ever been to Hoshiarpur before and we were slightly lost in what seemed like a large town. A cycle rickshaw *wallah* had taken us to this section of the town, near an old library building surrounded by pleasant gardens and large colonial-style banks shaded by tall green trees. But now we were wandering, going back and forth across a series of streets with tall white walls and imposing wrought iron gates. This upper-middle class Indian neighborhood seemed far from, and perhaps unconnected to, Ladakh. Children played in the streets in front of the neat white concrete houses and a small girl jumping rope in one street said something which caught our ears. "Did she just say something in Ladakhi?"

"Little sister," Nasir called out to her in Ladakhi. She turned around and smiled at us. It could not be a coincidence, finding a Ladakhi girl in this Punjabi town, I thought. Sure enough we had found the right address; she was staying, with her family, in the very household for which we were looking.

When we walked through the gates, some men came out to talk with us. We explained briefly what we were doing. Having walked into so many strangers' houses had made us better at explaining why we were there, introducing ourselves, showing the papers, etc. They replied pleasantly to my questions, and agreed, yes, their fathers had traded in Ladakh, and yes, they would be glad to talk with us. "But wait," said one man, "I'll just go to the next street, our neighbor there is from a family that also traded with Ladakh. And there is one other man we should call as well; just come, sit inside and wait."

Walking past a few rooms facing out onto the tiled veranda, we were ushered into the sitting room, a cool airy room with many windows.

The ceiling fan pushed air around, causing the lace curtains to sway slightly in the breeze. Floral upholstered couches were grouped around low, doily covered brass tables and a television stood in the corner covered with an embroidered cloth. The wife of one of the younger men came in to offer us a drink, and we sat sipping the juice as we waited for the men to assemble.

Once all of their neighbors had come, we began talking about the trading history of Ladakh. They had brought with them family heirlooms such as British colonial passports issued in Chinese Turkistan, and well-worn photographs of traders.

"This is my father, and here is his grandfather . . ." one man explained as he pointed at the picture and began to gesture around the room at his neighbors. "They would all travel and trade together in those times."

As I looked around the room at all of their faces, I thought about the enduring role that Ladakh played in the social lives of traders in Asia. The families of this neighborhood, a vibrant Punjabi community, had come together though their participation in Ladakhi trade. How amazing that more than sixty years after the economic transactions had ended, and in spite of drastic changes in regional politics, this social space created by trading relationships remained.

Identity and trading communities

In this chapter I will examine the ways in which historical trade through Ladakh was related to particular social networks. I am seeking to identify a group of late nineteenth- and early twentieth-century traders in Ladakh called the Arghun community. To do so I will discuss this community in relation to other regionally linked trading communities of the time period, and describe the variety of ways we can define these communities in social and cultural terms, such as kinship, religious, and/or ethnic groups. I have framed this discussion within an assumption that we understand human experience as having both symbolic and political dimensions (as discussed in Cohen 1974b). Viewing the humans as "two-dimensional" in this way allows us to explain how community formation processes can be a vehicle for political and economic interests, while maintaining the significance of symbolic elements of identity. I will argue that in the case of the Arghun community, kinship practices help to both organize and symbolize identity as simultaneously local and non-local in nature.

The Arghuns

In the culturally diverse historical Leh *bazaar* the Arghuns[1] stand out; this is an often invoked, but little examined, identity group involved with a majority of trade through Ladakh with Central Asia. Some ancestors of this Ladakhi community had originally come from Central Asia and other parts of South Asia, and married women in the Ladakhi community. The Arghun community, one of multiple communities of cosmopolitans engaged in trade in Ladakh, defies classic notions of ethnic identification, defined instead by their international kinship and participation in larger socio-economic systems.

The origins of the term "Arghun" are uncertain. In a 1931 publication the explorer George N. Roerich linked usage of the term in Ladakh to the Central Asian name "äkgü-arghun" for Nestorian Christians (Roerich 1931:29). This Nestorian connection is dubious; I have never seen the idea forwarded by any other authors, or an explanation of how the Arghun community of Ladakh would be related. Roerich himself could not provide the answer, writing only that the similarity between the words "is interesting to note" (Roerich 1931:29). Similarly unsubstantiated relationships of origin for the term could be drawn with the Arghan River in the Tarim river basin (Hedin 1940:155), and the Arganglas Mountain, part of the Karakorum Range in Ladakh. This term may even be indicative of pan-Turkic identity, as the word "Arghan" is a part of some modern Turkish names, including the Turkish ambassador in Jordan in 2002, Arghan Ozar. Regardless of the etymology of the term, in this chapter we are concerned with identifying the basis for social cohesion of the Arghun community.

A nineteenth-century British writer defined Arghuns as:

a class of half-castes, mostly the result of the *nikkha* marriages made by Turki merchants with Tibetan women. Having no land, they eke out a subsistence by doing caravan work on the Yarkand road: they are hardy and patient, and I don't think deserve the bad character that some writers give them. I am glad to see that Captain Ramsay in his *Dictionary of Western Tibet* speaks up for them. Though arrant cowards as regards fighting, no one can honestly say they are cowards amidst the great physical difficulties encountered in these regions, and the way they work in the only line open to them is certainly in their favor. Personally, I should class them considerably higher than the pure bred Ladakhi, their manner of life tending to make them more self-reliant.

(Bower 1894)

This author hints at a few common cultural stereotypes about Arghuns during the time period. Though in this passage he raises more questions about the community he attempts to describe, Bower's emphasis on a hybrid community (e.g. "half-castes") is somewhat similar to that found in modern definitions for the Arghun community. In these definitions most authors tend to conceptualize the Arghun community as a mixture of religious groups, of ethnic groups, or as a combination of the two. Religion and ethnicity both provided a basis for definition of social boundaries in historical Ladakhi social life when interwoven, bound together in the kinship networks that formed the fabric of Ladakhi historical trade. Thus in order to understand the Arghun community we must attempt to untangled the surviving narrative threads of this fabric, to examine how the historical traders in Ladakh articulated their own identities in religious, ethnic, and/or kinship-based terms.

Religious communities

Religious communities in the trade networks of late nineteenth- and early twentieth-century Ladakh were the most clearly defined, although not necessarily the most important, of the social groupings in the trade networks. There were a number of religious communities involved in the trade, with the presence of Muslim, Buddhist, Hindu, Sikh and Christian communities located within the overlapping regions of Chinese Turkistan, Ladakh, and North India.

There were numerous Muslim trading communities within the regions of Chinese Turkistan, Ladakh, and Kashmir, and smaller communities of Muslim traders were also located in the Punjab and Tibet (see for example Radhu 1997). There were also features of the trading network that were particularly Islamic. For example, many of the Central Asian Muslim traders and travelers were coming through Ladakh on their way to the Middle East as a part of their pilgrimage to Mecca, called the *Haj*. In 1925 Roerich's party to Yarkend observed several *Haj* groups on the Ladakh route in September, comprised of both men and women from Central Asia (Roerich 1931:42 and 44). This journey could take several years to complete, and was undertaken by some of the most prosperous Central Asian families. These families would combine the religious pilgrimage with business, trading goods as they traveled to support themselves along the way. *Haj* groups coming from Central Asia represented one of the few times that the local women of the area traveled along the trade routes, apart from when women moved to new towns with their families or for marriage. Buddhist communities in the trade networks were primarily based in Ladakh and Tibet, although there were some Buddhist communities in China as well. Many Buddhist traders also combined trade with religious and political concerns. Rizvi writes:

> A peculiar feature of Tibet's trade was that much of it – particularly with other Buddhist countries like Ladakh and Bhutan, also with China – was carried on under the guise of official religious missions.
>
> (Rizvi 1999:10)

In this model of trade, goods often played the role of tribute between powers or tithes to Buddhist monasteries. Buddhist individuals used these missions as opportunities for their own private trade, bringing trade items with them for personal profit. Another Buddhist religious forum associated with trade was the market center at a Tibetan religious function. Kenneth Bauer writes of Tibetan markets:

> For example, at Gartok (in western Tibet), traders from Hindustan, Ladakh, Kashmir, Tartary, Yarkhand [sic], Lhasa, and China proper gathered every summer (cf. Sherring 1906). The markets were often held after a religious function and were accompanied by entertainment and other forms of amusement.
>
> (Bauer 2003:70)

Buddhist religious scholars moving between Tibet and Ladakh were also a part of this system. While Ladakh has a significant Buddhist population, in majority in the Leh region and rural areas, one of the curious features of the Khan Archives is that there are few recognizably Buddhist names of traders in the documents. Most of the Buddhists in these documents were acting as *kiraiyakash*, or transporters, and came from rural villages. Yet there were many Buddhist participants and urban Buddhist families with elite roles in the trade networks; their relative absence in these documents should be ascribed to the fact that the documents primarily deal with the Central Asia routes trade that seemed to be dominated by Muslim Arghuns, rather than Tibet route segments of the trade were Buddhist traders were more common.

The Hindu community in Ladakhi Central Asian trade networks came mostly from the Hoshiarpur and Amritsar towns of the British Indian Punjab. These traders were not traveling for religiously motivated reasons, but primarily for commercial purposes. There is some evidence that the Hindu communities trading in Central Asia were treated differently than other traders on the routes of the region. In 1870 Henderson observed that the few British Indian Hindus who were based in Yarkend were subject to local laws that restricted their style of clothing and modes of transportation (e.g. not being allowed to ride on horseback), as well as requiring that they lived in one particular section of the town and paid higher taxes than the Muslims of the region (Henderson and Hume 1981:139–140). While there is no other proof of most of the former points, interviews with surviving traders indicate that Hindu traders did live separately from the rest of the trading communities. The last point, that the Hindu community paid higher taxes than Muslims of the region, may not be entirely accurate. As discussed in the next chapter, all subjects of British India had to pay higher taxes in Central Asia. Henderson, upon observing the higher taxes, may have assumed that this was a tax on "non-believers", as levied by some Mughal emperors of the past in South Asia.

Understanding the import of religious communities

Would these communities have conceptualized themselves as primarily an Islamic, Buddhist, or Hindu community in the late nineteenth and early twentieth century? Due to the dominance of religious group identity issues in modern political debates in Ladakh, and the modern world in general, expressions of religious community identity may seem most salient. However, if we assume religion, at the expense of the other cultural bases, as a primary motivator for group identities we risk an anachronistic reading of the social relations of the past. Religious difference certainly may have played some role in the social structure of the Ladakh trading networks in the early twentieth century. In 1938 Bahauddin Khan wrote, in response to an enquiry from the British Commissioner about another trader's complaint,

> As regards to S.C.O. I beg to request that his complaint is groundless and is due to the fact that he is Hindu and I am unfortunately a Mohammedan. Your good self will not find in your office any complaint lodged by him against a Hindu trader.

This missive clearly relates that there was some form of tension between Muslim and Hindu traders in Ladakh during that time period, making religious community a salient social category. Although Bahauddin finds this type of religious discrimination unfortunate, he acknowledges its existence. At the same time, there are hints that there may have been other issues being debated in this context. Bahauddin Khan continues in the next sentence to relate that he has worked with this individual and that they did not personally get along with each other. Additionally, he uses a surprising device in the course of this segment of the letter, the word "Mohammedan." While the use of this term may be the outcome of a writer writing in a second language or representative of common early twentieth-century nomenclature, it may also be significant. "Mohammedan," a common British colonial appellation for Muslims, is not a term favored by the Muslim community as it may be construed as misrepresenting the role of the Prophet Mohammed in Islam.[2] This raises the possibility that this letter was crafted to exploit British discourse about religious group identity, which privileged this form of group identity. This type of discourse dominates early twentieth-century British writing; for example British officers in Yarkend explain a fight that occurred in the *bazaar* as a result of Hindu–Muslim tension (Skrine 1973:149) with little analysis of actual motivation and in spite of general accounts of peaceful relations between the communities.

There is other evidence that religion was a salient social group signifier in these trading networks. Religious duties tied in with travel that encouraged trade situations, such as the aforementioned Islamic *Haj* and Buddhist trade missions from Tibet, are prime examples of the historical significance of religious identity based social organization. Religious difference also had social ramifications in the daily interactions of the trade system. Rasool Galwan, working for two traders in 1923, repeatedly referred to those traders as the "Hindus" (Galwan 1923:41–45), communicating that religious identity was a part of identity groupings in the social world of Central Asian traders. Galwan mentions that the Hindu traders would not allow him near their fire, as he was a Muslim (Galwan 1923:45), hinting at religious concepts of purity that shaped social relations in trade relations.

Religious communities were often linked within Ladakhi social groups. Intermarriage between these communities was common, especially in Ladakh between Central Asian and Kashmiri Muslim traders and Ladakhi Buddhist women. These marriages are highly significant, and as will be discussed later, played an important role in defining the Arghun community. They also show that religious identity was not the only source of cohesion for social groups; there were other salient social indicators. At the same time, it is imprecise to call these interfaith marriages; an interfaith marriage is a marriage between two individuals who retain their individual faiths in the marriage. These are actually inter-faith engagements, for in every case documented in Ladakh, the Buddhist woman who married a Muslim trader converted to Islam. Thus these interfaith interactions conformed to social structures based on religious group identity.

Ethnic communities

As the trading networks in late nineteenth- and early twentieth-century Central Asia were comprised of geographically diverse com-munities, most social scientists would consider the most highly visible form of social grouping along the trade routes through Ladakh as "ethnicity", a term popularly employed today to mean a distinct cultural group with its own practices and/or traditions. From an anthropological perspective, ethnicity is generally conceptualized as a non-state-based social group with common interests. Anthropological studies of ethnicity provide the basis for conceptualizing cultural groups within and between nations, although we should not consider them as separate from the nation. As Brackette Williams has pointed out, separating "ethnicity" and the "nation" as concepts ignores the role that nationalist ideologies and agendas can play in ethnic identification, when ethnicity is a label for communities pitted against an unofficially state-backed ideology of whom the "real" nation is com-prised (Williams 1989). Thus the identification of ethnic communities in the historical trading networks of Ladakh has been a task of iden-tifying historical statements of cultural difference that utilize the con-cept of non-state-based group categories, while contextualizing them in possible state-based ideologies of cultural difference. A broad definition of ethnicity has been aided by the expansion of definitions of ethnicity to groups that were not commonly labeled as "ethnic", such as the elite London businessmen of Cohen's study in "Urban Ethnicity" (1974a), described as having taken on ethnic forms with their distinct clothing, language, norms and customs. Yet, as seen below, even such novel descriptive criteria may not be wholly applicable to the Arghun community.

The culturally diverse bazaars of historical Ladakh certainly made an ideal setting for the study of ethnicity. The explorer George Henderson marveled in 1870 that:

> The conversation carried on of an evening round the camp fires was a wonderful mixture of tongues: English, Hindustani, Bengali, Kashmiri, Persian, Turki, and Thibetan. We talked Hindustani

to our followers and Persian to the Yarkendis, who, amongst themselves, talked Turki. By means of an interpreter who spoke Hindustani and Tibetan we communicated with our porters. Some of the men were from Calcutta and talked Bengali to each other, and our Kashmiri followers talked Kashmiri, which is said to be a mixture of all the languages of Asia.

(Henderson and Hume 1981:54)

The mixture of tongues around trading campfire is a warm metaphor for the cultural pluralism of this trading community, and an expression of cultural differences encountered by traders of late nineteenth- and early twentieth-century trading communities, as they sought economic profit in spite of the difficulty of inter-cultural communication. The inter-cultural exchange was not always as benign as Henderson's description. Galwan wrote in 1923:

Now a Chinese man has come in our room to drink water. And what water left in his cup, that he put back in our water-keeping pots. And the Gaffor has told to that Chinese: "You made our all water bad." That Chinese had get angry, and had beat the Gaffor with his hand. Gaffor had hit to Chinese eye".

(Galwan 1923:88)

In this passage we see that cultural misunderstandings arose in daily interactions, as the traders staying together in the *serais* had different concepts of socially acceptable behavior. The cultural differences between communities in the trade networks of Ladakh represent wide gaps in inter-cultural relations and communication, although many of these South and Central Asian traders had a common trading vocabulary fashioned of a mixture of words from several regional languages and dialects.[3]

Differing sources of information on these trade networks give very different ideas about the role of ethnic identity. In the Khan Archives ethnic identity terms such as "Ladakhi" or "Kashmiri" are seldom used. Instead, in order to identify a person after their name, sometimes their place of origin is written with their occupation, such as "Central Asia trader" or "merchant banker of Khotan". In interviews the innumerable cultural backgrounds of the traders were also emphasized; informants listed interactions with Yarkendis, Hors, Tungans, Hoshiarpuris, Kashmiris, Amritsaris, Kazakhs, Afghanis, Pathans, Tibetans, Chinese, Khotanis, Kashgaris, Arghuns, Punjabis, Lalas, Gaddis, and more.

These ethnic groups are difficult to precisely locate in relation to each other, as many of the ethnic terms used by informants are overlapping, non-discrete categories. A Hoshiarpuri is also a Punjabi (Hoshiarpur is a town in the Punjab), some of the Pathans were from what is now called Afghanistan (and thus perhaps Afghanis), Yarkendis are Hors, and Tungans are also Chinese. The reasons for these overlapping of ethnic categories in interviews included 1) multiple levels of description for places of origin, depending on the narrative, 2) the differing claims of historical and modern community identification terms in present day narratives about the past, and 3) the differing levels of interactions with people from other areas in the historical trade systems.

We can clearly see the confusion that arises from these multiple levels of identity discourse in narratives about the past through a discussion of two clusters of terms for ethnic communities involved in Ladakh trade networks; the people of Chinese Central Asia (including the Yarkendis or Hors and the Tungan Chinese), and the people of British Indian Punjab (the Gaddis or Lalas).

Chinese Central Asia: The Turkic "Hor" and Chinese Tungans

Who or what is a "Hor"? The use of the terms "Yarkendi" and "Hor" for people from the same region of Chinese Central Asia by Ladakhis was at first confusing. It seemed that the usages could be ascribed to simple language differences, as one informant explained, "Hor is Yarkendi and Yarkendi is Hor. In our Ladakhi language is called Hor. Like this [in English] is called Yarkendi". Thus according this Ladakhi informant the term "Hor" is simply the Ladakhi word for a person from the Yarkend region. Yet the term "Hor" has also been used to refer, in Ladakhi, to Central Asians in general, as well as being used in British literature to refer to a district in northern Tibet (Roerich 1931:333). Furthermore, the explorer Sven Hedin wrote in the early twentieth century that "Hor" is a general word for people of Turkic origins in Tibet, with its historical roots in Tibetan annals of about the eighth or ninth century, where the word Hor or "Jya-Hor" designates tribes from Mongol or Central Asian origin (Roerich 1931:335). Thus the term "Hor" may refer to older regional conceptualizations of ethnic group identity, and indeed was often used by informants to refer to the ethnic heritage of an individual, rather than where they were from.

Yarkendi, in contrast, was often used when referring to the national or regional origins of a people, grounded in a particular locale. For example, when asked what type of people live in Yarkend and

Kashgar, one informant answered, "Hors, Muslims . . . only Hors . . . and some Chinese."

This answer points to a conceptualization of a Hor identity that spanned across the two major trading cities of Chinese Central Asia. One older woman, a widow who had been married to a trader from Yarkend, confirmed this view of the difference between a "Hor" and a "Yarkendi" by explaining, "Hor is the name of people. Hor is not the name of country."

This quote again proclaims the difference between Hor as a social category for people, or an ethnic group identity, and Yarkendi as a designation for a person's geographic origins. This view is furthered by the fact that when asked who Yarkendis (thus literally people who lived in Yarkend) were, a few informants answered they were Kazakhs, referring to another ethnic group that was also present in that region.

There is also confusion in the accounts of present day Ladakh about the ethnic groups that came from Chinese Central Asia, due to the limited understanding of cultural diversity in the region. Like the Kazakhs mentioned above, Tungans are often confused with Hors since they are also called Yarkendis, as people living in Yarkend. One man explained:

[The people of Yarkend were] Tungan. So many Tungans came here.

How were they, what were Tungans?
Tungans, Hor, Kazakh . . . Kazakh . . . Kazakh. Kazakh, Tungan . . . The Tungans were Yarkendis . . . Yarkendis, they ran away and came. Then Hindustan took them there.

Why did they run away and come?
Don't know, God knows why they ran. Why they came here I don't have anything to tell.

This man, dimly remembering historical events that surrounded the Tungan community, could not sort out the place of Tungans within past cultural and historical settings. Yet another older man who had participated in more of the Central Asian trade remembered clearly that the Tungans were Chinese Muslims, who lived in Central Asia, as well as why the Tungans were at the heart of a key political struggle between Chinese and Central Asian armies. These ethnic differences may have been important in the trade networks of the late nineteenth and early twentieth century, but are considered relevant in limited ways in Ladakh today.

British Indian Punjab: Lalas and Gaddis

The trading communities from British India most commonly found in the trade networks of Ladakh were from the Punjabi cities of Amritsar and Hoshiarpur, such as the community mentioned in the beginning of this chapter. These trading communities were specifically Hindu in contrast to the majority Muslim and small Sikh and Buddhist communities engaged in trade through Ladakh to Central Asia. In the Khan Archive documents, these communities play a key role in the economic structures of the trading system, providing links to the European markets through the rest of India. While most informants in interviews were quick to specify that these traders came from Amritsar or Hoshiarpur, few referred to them by their region of origin. Instead, it was common to discuss them as "Lalas".

The term "Lala" is seen historically in trade documents, and often was incorporated into the names of people from that community. This results in referring to historical traders as "Lala" sometimes as their name, and sometimes to designate their belonging to the community. One informant referred to an individual named Shadi Lala by talking about both "Shadi Lala" and "*Lala*", provoking the question "Shadi Lala is one Lala or are all the Lalas called Shadi Lala?" He answered:

> No. Only one Lala was Shadi Lala. His shop was also in Kargil, now not in Kargil. It is said in Leh now still. In Leh Shadi Lala was a very big Lala of that time. That time their loads were carried.

The Lala community was not limited to Punjabi traders who lived in Ladakh and traded with Central Asia. A Kargili merchant mused, "These Lalas are old . . . Yarkend . . . These Lalas were also going to Yarkend. Coming here and were going there. Businessmen like Lala Shadilal, Lala Lahorimal, were very big traders of old times."

Lalas located in Yarkend and Kashgar were sometimes referred to as "Gaddis", a much less commonly used term in Ladakh today, which caused some confusion in interviews. Once, an informant commented, "There were so many Gaddis, hundred . . . two hundred, then the Gaddis reduced in number."

We then answered, "*The gardis [cars] were the same like we drive nowadays?*" This statement provoked general confusion, until we asked, "*What is 'Gaddis'?*"

The man then answered, "Gaddis are Lalas. Hindus. They went from here, Hoshiarpur, for trade."

Thus in addition to having their origins in the Punjab, one criterion for defining this group was also their religious beliefs.

The term "gaddis" may have also had a more general application than simply that for traders of Punjabi origin. At another point in the interview the same trader mentioned:

> There were hundreds, two hundreds of gaddis from Ladakh living there [in Chinese Central Asia]. Gaddis like Lala Ratan Chand, father of Madan. Bihari Lal, so many were coming for trade. There were very big *serais*. The *serai* of Godiya Chand, the *serai* of Ram Shankar. Very nice.

This statement, with its reference to the name of one trader, "Bihari Lal", raises the issue that some of these traders may have been from other parts of British India, as the practice of naming individuals after the region they came from, in this case Bihar, was common during this time period.

Arghun as ethnic identity

Thus although the 1941 Census of Jammu and Kashmir lists Arghuns as one of the seven castes and tribes of Ladakh with other ethnic groups of the region, such as the Brok-pa, I would argue that there are also strong reasons for questioning the categorization of "Arghun" as an ethnic identity when we consider the types of questions raised in relation to usage of so-called ethnic terms such as "Hor" and "Lala".

This is evident in a list written by Captain Hamilton Bower, a nineteenth-century British Indian army intelligence officer, of the members of his Tibetan expedition that included a British Indian Medical Service officer, a "native" sub-surveyor, a Pathan orderly, a "Hindustani cook", a Kashmiri, and "six Argoon caravan drivers" (Bower 1894:9). This list highlights disparities in the types of identities that were, and are, commonly used as descriptive terms for individuals or communities. Listing an officer as "British Indian" emphasizes the political identity of that individual, while the cook is simply an ethnic "Hindustani". Both the Pathan and Kashmiri of the party seem to be designated as ethnic group members; however these terms might have also been functional for British readers in the late nineteenth century, as a "Sherpa" might be invoked in mountaineer's literature today to refer to a porter. The sub-surveyor's only designation is that he is "native", i.e. not British, raising questions about the colonial differentiation between the roles of "Hindustanis", "natives", and

"British Indians". Thus we cannot assume that Arghun, or "Argoon" here, is simply an ethnic category; it may have been a functional, social, or political label as well.

Other labels existed in British discussions of Central Asian identity. Rasool Galwan, the Ladakhi trader who published an English account of his work in 1923, was an Arghun, although he never self-identifies himself as an Arghun or part of the Arghun community. Instead Arghun was a socially constructed category, which was reflected in conversation surrounding his work and daily life. Thus in his book Galwan relates being called an Arghun by others, such as the time when a Yarkendi man in Chinese Central Asia told him at one point, "among the Arghuns you are a good-luck boy" (Galwan 1923:39). Here we see that Arghun was an identity recognized by many different groups of people in the trade system. At the same time, this realization is complicated by the fact that Galwan also discusses members of the community called Arghun as "Ladakhis" in other sections of his book (Galwan 1923:27 and 95).

Scholars working in Ladakh today emphasize Arghun identity from a variety of perspectives. Rizvi dates the Arghun community's origins to the time of the Ladakhi kings in the early nineteenth century, before conquest by the Dogra regime, as an integral part of the *pashmina* trade, acting as agents called *khar-tsong* (court merchants) who were largely Arghuns (Rizvi 1999:51). In Rizvi's account Arghuns are descended both from Central Asian and Kashmiri traders who married locally in Ladakh. Ravina Aggarwal, an anthropologist who works in Ladakh, writes that Arghuns are literally mixed races or mixed religions and cultures, explaining:

> More specifically, Argon is the ethnic name for the Sunni Muslims, who are believed to be the progeny of migrants and traders from Kashmir and the Central Asian areas of Khotan and Yarkand.
> (Aggarwal 1995)

This quote outlines the popular use of the term Arghun in Ladakh today, linking religious identity and ethnic heritage. Both of these accounts emphasize the meeting of different groups of people as central to Arghun identity.

This theme was further emphasized in the course of my research when the term Arghun was often used by informants to denote certain ethnic boundaries in both the past and the present. A person of Central Asian descendent, whose father was considered "Yarkendi" ethnically and his mother "Ladakhi" was called Arghun. Another informant was a "Yarkendi" married to a Ladakhi Arghun, whose father was "Kashmiri" and mother "Ladakhi"; such a person could also be defined as Arghun, but also as Ladakhi. Repeatedly in family histories from the Arghun community, we see an emphasis on the hybrid nature of the community. From such descriptions, I would describe the basis of the Arghun community to be much more closely intertwined with the idea of a cosmopolitan identity, discussed in detail in the next chapter, than a classic ethnic identification. Part of what defined the Arghun community was their international kinship and participation in larger socio-economic systems.

Therefore, to understand the Arghun community, we must focus on kinship groups, illuminating Arghun identity in formation, rather than as a static ideal ethnic designation. The role of kinship as a social signifier for Arghun group organization, in contrast with that of both religious and ethnic identity, shows partially how this cosmopolitan social group can be perceived simultaneously as both a local and non-local identity.

International kinship groupings

In the late nineteenth and early twentieth century, South Asian merchant communities were often formulated through lineage alliances. The roles of the family, and kin group in general, were particularly central to social organization of trade networks, as Claude Markovits comments, "virtually all merchant firms were family firms or 'partnerships' between two families of the same caste, often related by marriage" (Markovits 2000b:310–311). Markovits also notes that a study of trading firms in the late eighteenth century reveals similar features, and that "the identity of the family and that of the firm was synonymous to such an extent that there was no specific term for the latter" (Markovits 2000b:310–311). While Rizvi has commented that Ladakhi caravan men formed a "more amorphous community" than their counterparts in British Indian trading communities, which had "particular caste-based communities – Vaishyas, Jains, Agarwals, Mahajans, Khattris, Gosains . . ." (Rizvi 1999:16), there are still a number of structural similarities observable by focusing on the role of the family and identity of kin groups within Ladakhi trading networks. Furthermore, marriage strategies employed by Ladakhi Arghun traders places their community within a broader tradition of trading diasporas, as kinship networks are common in other interregional trade networks as well (see for example Engseng Ho's work on Hadrami Arab traders in *The Graves of Tarim*, 2006).

The kinship patterns of Ladakhi trade participants points to a distinction between social groups within the Ladakh trading communities, between the temporary participants with limited roles, such as the *kiraiyakash*, and the more wealthy merchants and trade middlemen. Although both groups utilized kin groups as a particular strategy in trading interactions, they did so differently. The kinship structures of *kiraiyakash* families were central to their participation in the trade as their participation was intimately linked to household functions, such as providing food and livestock to traders traveling through their village, as will be discussed in the next chapter.

In contrast, the merchants and trade middlemen participated in kinship systems that created kin group bonds that spanned religious, regional and national boundaries. In these international trading communities kinship networks were not simply a tool used in response to trading situations, but a strategy to increase trading opportunities for the family structure. Bahauddin Khan, the trader of the Khan Archives, had originally come from Central Asia to Ladakh with his father, and was later stationed in Ladakh to establish family business there as a trade middleman. Like most traders who would eventually be called the Arghun community, he married a woman in the Ladakhi community, and established a local household. Many Central Asian families in this trading network had similar families across regional and national boundaries, with sons in areas now in India, China, and Pakistan; this was particularly common among the elite of the trading communities. The end result was networks of family members that did business with each other across regional and national boundaries. This created situations such as that of an *aqsaqual* (elite trade official) stationed in Yarkend in 1931, whose ". . . eldest brother was *aqsaqual* in Kashgar, another was *aqsaqual* in Leh, and a third was at the head of a big trading establishment in distant Lhasa" (Roerich 1931:86).

When viewed over time, this kinship strategy would seem to be focused on a goal of assuring that one would have sons who were native to the trading areas and spoke the language of the region; however it was not limited to the establishment of vertical descent groups. During the nineteenth and early twentieth centuries, marriage in most parts of the world, including South and Central Asia, was a social and legal contract between two families rather than two people. Thus traders who married women in local areas married into local families, solidifying social relations with the fathers, uncles, and brothers of their spouses. International families like the Khans, Khwojas, and Shahs had close relations in towns throughout the region, such as Leh, Srinagar, Yarkend, Khotan, and

Lahore. Their kin connections were the basis of a complex web of social networks, which contributed to their political power and economic strength. These kinship networks were such a basic foundation of the trading network that one elderly man who traded in Central Asia in the past, when asked if he had socialized with the Punjabi traders while based in Yarkend answered:

> Why would we meet? In Yarkend there were so many people who were British subjects. Lots of Ladakhis were there . . . Sheikhs from Nubra, people from Nubra, Baltistanis were settled there. Very nice. The Khwojas were there . . . [and] their wives. They became traders. Their houses were in Kashmiri Kocha. Their gardens were everywhere.

This trader, beginning his explanation of the social circles they associated with in Yarkend, begins with an explanation based on political identities, then frames the interactions in ethnic terms, and finally slips into explaining the social groupings in terms of families and households. While neighborhoods, like the *Kashmiri Kocha* that were quarters for Kashmiri traders, may have been organized along ethnic lines, social interactions were organized within kin groups.

Marriages between Central Asian and Kashmiri Muslim traders and Ladakhi Buddhist (and later Christian) women united families across religious and ethnic groups. The social implications of these marriages have a great deal to offer to future anthropological studies when we consider, for example, the possible religious implications of a Muslim community formed by families of such diverse cultural backgrounds and comprised of female members with diverse religious backgrounds.

In spite of the positive economic and political outcomes of these intercultural marriages some kin groups engaged in trade in Ladakh did not espouse this method. There were some limits to the kinship extensions of these trading networks, as informants never mentioned historical incidences of marriages between Muslim and Hindu segments of the trading communities, or even of Punjabi and Central Asian participants. The Punjabi traders, based in Amritsar and Hoshiarpur, seem separate from other trading families within this network. The geographic limitations of this study, however, may have contributed to this view of the separate kinship systems of Punjabi traders. All of the Muslim traders in the Punjab no longer had descendents living in India as most had emigrated from India during Partition. Informants in Amritsar remembered a few Central Asian traders who lived there before and there may have been some intermarriage within this community. The Punjabi traders engaged in trade with or through Ladakh certainly were involved in their own kinship group based networks. Many of the present day families in the region continue to have business associations in Ladakh, which have been passed down from father to son. Furthermore, the Punjabi firms of Amritsar and Hoshiarpur exhibit some horizontal kin affiliations, with multiple related households being engaged with the trade in Ladakh.

Differences in the structures of Punjabi trading ventures compared to those of comparable Ladakhi, Kashmiri, and Central Asian firms may also have played a role in these different kinship patterns, as many Punjabi traders and trading firms used the services of employees for travel to Ladakh and Central Asia. These employees were agents for family firms from Amritsar and Hoshiarpur who would often temporarily be stationed in Ladakh and Central Asia. One descendent of an owner of an Amritsari firm explained:

> My father never went to Leh. Even though he was doing this business, we had a, *munim* you call it, a man who visited Leh. A clerk. He [the employee] used to go after every two months. My father never visited to Leh. He went up to Srinagar only. To collect [money].

This informant also mentioned that although his grandfather also traded in Ladakh, he never went to Leh either. This changed in the mid-twentieth century, as some of their employees reportedly started up their own family firms for trade, and the descendents of Punjabi traders began to conduct their own business directly in Ladakh.

The political borders between Central Asia and British South Asia in the nineteenth and early twentieth centuries may have played an important role in limiting the kinship interactions between these communities. The boundaries of this community were tightly controlled, represented by the presence of a British consular post in Kashgar, and general political control expressed in the documents over trade between British subjects and surrounding areas. These political tools for controlling involvement in trade may have acted to formalize British Indian trading networks to such a degree that only professionals, such as the agents of firms, were able to navigate the legal obstacles.

Relationships between these separate kin groups did, however, help shape trade networks between Ladakh and the Punjab. The same informant who mentioned that his father and grandfather never went to Ladakh explained that at the same time:

> [Ladakhi] customers used to go there to Amritsar. There [they had few] goods, they were farmers, they had very good faith on our elders like my grandfather and my father, they had a very good reputation. They have a lot of faith in us. We used to bring money and deposit it here and whatever they wanted we would send them.

Other informants in Amritsar mentioned that at the time of partition the trade relationships between their fathers and other traders meant that they aided the traders and their families when fleeing to Pakistan or in the case of a few Yarkendi traders when immigrating to Turkey as discussed in the next chapter. Thus family firms in British India trading in or through Ladakh did have business that was conducted along kinship group alliance terms.

Arghun identity

While religion and ethnicity could both be viewed as possible bases for the types of social networks found in trade through Ladakh, neither seems to define the types of social networks associated with trade. Religious identity is present in the structure of trade, as well as written discourse of traders, as religious travel duties increased opportunities for trade, such as the Islamic *Haj* and Buddhist trade missions from Tibet. Religious identity is central to modern discourse about Ladakhi identity, however in these historical cases we have seen that religious intermarriage and trade between religious communities made traders from diverse religious backgrounds part of the identity groups.

The concept of ethnicity as a basis for social networks of traders is also not wholly applicable; in the historical documents, ethnic identity terms are seldom used and when they are it is as overlapping, non-discrete categories such as in the Yarkendis-Hors-Tungan and Punjabi-Gaddi-Lalas examples. While identity terms were used to locate individuals within particular interactions (e.g. in relation to colonial officials or other travelers) in a manner reminiscent of Cohen's situationalist descriptions of ethnicity (Cohen 1974b), ethnic terms were not the only type of identity groupings used for this purpose. Overall the historical data does not convey a strong notion of ethnic community as the primary identity grouping for traders working in Ladakh.

Thus while both religion and ethnicity were socially salient identity groups in Ladakh, historical communities of traders were formed, and reinforced, primarily through kinship networks that crossed ethnic and religious boundaries. The Arghun identity group as a whole was historically formulated by participants through these networks of international kinship, which was reinforced through the interactions with economic and political structures of the Central/South Asian trading system. These political and economic interactions are presented in further detail in the following chapters.

4 Social strategies for profit

Ethnographic present: The Kiraiyakash's village

On the way back from a trip to Kargil, we stopped in a small village to find a *kiraiyakash*, a transporter of trade goods, whose name and thumbprint we had found on an old receipt. As soon as we stepped out of the jeep we were surrounded by curious children of all ages, as in many of the other small towns we visited. We asked one of the children where the nearest house was, but before we could set out over the empty fields, a man came up and asked us who we were looking for. *"Someone who worked as a kiraiyakash in the old times, named Tsering Tashi,"* we answered, *"or his family members."* The man shrugged and called over others who were working in the fields. After a few minutes of conversation amongst themselves, one man separated from the group and approached us. "My father's name was Tsering Tashi," he stated carefully. Our conversation began.

Both the man and his father had worked as *kiraiyakash*, and after we explained why we were there, he agreed to answer a few questions. We settled in a small cleared area next to where the jeep was parked, and a number of other men joined their friend to discuss their memories of trade. Children gathered around curiously to listen, and we began the interview right there on the side of the road. "Being a *kiraiyakash*," the man began, "means the taking of goods of *Lalas* on horses and *dzo* to Ladakh." He continued to explain that residents of their town would transport goods from one local area to the next, where they would then be transferred to other villagers for the next segment of travel between Leh and Srinagar. The *kiraiyakash* recalled, ". . . at that time a horse's charge was only rupees five or six from Kargil to Leh."

"Only five?"

"Yes, only five rupees. At that time money had good value. If we bought one rupee of barley, with one rupee we got one *khal* [about

Figure 4.1 In another village outside of Kargil, children surround the elders discussing their work as *kiraiyakash* in historical trade systems. Kargil area, 2001.

twenty-two pounds] and five *bo* [another 2.2 pounds, in a different measure].[1] If we bought rice we got eight *seers*. Money had that much value."

He paused, and then began explaining how the *kiraiyakash* could profit in other ways, by bringing local products with them to trade while they carried the goods for merchants. "We brought their wool . . . and we also took barley from here, and brought it to Sakti. And from there we bought salt from the Chang-pas. When we gave one *bo* of barley to them, they gave us two or three *bos* of salt. We did that much trade. Why at that time were we *kiraiyakash*? Because at that time there was no vehicle for transportation, at that time we used horses."

"Why did all the people of this village work as kiraiyakash?"

"What else could we do then?" he said, as we all looked around at the small houses scattered throughout the fields. "There was no contractor work, and no government jobs . . . those who had horses were *kiraiyakash*."

After talking about the work and profits of trade for some time, the man gestured towards an area away from the road, and began talking about the Yarkendi visitors who came in caravans. "There was a stop, they stayed here. . . . Over there," he repeated as he pointed again across the field. "Now they destroyed the building and built a government office there."

"What were the people of Yarkend like?"

"Yarkendis were very strong-built men with red cheeks. Their horses were very big, very strong, and each horse had their own saddle. Even their donkeys were very big – the loads carried by their donkeys were equal to the loads carried by our horses. The clothes of Yarkendis were very warm. Their pants were very warm; they put cotton inside between the two layers. They had special kinds of robes, very warm, with tall collars ... They were very nice people, they came from far-flung areas. [They would do] whatever we told them – to give the goods like this, cheap, or whatever. They used the words like "*samar karkenbarasma*" for "give hay". If they wanted wood, they told "*otan karkenbau*" or "*otan baraidaio*". For water they used "*shu*", for pot "*kazangs*", for bread they used "*nan*". "*Nan beradaima*", "*bermadaidai*" – if they asked for bread then they used these words. "*Kerkan*", for *tsampa* [barley flour]."

We didn't know any Uighur ourselves, so it was hard to judge the accuracy of the terms. But we were impressed with his ability to recall these terms so confidently over sixty years later, and asked, *"Do you know any Yarkendis?"*

"No, how could I know them? I was only eight years old at that time. After that they didn't come. After that Yarkend was destroyed ... [But, back when they came] they had everything with them. If we asked them for gold, they had even gold with them." At this the farmer looked at us and made a gesture as if he was pulling handfuls of gold out of his pockets. He then smiled and showed empty hands, "Their gold was not like ours."

Trade networks

In the last chapter, social groups associated with the trading networks of Ladakh were discussed in socio-cultural terms, recognizing the Arghun community as a kinship-based social grouping, with little attention paid to the particular economic structures of the trading system that necessitated such an approach. While there was profit to be made with sporadic participation in regional trade networks in Ladakh, the political and geographic features of the system made substantial economic gain possible only for traders with widespread contacts, who were connected to a broad system of participants. This is best understood through examination of the economic implications of Ladakhi traders' social networks, with particular attention to statuses and roles within the trading networks. The information in this chapter shows that while the cultural significance of particular social roles varied from place to place within the trade system, many social features of this system were in response to specific economic pressures and thus existed in multiple cultural settings.

Rizvi has argued that the traders of Ladakh were not "locals made good," that in other parts of South Asian trade networks local people working as middlemen raised their standard of living, but in Ladakh there was a divide between subsistence traders who made their living and the caravan class who were the elite (Rizvi 1999:17). While this may have been true on the Tibetan route (especially with the *pashmina* trade) and in earlier times, the historical data associated with the Central Asian and South Asian routes through Ladakh offer evidence for the existence of a variety of social roles in the economic interactions, including the creation of a local middlemen group. The trade system functioned through the use of multiple types of currency, communication facilities, transport methods, and taxation systems; these complexities necessitated labor specialization and social strategies for profit.

Types of currency

As the traders based in Ladakh were geographically poised between two major economic powers of the nineteenth century, China and the British Empire, there was a great deal of variation in the types of currency used. The British Indian currency of *rupees, annas* (one sixteenth of a *rupee*), and *paisa* (one quarter of an *anna*) were commonly used in Jammu and Kashmir in the nineteenth century, and a common form of currency for trade in Ladakh. This linked Ladakh's trade to a number of other nineteenth-century economies, as Indian *rupees* were used across mainland Asia, as well as the British colonies of Somaliland, Ceylon, Mauritius and the Seychelles Islands (Clauson 1944). Trade documents show that the British Indian Punjabi and Kashmiri traders in Ladakh used this currency, whether in the form of an actual payment or as units for credits to traders' accounts.

The Central Asian traders in the Ladakh system used a wider variety of currency forms. Some Central Asian traders would maintain credit accounts with Ladakhi or Punjabi traders in rupees, while others used bank drafts, Chinese government-backed currencies, or promissory notes drawn on Chinese banks. These were not very popular with traders by the 1920s, however, as political upheaval in Chinese Central Asia led many to question the stability of regional financial institutions and government administration. One trading family recalled, for example, that their grandfather found the currency he had received was no longer legal tender; years later the family burned large stacks of this currency that had languished in their storeroom for decades. According to interviews, many Central Asian traders relied on gold as a form of payment to villagers who gave them food and shelter. In addition to having a value that was independent from uncertain political and financial backings, gold may have been popular because many of those traders were on their way to Mecca to go on *Haj*, and planned travel through a number of countries with differing currencies. A final currency in use in the Ladakh trading networks, the Mexican dollar, was popular in Central Asia due to the purity of the silver.

Communications and transport

There are four distinct categories of economic transactions when capital was exchanged in the historical Ladakh trading networks: the buying, transport, customs taxation, and selling of merchandise. As buying, transport, and selling of merchandise are all standard economic features of a trade system, I will briefly discuss features of these interactions specific to this system; their cultural significance will receive further attention in the next chapter. The role of customs taxes in this economic system demands more particular attention, however, as they provided an economic niche for the development of elite trade middlemen in Ladakh's trading networks, a community that most clearly emphasizes the relationship between profit and social networks.

Both the buying and wholesale selling of merchandise were business transactions conducted in highly formal business settings between professional traders. Ladakhi traders formed long term business connections with traders of other regions and in through these relationships, with the help of a network of communications, standardized market values for common commodities between different regions. Most of this communication in the late nineteenth and early twentieth centuries was conducted by telegraph. Ladakh obtained access to many local communication facilities earlier than other rural areas in Himalayan Central and South Asia. Official government post offices, telegraph offices, and later telephones all played an important role in the communications of traders involved with inter-regional trade in Ladakh, although the telephone was not an instrument of general usage until after independence in India.

The Imperial Post Office first opened in Leh on June 1st, 1875, though it ran on an experimental basis until January 1st, 1876; a permanent

Towns	Facilities
Sonamarg	Post office and telegraph office
Dras	Post office and telegraph office
Kargil	Post office and telegraph office
Leh	Post office and telegraph office
Skardo	Post office and telegraph office
Kagan	Post office
Khaltse	Post office and telegraph office
Terkati	Post office
Malshaibagh	Post office and telegraph office
Tolti	Post office
Shigar	Post office
Khalapu	Post office

Figure 4.2 Table of early twentieth-century communications facilities.

facility was then opened in August 1876.[2] The post office was open throughout the year, with regular runners only in the summer time. At other times of the year mail delivery service was dependent on weather conditions.

The telegraph came to the Dras–Skardo area in 1882; many traders working in the Ladakh region were familiar with the capabilities of this communications system by the time the Kargil–Leh line and Leh telegraph office were opened in 1900–01. Telegraphic communication became a key way for traders in Ladakh to maintain business with other regions in a timely fashion. Traders buying wool in Chinese Central Asia were able to check the wool resale rates in British South Asia before deciding on purchasing prices, and wholesale merchandisers from British India kept informed about the general prices of their goods in Central Asian markets.

In 1932 the highest ranking Jammu and Kashmir government representative in Ladakh, the *Wazir-i-wazarat*, requested the construction of telephone lines to Leh because of "certain mischief-mongers at Leh" (Chohan 1994:74). He expressed a belief that telephone communication would enable him to keep in daily touch with the town when he was in other areas and quickly address any problems. At this time the Superintendent of Telegraphs of Jammu and Kashmir denied the request, citing expense, however in 1932–33 the Maharaja of Jammu and Kashmir gave leave for installation of "special telephones" in Kargil, Skardo and Leh, in response to political unrest in the region. These facilities were solely for official administrative use and there is no record of telephone communication by traders in Ladakh before Indian Independence.

While news could come quickly through telegraph, goods and traders traveled slowly over the difficult mountain terrain to reach Ladakh. The shipment of goods from South Asia to Central Asia (or vice versa) was a long process that involved a number of transporters, which resulted in high transit costs. Whether the transporters were local villagers in the role of *kiraiyakash* or professional long distance porters such as the caravan men in Rasool Galwan's autobiography (Galwan 1923), the transporters of goods through Ladakh had to be well informed concerning regional conditions, and familiar with the terrain. Landslides, sudden snowstorms, and bandits were just a few of the hazards faced by those transporting goods through Ladakh.

The terms of transport arrangements were formalized with the issue of a transport agreement receipt, a *challan*, which was usually filled in triplicate so the sender of goods, transporter, and receiver all had copies.

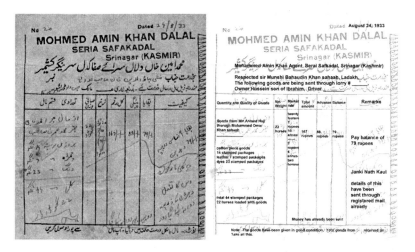

Figure 4.3 Example of a *challan*, original on left and original with translation overlay on right.

The *serai*, an inn and storage place for goods, was the economic and social center of traders in North Indian and Central Asian trading towns. In the early twentieth century there were three *serais* in Leh; all have now been demolished. Many Ladakhis remember *serais* in Leh and recounted that the main *serai* had rooms with attached kitchens on the second floor for traders. Stables below on the first floor housed horses and other pack animals, with a separate yard for camels. In the central *serai* courtyard, where the traders would keep all their goods, there was a prayer platform. Large gates guarded the entrances as the goods stored within were valuable.

Serais were not simply hotels; they functioned as trading areas, transport centers and taxing posts. European explorer De Bourbel (1897) noted that *serais* were exclusively for local traders and merchants; British and other European travelers would stay at the *dak* bungalow, government guesthouses that were constructed and maintained at regular intervals on routes such as those through Ladakh. The *dak* bungalows

Figure 4.4 The Munshi Aziz Bhat *serai* in Kargil, still standing, exhibits similar features with traders' rooms on the top floor and stables on the ground floor. Photograph by Abdul Nasir Khan.

along major routes, especially the Srinagar–Leh road, were staffed in the summer months to facilitate the movement of colonial government officials and their guests in the area. On the route between Sonamarg (Kashmir) and Leh (Ladakh) there were 32 *dak* stages so that official travelers had regular rest and facilities (Chohan 1994 and Neve 1918). These were in addition to several other types of structures built to support government administration. The *dak* bungalows were supported by the postal system as well. Postal runners would stop at each of the *dak* stages on the route between Leh and Kashmir, using the facilities and offering postal services to travelers.

Customs taxes

Many of the British administrative affairs in Ladakh, as well as those of the Jammu and Kashmir government, were concerned with the taxation of goods coming from and going to Central Asia. Historical account books from Ladakh indicate the role of taxation on international goods was far more complex and integral to the economics of the overall system than previously realized by scholars studying trade in Jammu and Kashmir in general and Ladakh in particular. This feature of economic structures in the trans-regional trade system necessitated the formation of specialized trade professionals with many social and political contacts in the region.

The 1870 trade treaty between British India and the Government of Jammu and Kashmir that designated the trade routes to Central Asia through Ladakh a free trade zone meant that any goods traveling from Central Asia to British South Asia, or vice versa, were exempt from customs taxes if the goods were sold outside Jammu and Kashmir. Goods designated for travel through the region without sale in local areas were sealed with a wax seal or stamp of a company to prohibit tampering with their contents. These are referred to as "stamped packages" in transport agreements such as the example shown earlier. When traders, or their agents, brought these sealed goods into Jammu and Kashmir they had to pay the designated customs tariff for their goods. The contents and value of each shipment were assessed and documented, then customs officials demanded payment based either on a rate per unit or a percentage of value. Customs officials located in large *serais*; inspectors from Jammu and Kashmir Customs and Excise offices and the resident British customs official there oversaw inspection and documentation. *Charas*, a *cannabis* substance traded along the Ladakh route, also needed to be inspected and documented by a special *Charas* officer, who regulated *charas* duties and enforced regulations for the

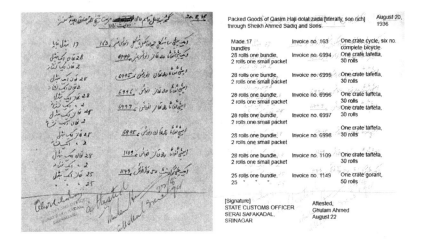

The following is the translation overlay text from the right side of the figure:

Packed Goods of Qasim Haji dolat zada [literally, son rich] through Sheikh Ahmed Sadiq and Sons.   August 20, 1936

Made. 17 bundles	Invoice no. 163	One crate cycle, six no. complete bicycle
28 rolls one bundle, 2 rolls one small packet	Invoice no. 6994	One crate tafetta, 30 rolls
28 rolls one bundle, 2 rolls one small packet	Invoice no. 6995	One crate tafetta, 30 rolls
28 rolls one bundle, 2 rolls one small packet	Invoice no. 6996	One crate taffeta, 30 rolls
28 rolls one bundle, 2 rolls one small packet	Invoice no. 6997	One crate tafetta, 30 rolls
28 rolls one bundle, 2 rolls one small packet	Invoice no. 6998	One crate tafetta, 30 rolls
28 rolls one bundle, 2 rolls one small packet	Invoice no. 1109	One crate tafetta, 30 rolls
25 rolls one bundle, 25	Invoice no. 1149	One crate gorant, 50 rolls

[Signature]
STATE CUSTOMS OFFICER
SERAI SAFAKADAL,
SRINAGAR

Attested,
Ghulam Ahmed
August 22

Figure 4.5 Invoice with Custom Officer's Stamp, original on left and original with translation overlay on right.

transport of this drug. Customs officials would oversee these transfers of money, as well as check the accounts of involved businesses.

Once the goods reached the customs check-post at their point of departure from Jammu and Kashmir, these documents were produced to prove all the goods were still in transit and show how much had been paid previously so that the full amount could be refunded. The British Joint Commissioner in Leh would provide customs insurance forms that could then be cashed by the traders to regain money they had paid earlier when bringing the goods into Jammu and Kashmir.

One informant who had worked as a trader remembered this system in terms of the goods themselves, as each type of good had a customs rate. He reminisced:

Malmal, mostly malmal. Malmal and silk. What's that called? . . . [Muttering to himself] . . . Chinese silk. [Long pause] Shanghai, yes . . . Shanghai. At that time called *Shingqalan*. That cloth was called *Shingqazam*. That Chinese cloth was very famous in Turkistan. And that was customs free. In Srinagar it had a customs cost, and in Ladakh when it reached to customs there was a refund. The customs money. And from there, it went to Yarkend. And from Yarkend *charas* came. *Charas* and silk. And in Leh they took customs of *charas* and that time when it reached to Kak Sarai [in Srinagar] the customs was refunded.

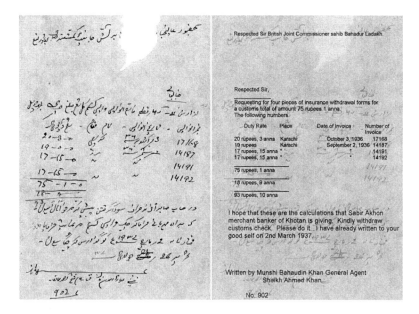

Figure 4.6 Request for withdrawal forms, original on left and original with translation overlay on right.

Today, traders' descendents who are based in Ladakh are much more aware of the system of customs during the late nineteenth and early twentieth century than those whose families were based in Kashmir. When asked about the customs systems of the past, one descendent of a Kashmiri trading family answered:

> I think in old times there were no customs. I didn't hear about those customs. But it was told that people went to Punjab from here for labor work, or Shimla, Jammu, etc. Coming back after working there so [perhaps] they told that we cleared the customs or paid the customs. So we don't know what customs are. Then after, slowly we knew that customs is collected at posts where according to the goods and they knew at that time no customs system.

Current variation in awareness of this historical system hints at a high degree of specialization in the trade industry in relation to customs taxes. According to document evidence the customs tariff arrangements provided employment for countless British and Kashmiri customs officials, as well as trade middlemen that specialized in working with customs invoices, insurance forms, and refunds.

Specialization in dealing with the customs forms and invoices for reimbursement is often termed in the trader's papers as the "buying and selling" of invoices. This system was a lucrative parallel economy in the historical trade systems of Ladakh. There are a series of letters from 1937 in the Khan Archives that clearly illustrate the need for social and political connections for trade middlemen to proceed smoothly through the system of reimbursing customs invoices for the tax refund. In one trade document from March 1937, a trader wrote, "[w]ith the sudden death of the customs officer we have a great loss, because all our payments were hindered." In a series of ongoing correspondence, the death of this customs officer continued to complicate customs refunds for the traders throughout the month. Later in the month the same author writes that his firm hopes that the transfer of invoices has gone smoothly, and that they expect extra expenditure. A month later the same writer, commenting that the invoices surely must have been taken care of by now, bemoans the fact that "the transfer of invoices has become very difficult." Thus we see that the death or removal from post of just one officer could cause at least a two month delay in regaining trade profits, a serious problem for any small trading firm that needed to maintain an even flow of capital. This indicates that receiving customs invoice reimbursements was a highly bureaucratic process, facilitated primarily by personal relationships between traders and officials. Perhaps this is why the same author of these documents, in spite of the difficulties associated with reimbursements from customs officials, writes:

> So, please send us detailed information about what sort of expenditure is required in addition to previous expenditure done for these invoices and how many days you need. Because we think that we may purchase all the invoices whether they are more or less, so that [we] would gain in commission custom invoices by this way.

The buying of other traders' invoices, especially small ones, would have been a lucrative pursuit for trade middlemen who were already engaged in collecting customs tax reimbursements. With the time and perhaps money invested in forming social connections to officials in the system, few traders with small shipments would have been able to make a great deal of profit on customs reimbursements. A middleman who was able to purchase many customs invoices at a discounted rate and reimburse them as a group would have been able to make a profit.

Trading firms located in multiple regions would either sell their invoices to trade middlemen in Ladakh, or authorize them to deal with invoices on their behalf, most probably for a set fee as one trade document in the Khan Archives detailed the payment of agents who had finished customs invoice reimbursement work.

The descendents of traders in Ladakh today are largely unfamiliar with the practice of buying and selling invoices. While these informants were often well informed about the types of goods and transport systems used historically, none of those interviewed recalled this system. For example, in one interview the conversation on customs invoices proceeded as followed:

> *At that time what did invoice mean?*
> Informant #1: I don't know completely.
> Informant #2: Invoice means, I think the agreement between consigner and consignment. The agreement done between both. Like you are buying and I am seller, the agreement doing between both makes the invoice, making *hundi*, it means that. The deal going between two of us, we make the invoice, that is.
> *They were writing that "we sell and buy invoice", what does it mean? Buying and selling, how did they make money out of this?*
> Informant #1: We don't understand it completely . . . you better ask someone else.

Repeatedly informants were doubtful, skeptical, or confused by the idea that their fathers and grandfathers had engaged in such trade. Some of them theorized that this was a form of grey market in the trade system, not quite illegal but not entirely official. This conceptualization of the role of buying and selling invoices is not supported by any information in the documents. None of the traders indicate that profits were made by misconstruing invoices or shipping orders, and many requests were sent publicly through government operated telegraph offices. Instead, it seems as if the buying and selling of customs invoices was a legitimate business practice that trading middlemen engaged in to increase their profit strategies.

Profit strategies and social hierarchies

The economic transactions outlined above meant that a number of traders, with varying levels of economic investment, capital, professional experience, and local interests, had to work together to achieve their profit goals. We can see some of the roles in this system in the documents featured in the illustrations above. These *challans* show how the trade middlemen, shop owners, transporters, and wholesale goods supplies each had their own sets of contractually defined rights and responsibilities. The specific professional clusters within this trading system can be conceptualized as social groups, as each had significance in local and regional social hierarchies. This is particularly evident when examining four careers within the trading networks, those of *aqsaqual*, trade middlemen, *kiraiyakash*, and *munshi*.

Aqsaquals

Although in Persian *"aqsaqual"* literally means a "white beard", the term was used in the trade systems of Ladakh to signify a political post. *Aqsaquals* were usually minor government officials posted in an area by a regional government to oversee traders from their region, interact on an official level with local governments, and represent the general trade interests of their region of origin. The owner of the Khan Archives documents, Bahauddin Khan, was originally posted in Leh as an *aqsaqual* for the local government of Khotan according to his descendants. Bahauddin Khan's case, as well as those of several other *aqsaquals* discussed in published literature from the time period, suggests that while *aqsaquals* were government officials they were also free to conduct their own private businesses. Indeed, because of their trading and political connections these trade network participants were well situated to make a profit within the trading networks of South and Central Asia.

There are several accounts by European travelers in Central Asia that mention *aqsaquals* in the towns that they visited. The manner in which these trade officials are discussed often indicates that they occupied an elite status. For example, in 1931 Roerich writes in Yarkend:

> The house of the Ladak [*sic*] *aqsaqal*, Abdul Razak, proved an ideal place for our stay in Yarkend. It was clean and had a spacious garden with roomy courtyards and good stables. The owner had a very fluent knowledge of Lhasan Tibetan, having spent several years of his life in Lhasa.
>
> (Roerich 1931:86)

Roerich continues to describe this man's life, discussing that his family members were *aqsaquals* in multiple areas of Central Asia. He concludes:

The *aqsaqal's* assistance proved invaluable to us. We spent the evening with the *aqsaqal*, who possessed a vast experience with tribes and different regions of central Asia.

(Roerich 1931:86)

These passages, along with later passages in Roerich's book that describe further stays with other *aqsaquals* in the region, relate interactions with an individuals whose wealth, education, residences, and social connections all indicate an elite status in the local community.

This elite status was both social and political in nature. Eleanor Lattimore's discussion of the British Indian *aqsaqual*, who oversaw the Indian traders in Yarkend, provides an example of the juxtaposition between these two sources of status. Lattimore provides an unflattering description of this trade official:

He was the first of the breed we had encountered and we made the mistake of treating him as we treated Chinese officials, with deference and respect. The Chinese appreciated this attitude, entertaining us with feasts and making us presents and, as our hosts, trying to see that we weren't cheated and arranging our transportation as cheaply as possible. To the Aksakal [*sic*], however, who was evidently completely unaccustomed to deference from the "ruling race", our courtesy seemed a weakness of which he could take advantage, and he pocketed exorbitant commissions for himself on everything we bought in Yarkand, our supplies for the journey to Leh and the hire of the fourteen ponies and four men who formed our caravan. Later, we heard from a British officer here that an Aksakal, far from having the dignity of a Chinese official, was a person to whom you gave an order, and whom you could tip, like a butler.

(Lattimore 1935:278–279)

In this case the so-called "weakness" of the *aqsaqual* is perceived in relation to his political status as a colonized person. From another perspective his reported distrust and lacking standards of honesty could be ascribed to rebellion rather than weakness. The concept of an *aqsaqual* as a butler, the head of servants in a household, also highlights the complicated status of socially elite individuals within the colonial political system. The shifting nature of this status will be addressed in the next chapter when discussing cosmopolitanism.

Trade middlemen

Many *aqsaquals* like Bahauddin Khan also worked as trade middlemen in the regional trade networks. These individuals acted as links between traders from other regions in local areas. Today there are many global firms that specialize in "localization" services for other global firms, offering services such as language translation, cultural training, and providing social networks in host countries. The trade middlemen of the trading networks through Ladakh performed similar tasks for traders Central and South Asia. Part of this work involved dealing with the local bureaucracy, such as engaging in the buying and selling of customs invoices as described above. Often these traders, especially those in Ladakh, linked Indian firms with their agents stationed in Central Asia, helping to convey information, capital and goods between the two.

Traders in Ladakh also acted as forwarding agents, as one informant explains:

> For example, goods came from Srinagar and if it was sent to Leh, then we stocked the good and from here [Kargil] we sent it to Leh. The *arthi*, now it is called forwarding agent. Forwarding agent . . . We were forwarding agents. Those days we used to work as the

Figure 4.7 Telegrammed instructions to a trade middleman in Ladakh.

forwarding agents, because the traders from Kashmir, they used to stock their things in Kargil. . . . it had to go to China or from Ladakh . . . so Kargil was in the central place.

Many of these trade middlemen in Ladakh worked on a commission basis and grew wealthy through this work. The work of the trade middlemen in Ladakh, in both Kargil and Leh, emphasized a need for broad social networks in order to perform their work properly. A series of documents in the Khan Archives after the death of Bahauddin Khan display how difficult this position was to maintain in the hands of his younger, more inexperienced son. These documents show that Bahauddin Khan's son Shamsuddin Khan faced disputes concerning property value and ownership of goods after the transfer of business upon his father's death; these complications eventually required legal mediation by British officials.

Middlemen were engaged in most of the economic strategies described earlier in this chapter. Primarily, they were required to be constantly up to date on prices and knowledgeable concerning methods of transfer for customs invoices. In order to complete these tasks they had to have a holistic perspective of the economic structures of the trans-regional trade networks, from a specifically local perspective. Thus the professional position of trading middlemen represents a cosmopolitan elite social status, as these men negotiated diverse cultural perspectives and interests while maintaining their own local position. Their work embodied complex negotiations between cultural difference and shared interests in daily practice.

Kiraiyakash

The *kiraiyakash* interviewed in the beginning of this chapter were participants in the Ladakh trade system that acted as transporters of goods, or pony-men. In the historical documents, most *kiraiyakash* who participated in the trade were listed as residing in small villages, often outlying Kargil town. These *kiraiyakash* were part-time trade participants, who were hired for a particular journey. While they are referred to as *kiraiyakash* in the historical transaction records, most of the pony-men did not self-identify by this title, but rather communicated their participation in local terms as a task. A second generation informant from a Mulbek family explains:

> That's called *kor la cha cha* [to take loads]. . . . Father told that they took loads from here to Kargil. They brought loads from Kargil

and reached Mulbek. From Mulbek they took loads to Leh . . . [They] only took loads and came back with some money. They received the money, and with that money [they] bought some essential goods for running the home.

A shortened form of the term *khor la cha cha* was also used by the more wealthy traders who hired them for transport:

> *Kiraiyakash* were laborers . . . suppose someone had horses, some one had *dzo*, another had a yak . . . so from here shopkeepers or traders told them, "You go to Srinagar from here with your horses, *dzo*, donkey or yak. There is this much [in] our loads". We called them *khor*. "So [you] load them and bring here, we will give you the labor charge". So this type of labor is called *kiraiyakash*.

Whether focusing on their participation in the trade networks as a whole, and calling them *kiraiyakash*, or viewing the work from an emic point of view and calling the task *kor la cha cha*, all informants agreed that they were paid for these services in a variety of ways including exchange of small goods and cash payments. Most village participants did not have the capital needed to invest in any long distance trade and were simply supplementing their household income with the provision of labor and transport animals. This was a common arrangement, and as an informant in Mulbek explained, an important part of the local economy:

> Almost everyone had donkeys and horses [in those times]. It was not that someone had many more or less. Everyone had five or six; we had to keep them for survival. If they didn't carry loads, then there was no income. No money. And we had to buy barley then . . . and [it was] for bringing rice. They went to Sonammarg with animals, *dzos*, and cows. And after dropping their loads in Leh they went to Sonammarg, then they brought *soa*, barley from Srinagar, and survived on that. They were also bringing rice from Srinagar – a very good kind of rice were getting there. For one *rupee* we were getting even five, six, or seven [kilograms] in those times, [when] we were bringing [the goods] from Sonammarg.

Thus participation in the trade system provided local villages with the necessary cash to buy basic household items they needed; these remote villages participated in a cash-based economy. The pervasiveness of this economic system in the countryside of Ladakh, and the importance of local contributions, contradict common idealized notions of historically isolated and self-sufficient villages in Ladakh.

The role of *kiraiyakash* as agents in trade transactions is expressed in various stria of meaning in historical documents. There are a number of *challans* that outline *kiraiyakash* responsibilities in highly formal terms. From these documents we can conclude that working as a *kiraiyakash* involved some degree of economic risk taking, as the *kiraiyakash* were contractually obligated to pay the cost of any lost or damaged goods. The dates of the documents and knowledge of trade route limitations in Ladakh indicate that this was temporary seasonal work, and earnings were a sporadic source of income. The implication of this second economic feature of the *kiraiyakash* role is that there were no professional full-time *kiraiyakash* in Ladakh. Perhaps this is why the economic contributions of villagers in Ladakh within the trade system have often been difficult for historians to document. Yet in spite of the lack of a full-time profession, the *kiraiyakash* did occupy a distinct labor position. The men engaged in this type of trade would have repeat interactions with the same traders, building up business networks of their own in the system. As mentioned in the last chapter, kin groups were employed as an economic strategy to maximize household productivity. Fathers would bring their sons into the networks as *kiraiyakash* to increase the wages earned in their household to meet household needs. Family members would also share specific strategies to increase trading potential. An older *kiraiyakash* recalled learning a few words in Uighur, at the advice of his grandfather, who told him that it would increase his opportunities for earning money in the trade system. He said:

Grandfather was carrying many Hor goods . . . And he completely talked in the Hors language. And I also learned. He told that "Grandson, this will help", although now I have forgotten because the coming of the Hors stopped. *Bir, thokom, altaija, yatai, seki, untot, analtai, anyatai*, these are names for from one to hundred. I knew, now I have forgotten.

In such a way *kiraiyakash* kin networks could increase the potential for their participation in historical trade networks, and bring more capital into their households. The *kiraiyakash* also had to be knowledgeable about the treacherous terrain in Ladakh to effectively transport goods within the stipulated time period. Thus while there were not professional *kiraiyakash*, there was certainly a recognizable segment of the population with an identifiable common set of social networks and career skills.

The documents provide additional information about the perceived social class of the *kiraiyakash* within Ladakh and the rest of the trade networks. In contrast to every other pre-printed formal document, which contained a place for the signature of the traders involved, contracts for transport with *kiraiyakash* contained a section that prompted writers for the "Thumbprint of *Kiraiyakash*". Informants explained this was because it was assumed that *kiraiyakash* were the only uniformly illiterate population regularly engaged with the formal aspects of trade through Ladakh. Many *kiraiyakash* did indeed choose to record their thumbprint in this space, which suggests but does not prove their illiteracy. A few *challans* provide a slightly different view, as they have the written signatures of *kiraiyakash* in Bodyig, the Ladakhi language written in the Tibetan script. These *kiraiyakash* were simply literate in a language other than the most common language of trade documentation, Urdu.

Munshis and Patawaris

In contrast, there was a section of the professionals involved with trade whose function was to be highly literate in Urdu. Many of the traders engaged the services of *munshis*, or secretaries that were responsible for tasks such as accounting, bookkeeping, legal documentation, and correspondence. The *munshis* of the trade system in Ladakh are like ghost writers; they are not explicitly named in any of the documents, but are the potential authors of all these papers. Interviewing participants indicated that this profession was common in the late nineteenth and early twentieth-century Ladakhi trade system. There is also evidence of the writers in the documents themselves. The highly formalized and professionally specialized language in most of these documents is a clue of authorship by *munshis*. In order to understand the relationship between language use and trade in Ladakh, we return to another occupation mentioned earlier in this book, that of the *patawaris*. The language of the historical trading documents was often dubbed by informants as *patawari* Urdu, without going into detail about what a *patawari* actually does. Although *munshis* and *patawaris* are two different occupations in South Asia, the present day notion of a *patawari* as one that derives power through their skill in using language is relevant to help conceptualize the historical role of *munshis* in the trade system.

A *patawari* is literally a land settlement officer or a lower ranked revenue officer of local governments in India. *Patawaris* play a key role in the society and social imagination of many South Asians in India,

Pakistan, and Bangladesh today. In the past *patawaris* were officials in the *zamindari* system of South Asia, responsible for many bureaucratic tasks associated with land ownership including measurement, recording ownership and boundaries, recording leases and mortgages, and storing all these records. There were reports in the colonial period of village *patawaris* also responsible for collecting and maintaining information in the village birth/death register. There is a juxtaposition between the lower government rank of the *patawari* and the importance of their work to the people of the village, which may account for the negative role that *patawaris* have traditionally been cast in the social imagination of South Asia. As one NGO's report on village bureaucratic structures in Pakistan reveals:

> The *Patawaris* judgments and recordings directly affect people's daily life, primarily by making decisions in land disputes. Before the abolishment of the land revenue system, the Patawari also determined the amount of the burdensome land revenues. This also gave a favorable position for taking bribes. His assessments and measurements were difficult to control from outside. According to Basho villagers, "A feet's length (field's size) is dependent on *Patawari* bribes!"
>
> (Steinsholt et al. 1998:19)

The suspicion with which *patawaris* are often viewed traditionally in villages was also once linked to the now defunct practice of establishing hereditary *patawaris*. Even today, there are reported cases of corruption with *patawaris*. The May 17, 2001 edition of the Chandigarh's Tribune newspaper reported that retired *patawaris* were facilitating the selling of land to multiple owners:

> Sources say the new generation is not well-versed with the Persian and Urdu terminology used in revenue records and hence many such words are difficult to decode. Sources say many land disputes arise due to lack of knowledge of Persian and Urdu by the new generation of revenue officials.
>
> (Walia 2001)

I mention these aspects of *patawaris* as background information on former perceptions of the post. The direct bearing of this information on the role of language in historical trade documents, and the trading networks of Ladakh as a whole, is that of the role of the *patawari* as a government official whose mastery of the subtle language of bureaucracy has elevated him to a local rank beyond his actual government rank.

The *patawari* is strongly evocative in South Asian culture, not only as the archetypical corrupt *patawari*. A more positive notion of the *patawari* is evoked in numerous biographies of intellectuals and scholars, whose claims to the intellectual arts are substantiated by reference to their, or perhaps their fathers', *patawari* training. This second notion of the *patawari* is of a well educated official versed in Persian as well as Urdu, Sanskrit, and later English; they were often the most literate men in their villages, multi-lingual professional men of letters. The *munshis* of the trading system of Ladakh evoke similar conceptual assemblages. Although not the most elite group within the trade system, as they rarely had their own international networks and were paid salaries rather than having business ownership, *munshis* derived their power through their faculty with language. Viewed sometimes with suspicion and other times with admiration, this final social group of participants in Ladakh is the most anonymous. In spite of their role in producing all the communication of the trade system, the historical voices of *munshis* as individuals remain obscured.

5 Living in a material world
Cosmopolitan elites

In this chapter I will argue that the Ladakhi Arghun community formed a cosmopolitan elite through interactions with commercial goods in the trading networks of Ladakh. The presence and use of trade goods shaped social relations through material connections to other commercial and cultural systems that were only available to a limited section of trade participants. This is particularly evident when we consider the role of material culture in the shape of three specific trading commodities – cotton piece goods, synthetic dyes, and *charas*.

A material world

Inanimate objects are not socially inert; identity can be intimately linked to particular commodities. For example, in the article "Ethnicity on the Hoof: On the Economics of Nuer Identity," John Burton writes, "... the enigma 'who are the Nuer' could be partially resolved by answering the related question, 'where are their cattle?'" (Burton 1981:161). While the Nuer example involves an animate commodity, the point remains; among the historical Nuer of Southern Sudan identity was intimately linked to particular objects that constructed social relations in the community. Burton also argues that understanding the role of commodities in identity formation of the Nuer challenges "static ethnic designations" that some anthropologists have traditionally relied upon, a view that obscures economic realities and falsely constructs the concept of a tribal community as an indisputable category (Burton 1981:157). Thus if we conceptualize community identity in relationship to commodities, we must consider identity to be as dynamic as the markets these commodities move within. If commodities are considered a part of community identity formation, then close attention to the processes by which relationships are constructed between commodities and systems of cultural meaning can help anthropologists understand culture from a dynamic perspective, rather than as a fixed entity. These relationships can be manipulated by communities with political and social agendas. For example in the work of Suzanne Brenner the historical consumption of cheese in Indonesia was an act that for participants signified a relationship with "Dutch-ness," an elite identity with the context of a colonial society (Brenner 1998). Trading groups, as explored in the work of Abner Cohen (Cohen 1974a), may utilize commodities as symbols to re-formulate traditional concepts of shared identity in new political and economic settings. Thus the task of studying material culture may seem to be one of examining how commodities in trade interact with traditional cultural symbols to re-articulate, re-define, or challenge social relations.

The role of the commodity in the cultural sphere, however, has further dynamic qualities. In *Sweetness and Power* Sidney Mintz has showed how trade of the commodity of sugar actively shaped political and economic relations between multiple cultural groups (Mintz 1987); a commodity that travels between regions creates a network of meanings between all those that come into contact with it, not only the producers and consumers. Similarly, Brian Spooner's essay "Weavers and Dealers: The Authenticity of a Persian Carpet" (Spooner 1986) highlights how varied social relations can be linked to the economic sphere and objectified in an item in multiple stages: in production (locally), distribution (between local and international merchants), and consumption (internationally). These works have helped shape my interpretation of material culture in Ladakh trading networks – while I consider particular commodities to have the ability to shape relations between groups of people that may not have actually met in the trading systems, the meanings or ideas associated with these goods are not assumed to be uniform at all stages of the economic system, or for all participants.

At the same time, I have kept in mind a key quote from Daniel Miller's work on material culture, where he cautions readers not to assume that "commoditization implies any particular change in society," pointing out that that the presence of new commodities in a culture is often assumed to be anti-traditional without any detailed understanding of the actual consumption patterns over time (Miller 1995b). This is a particularly relevant point to consider when we see, for example, European and Japanese consumer goods in the material culture of early twentieth century Ladakh. While many possible social and cultural meanings can be associated with these goods at different stages of their trade, we must look for evidence that suggests their reception by those in the

Ladakhi trading system, rather than assume that the goods have inherent significance or predefined sets of meanings associated with their presence.

Ladakhi consumers and social identity

Commercial goods shaped the historical social relations of Ladakhi Arghun traders both within Ladakh and outside the region, through partner trading communities of the British Indian Punjab and Chinese Central Asia. The presence, value, and use of these goods contributed to the construction of the Arghun social status as cosmopolitan elites through the creation of linkages to broader social and political trends. There are two separate types of goods we should discuss in local Ladakh markets, the common household products sold at general merchant stores and by small traders, and elite luxury goods. While both types of goods had consumers in the early twentieth-century Ladakhi population, there was a great deal of social stratification in the purchasing power and tastes of the community.

Many of the trade goods that flowed through Ladakh during the early twentieth century were sold outside of Ladakh. Ladakh was considered a transit stop for most of its trading history. Most traders who currently have retail shops in Leh with historical connections to commercial activities in the town did not have a retail presence in Leh until after the cessation of trade with Central Asia. The pre-independence government of the Maharaja of Jammu and Kashmir had charged high customs duties for many of the goods coming through Ladakh, which were reimbursed only if those goods were transported sealed out of Jammu and Kashmir. This was part of the Commercial Treaty of 1870 between Jammu and Kashmir and the British Indian government, which mandated that the Government of India would refund the State Government of Jammu and Kashmir for all duties charged in exchange for the right to free trade through Jammu and Kashmir with Central Asia (Kapur 1992). Thus the Ladakhi community was considered a market worth targeting only after the formation of borders and subsequent development of the region as key frontier zone for India. Yet, in spite of these general market patterns, a significant amount of consumer goods were sold within Ladakh. This is evidenced in the types of goods on display in local houses in Ladakh today, in the storehouses of Mohammed Aziz Bhat in Kargil and in bills of sale in the Khan Archives from Leh. Who in Ladakh could afford these goods?

Some scholars of Ladakh assume that the generally agriculturally engaged Ladakhi population was without the means to participate in market exchanges in the early twentieth century. There is evidence to dispute this commonly held perception. A few traders established shops with imported goods in Ladakh itself; for example one merchant who runs a photography studio in Leh town relates that his ancestors had a general merchant store in Leh in the early twentieth century. While they had come to Ladakh to trade in *pashmina*, this merchant's ancestors apparently found a decent market in Leh, as they were also engaged selling goods such as rice, cooking oil, and utensils in the town. The business reflects the presence of at least some forms of capital that could be used in market exchanges by Ladakhis. Trade networks themselves provide further evidence for the possibility of viable consumer markets in the region; many Ladakhis, especially villagers, supplied travelers with food and animal fodder that were traded for fixed exchange items such as *pashmina*, gold or currency.

Descendents of other traders from Srinagar based in Kargil in the early twentieth century explained that in their grandfather's time, *pashmina* was thus traded by locals for goods at their general store:

> *Pashmina* was from there, and [here] they bought groceries like tea, etc. That time there was no money; there was a shortage of money.
> *What was the currency used?*
> Two *annas*, that was of bronze, and other was *paisa*, 25, 50, beside that there was a bronze *paisa* there was a hole in that and a big one.
> *So you were giving paisa to them [for the pashmina]?*
> Paisa, or goods which they needed – tea etc., grocery etc.
> *You were also taking paisa from them, when you sold goods to them?*
> No. No we were not taking money, we were giving them goods for goods.

This economic system was based on the resources that local Ladakhis could provide that were valuable commodities in the international market. Supplying traders also brought forms of cash into local pockets for the purchase of imported household items, such as cloth, soap, and other consumer products.

Many of these local participants were *kiraiyakash*, or pony men, a class of trade network participants discussed in detail in the last chapter. Thus as consumers the Ladakhi people did provide a small market for goods. The types of goods at this level of the system, however, were different from the types of goods consumed by elite Arghun trading communities in Leh and Kargil.

Commercial goods and the Ladakhi elite

The Ladakhi Arghun trading families, like the family of Bahauddin Khan, were not only the consumers of general mercantile goods in the early twentieth century, but also purchasers of more expensive, technologically advanced, and internationally traded goods. This consumer identity helped to shape the Arghun elite identity within and outside of Ladakh.

In the Khan Archives elite goods appear in early twentieth-century receipts for the private purchase of items such as a potato masher, a brooch, Ajax hot water bottles, Kiwi brand boot polish and Gillette brand razors. These were commonly purchased through large British dry goods companies with offices in major metropolitan areas such as Bombay and Calcutta; the orders were presumably based on catalog information, sent by mail, and items were shipped with invoices paid on receipt. Other evidence for similarly imported items is also present, such as notes written on the back of a "Neptune Navy Cut Magnum" box of cigarettes produced by the British-American Tobacco Company in London. These are luxury items that only wealthy members of Ladakh society would have ordered in the early 1940s. Elite families in Ladakh had access to goods that others did not have the financial or networking resources to own themselves. Thus we see in a trader's correspondence in Figure 5.1 that the *Wazir-i-wazarat* found it necessary to request the use of a rifle from Bahauddin Khan.

The language of this letter represents Bahauddin Khan as a high status individual by the Wazir, who would have been of high political status himself.

From the material culture excavated at the Munshi Aziz Bhat Serai comes further evidence of elite goods, such as a Petro-Max lamp, a phonograph, and firearms. These items would have been highly expensive in the early twentieth century, and bought by the wealthiest families of Ladakh. Archival contents suggest that some of these elite goods were imported into Ladakh for non-Ladakhi use. One letter from a British banking agency in Srinagar to Bahauddin Khan requested that he forward cartridges for a gun, such as the one pictured below, for use by a British Officer who was traveling in Ladakh to attend a local festival. The social import of such a request is an acknowledgement of Bahauddin Khan's status in regional trade networks as both a reliable person who could be charged with such a task, and as a well connected individual involved in a series of non-commercial, yet economically significant, transactions that bound the trading networks together even more closely. Thus traders in Ladakh had a multi-faceted role to

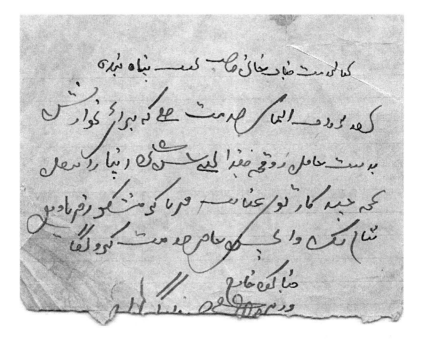

Figure 5.1 Letter to Bahauddin Khan. Translation: "To Respected Sir Khan
Sahib protector of servants, after greetings, requesting that kindly
send your rifle with some cartridges through Hussein Shah with whom
this letter is being sent, by the evening it will be sent back for your
service. Your Servant, Wazir" [rest of document torn away].

play in the local economy, including the role of procurers of fine goods
through the use of their extended trade networks. This role indicates
the specialized access to goods that trading families had through international connections, access to capital, and recognized status within
the community.

Not all the commercial evidences of elite status are in the form of
material objects. Correspondence indicates that the families of
Ladakhi cosmopolitan elites were able to access modern health care at
the Moravian Mission Hospital in Leh. From oral accounts of the lives
of Ladakhi traders there is evidence of other elite consumer services;
descendents of the trader Shamsuddin Khan recall that their father
had sent some of his clothes for dry cleaning to Jammu in the 1940s.
The concept of sending laundry for dry cleaning from Leh to Jammu,
in spite of the time, distance, and cost involved is amazing, yet other
informants confirmed that they had heard of this happening as well.

The Ladakhi Arghun traders were certainly elites within their community. These families were earning large amounts of money and conspicuously spending their income. Long distance traders like Munshi Aziz Bhat and Bahauddin Khan commanded large businesses, owned a great deal of property, and were generally referred in respectful language reserved for elites. They held posts of political importance and their children would receive an education superior to many other children in the area.

This elite status, however, is contextual. Consider, for example, the experiences of Ahmed Khan, the ancestor of the Khacho family of Kargil, who collected numerous letters of references from travelers he assisted as a government official (*thammadar*) of his region. The documents from the Khacho family express the multiplicity of statuses which accompanied the role of Arghun elites in late nineteenth- and early twentieth-century Ladakh.

The British Commissioner of Leh acknowledged Khan's position as a "civil servant of the Kashmir Govt."; the explorer Younghusband, however, simply wrote of the man in terms of meeting his own needs, writing Ahmed Khan's name incorrectly as Mohammed Khan in the process. Ahmed Khan's letters express the variety of attitudes of British officers and explorers who interacted with him, as the authors of the letters conceptualized their social relations to Khan. This variation signifies both the power inequalities embedded in the colonial system of the time period, and the status that Ahmed Khan had within his own community because of his political appointment, education, and wealth.

In the Khan Archives this shifting status of the Arghun elite was articulated in correspondence between Bahauddin Khan and the British Joint Commissioner in Ladakh. A social relationship between fellow elites was expressed in some letters through discussions of polo ponies and whether or not they would be able to play the game together soon. In some documents where Bahauddin Khan discussed polo games, he also requested a favorable ruling in a case before the British Joint Commissioner; yet other documents show that members of the same family had to write formal petition letters to the British Joint Commissioner over legal matters. These letters represent the vagaries of social status within the elite circles of Ladakhi Arghuns; they simultaneously socialized with British colonial officers, and had to appeal to them as subjects in economic and political matters. Arghun navigation of this multiplicity of social contexts helps define this community as cosmopolitans, individuals who embody interactions between complex cultural systems in their daily lives. The recognition

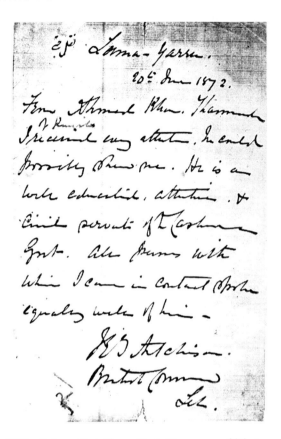

Figure 5.2 Affidavit from Hutchison. Text: "Lamayuru 20th June, 1872. For Ahmed Khan. Thammadar of Kargil. I received every attention he could possible show me. He is a well educated, attentive, & civil servant of the Kashmir Govt. All persons with which I came in contact spoke equally well of him. J.C. Hutchison. British Commissioner Leh."

of the choices and decisions Arghuns made in navigating these social relationships highlights the fact that the relationship between cosmopolitanism and elite status is not primarily a modern one.

Cosmopolitanism

Some authors view the cosmopolitan experience, with an emphasis on bringing together multiple cultural backgrounds, as contrasting to

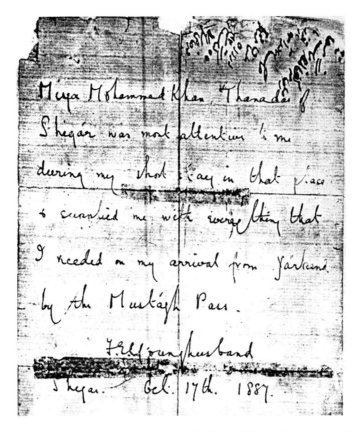

Figure 5.3 Affidavit from Younghusband. Text: "Mirza Mohammed Khan, Thandar of Shigar was most attentive to me during my short stay in that place & supplied me with everything that I needed on my arrival from Yarkend by the Mustagh Pass. F.E. Younghusband Shigar. Oct. 17th 1887."

that of pluralism that emphasizes the differences within culturally diverse settings (Gutmann 1993). Ascribed to the cosmopolitan is a type of cultural universalism that leaves no room for regionalism or local ethnic identities (Walzer 1987). Cosmopolitanism is often alluded to in the context of discussing globalization, for a cosmopolitan individual is one who participates naturally in a transnational public sphere. This definition of cosmopolitanism has been applied to studying the role of citizens in modern democracy (e.g. Bohman 1999). To be cosmopolitan most often means to participate, at times when others are not participating, in a pluralistic and diverse public sphere. Thus cosmopolitanism as an experience is often linked to the idea that there is a distinct community within a state, city, or region that is identified as cosmopolitan. The term carries with it a sense of separateness; cosmopolitans are a group of people who are experiencing cultural diversity in a particularly identifiable manner – a manner which is specifically identifiable when viewed from the outside.

James Bohman, when writing about cosmopolitans, emphasizes that members of cosmopolitan societies must realize that there are multiple conflicting interests and cross-cutting social issues in the social worlds that they occupy (Bohman 1999:193). Cosmopolitans are not simply world citizens then, but world citizens who have managed somehow to recognize separate cultural spheres in their own lives. The cosmopolitan is one who actively creates a cultural world, straddles what seems like cultural divides to others around them, and is thus constantly engaged in renegotiating their role with these larger cultural spheres. This requires recognition of shared interests with people in other areas, without requiring that the interests be expressed in the same way.

Cosmopolitanism is an abstract and constructed category – dependent on how we interpret and understand information about the world. This is not to say that cosmopolitans are not real. Even the concept of a table crucially depends on cultural knowledge that allows us to interpret collections of pieces of wood (or metal, or plastic, etc.) as tokens of the type "table" because they are arranged in particular ways and used for particular purposes. Thus, discussing what cosmopolitanism is requires defining the cultural knowledge that allows us to create this particular category of social experience. Despite the constructed nature of this concept, defining cosmopolitanism is still a valuable endeavor, practically speaking. Philosophical pragmatism tells us that a concept is meaningful or significant only insofar as the application of it is useful.[1] Recognizing individuals as cosmopolitan is useful for addressing how populations can understand cultural difference within a global context. The conceptualization of cosmopolitanism in this book allows us to understand practically how culture areas are linked together within individual lives, the lives of cosmopolitans. This model of cosmopolitanism enables an examination, in particular cultural settings and time periods, of individuals as embodiments of the values associated with globalization today. Identifying cosmopolitans thus reveals the possibility of negotiating diverse cultural perspectives and interests without devaluing cultural difference, with the realization that these negotiations are neither the reflexive prerogative, nor chance product, of modern globalization.

A systematic search into the concrete expression of this view of cosmopolitanism necessitated the following set of questions. How do people become cosmopolitan? Why do we tend to perceive cosmopolitanism as a modern phenomenon? And, how is cosmopolitanism "lost"; that is, what particular economic and political contexts are so closely related to cosmopolitanism, that people experiencing de-contextualization from those settings are no longer considered, or perhaps consider themselves, cosmopolitan?

Elites in many communities, especially in colonial settings, have a long history of living a cosmopolitan life, negotiating their cultural practices and beliefs within the context of seemingly contradictory cultural identities (see for example Haskett 1988). In the cosmopolitan social world, however, an identity such as "elite" is contextual, embedded in various other commercial and cultural systems than those of their immediate surroundings. This aspect of the cosmopolitan nature of elite identities in Ladakh is difficult to trace, however, through historical documents alone.

Cosmopolitans in a material world: A commodity-centered perspective

The movement and consumption of goods communicates more clearly the role of cosmopolitanism in this elite community. Interactions with goods, whether as consumers, producers, or transports, are well documented and can be conceptualized as part of the contesting identity issues that they represented. To closely examine the process by which this occurs, I utilize Spooner's model of how social relations are objectified in multiple stages (1986). This analysis highlights the complex social world of a commodity by distinguishing the social relations of the object's contexts of production, distribution, and consumption.

While the consumption of the goods described earlier in this chapter provides an intriguing picture of life in Ladakh in the early twentieth century, this representation of material culture scratches the surface of the trading system in Ladakh. Common goods transported through Ladakh, not always for sale in the region, were far more significant in the formation of a cosmopolitan elite community. Through these goods Arghun traders were able to locate themselves within larger social networks associated with national economies, global markets, and international colonial empires. This section focuses on the role of three specific trade commodities: piece goods, synthetic dyes, and *charas* (a cannabis product). The evidence presented below will compare the process by which social significance was attributed to these goods' contexts of production, distribution and production in the global arena, and their possible roles as material representations of cosmopolitan cultural hybridity. These commodities have been selected to help to clarify how the elite consumer and middleman groups formulated selective local perceptions of the importance of varying cultural systems articulated in trade goods.

We can define Ladakhi Arghun communities as cosmopolitan through recognition of their roles as cultural brokers in segments of the trade system. Regional trade participants were not simply drawn into uncontested global meanings of material culture. Instead, they negotiated a sense of belonging to larger social networks within their own cultural frameworks, creating a symbolic system of commercial goods that was distinctly local in nature. Their choices and decisions associated with trade helped shape the global role of these commodities, and were in turn shaped by participation in various regional, national, and international public spheres.

One site of articulation of this participation is represented by the correspondence between traders in the North Indian trading networks. A number of telegrams and letters in the Khan Archives were requests for news or prices from different areas in the trading networks. Requests for the prices of goods in a certain area enabled traders to ensure that the market prices were roughly standardized in towns within the same trading network. This correspondence was also a way for traders to keep abreast of current events; they wrote to each other about the political events impacting their extended international networks and demanded news of political and social events in other areas. The Ladakhi Arghun traders' work seems to have necessitated the cosmopolitan lifestyle; balancing their business interests in the political, social, and economic spheres of Chinese and British territories required dialogue with their counterparts in a variety of regions. This participation in discussions of world events was further supported by the elite nature of the Ladakhi Arghun community, whose access to trade commodities enabled them to read newspapers, magazines, and books from around the world. Material culture evidence from the Khan documents indicates that in 1937 Bahauddin Khan's son Shamsuddin Khan was a subscriber to *Dilgudaz Magazine* from Lahore, a commercial and literary magazine that would have given him information about the events and news in British India. Books from the Kargil *serai*, now housed in the Munshi Aziz Bhat Museum, show that elite traders purchased books in English from around the world. These include biographies of famous individuals and accounts of colonial service in other parts of the world, as well as popular novels such as *David Copperfield*.

Another way Ladakhi Arghun traders were able to frame the significance of their trading decisions within multiple cultural viewpoints was through their participation in the international kinship networks discussed earlier. The dialogue between the diverse interests of family members internalized discussion of multiple culture viewpoints, making it an integral part of the Arghun community. The Arghun traders who brought goods through Ladakh were not cultural automatons. Each trading decision was made in response to this variety of perspectives of the significance of the individual commodities. Today we might consciously choose a Fair Trade coffee in the store due to its association with socially responsible methods of growing and distributing coffee beans; embedded in this decision is our cosmopolitan recognition as a consumer of the ways in which our lives are linked to the lives of people in other countries. In such a way traders who were transporting and marketing these goods in Ladakh were the cosmopolitan decision makers who influenced global events.

Cotton piece goods

Piece goods (also sometimes referred to as "dry goods") are finished fabrics usually sold to consumers in units of lengths; they are often presented in stores as bolts of cloth that a clerk will cut upon request for the buyer. Piece goods were a high profile commodity in early twentieth-century trade through Ladakh, frequently noted by European travelers through the region. In 1931 Roerich wrote:

> The returning [to Chinese Turkistan] caravans carry loads of European-made goods: products of Manchester looms and Bradford woolen mills, British and German dyestuffs, various articles of *haberdashery*,[2] and Indian products and spices, such as saffron, which is exported in great quantities from Kashmir to Turkestan and Tibet.
> (Roerich 1931:22)

Many Ladakhi informants also particularly mentioned the import of cotton piece goods to Central Asia through Ladakh when asked about the commodities of trade. One reminisced, "Cotton. *Latha* was fine cotton that comes from England. Yes. *Chabis latha* was very famous in those days. *Chabis latha.* And one *latha* was coming from Japan, *Hazari latha.*" There are a number of documents in the Khan Archives that refer to the transport and sale of piece goods and cotton piece goods seem to have been readily available in Ladakhi markets. One of the surprising trends in the trade with Chinese Central Asia is the large amount of Japanese cotton piece goods that were transported through Ladakh by British Indian traders. This is indicative of consumer choices within Indian markets during the time period that reflect the cosmopolitan roles of Arghun traders.

In the nineteenth century, Britain had the largest cotton textile industry in the world, and India consumers since 1843 had been its biggest market (Markovits 2000a:312). In contrast mid-nineteenth-century Japan did not have a large domestic cotton manufacturing system. Whereas the silk industry in Japan developed rapidly during this time period, the cotton industry had a few privately-owned cotton mills in 1860–1870 using equipment of European manufacture, with a total output roughly the same as a "single fair-sized Lancashire mill" (Allen 1972:71–72). It was only in the 1890s that the Japanese cotton industry began to grow within the Asian economic arena. First Japanese mills captured the Korean market for cotton yarn in 1894–95, and then Chinese markets in 1896 when the Chinese government "placed a ban on Indian goods in consequence of the outbreak of an epidemic in Bombay" (Allen 1972:72). Thus the growth of Japanese cotton production was very much a regional Asian phenomenon.

In the early twentieth century Japanese cotton piece goods had begun to enter Indian markets and steadily grew in popularity in India. Japanese piece goods were less expensive than all varieties of British piece goods by 1930, yet British piece goods "continued to constitute the bulk of India's imported cotton piece goods" due to protective tariffs on the British cotton imports in India, which set a 10 percent lower tariff rate on cotton goods coming from Britain to India (Banerjee 1999:167–171). In such a regulated market, Japanese piece goods had a severe disadvantage in British Indian trade. However, Indian consumers were not only concerned with the cost of goods; there were other features of the market. Considering the social movements of the time period, we can view the presence of Japanese cloths as proof of the cosmopolitan choices made by trade middlemen in areas such as Ladakh.

Textiles in early twentieth-century India were a socially meaningful commodity. Textile imports played a central role in the Indian independence struggle as encouraging the use of *khadi*, a fabric of handspun thread of Indian production, was the symbolic keystone of Gandhi's movement in the early twentieth century. Indeed an early version of the Indian nationalist flag in the 1920s featured the *charkha* (a spinning wheel that symbolized domestic production of cloth), which was later replaced with the Ashoka Chakra[3] on the flag today, on *khadi* (Virmani 1999). This rejection of the British textile industry was symbolic; the classic English industrial revolution was based on textile production, and textile production and surrounding industries "gave Great Britain its industrial supremacy before 1885" (Travis 1993:13). Thus a refusal of British cotton piece goods was a rejection of the international role of industrial Britain.

Japanese manufactured cloth may have appealed to consumers for related reasons; artifacts of trade in Ladakh show that Japanese piece goods were marketed with Indian nationalist concerns in mind as they were named in Hindi to appeal to public sentiment. The decline in sales of British produced cloth, and subsequent rise in popularity of Japanese piece goods also shaped the context of textile production in Japan. Although textiles were previously a small sector of Japanese industry, by 1934 exports of textiles and textile machinery had paved the way for the subsequent growth of the twentieth-century Japanese export market (Allen 1972:231). Contesting meanings of items such as cotton cloth, traders within South Asia distributing piece goods impacted public perceptions of these technologies in their contexts of production within England and Japan.

The traders who brought British and Japanese cotton piece goods through Ladakh were a part of this political movement; Ladakhis participated in many of the same historical fights against colonialism as did other Indians. A Ladakhi Arghun freedom fighter in the Indian struggle for independence, Munshi Abdul Sattar, was in the same social class as some of the largest trading families of Leh; one of his children later had an arranged marriage with the child of a major Ladakhi trader. Thus Ladakhi traders, participating in social movements of their times, challenged British imaginings of technological superiority, helped build symbolic vocabularies of resistance against colonialism, and took part in the creation of Japan as an export power in world markets.

Synthetic dyes

George Henderson, a member of the 1870 Forsyth Expedition to Chinese Central Asia, remarked in his report with great enthusiasm that in exchange for valuable goods of Chinese Turkistan such as "gold dust from Khoten [*sic*], silk, extract of Indian hemp, and horses," Indian traders could offer items such as aniline dyes "which are in great favor," clearing over one hundred percent profit (Henderson and Hume 1981). Aniline dyes were worthy of gold dust in the late nineteenth century because they represented one of the most exciting new commodities in world markets of the time, capable of fueling economic, social, and scientific change. Since the invention of the first synthetic dye, by William Henry Perkin who discovered "Mauveine" in England in 1856, the world had been awash in new colors.

There is a great deal of evidence of the transport of dyes through Ladakh to Chinese Central Asian markets. A number of documents in the Khan Archives represent shipments of crates of dyes from the 1920s to the 1940s. Among the goods in Munshi Aziz Bhat's *serai* were a variety of dye boxes representing those available in early twentieth-century Ladakh, including magenta from Farbenfabriken Bayer, scarlet from I.G. Farbenindustrie, a green from Commercial Dyes and Chemicals, an unmarked color from Northern Colour Industries Eagle Brand, and unmarked colors of Har Bhagwan Rangwala Batakh Brand (Duck Brand) and Pachkari Brand.

These dyes produced in Germany, USA, India and England, were transported through British India, circulated in Ladakh's markets, and were destined to travel on to Central Asian markets.

The Khan Archives show evidence of synthetic dyes circulating in Leh and Kargil markets at least as early as the 1920s and 1930s, although it may have taken longer for their use to become commonplace in Ladakh, as many were shipped to Chinese Central Asia. As Monisha Ahmed, an anthropologist who works in the Rupshu area of Ladakh

Figure 5.4 German dye box from Munshi Aziz Bhat *serai*, 2000. Photograph by Abdul Nasir Khan.

found in an interview with an informant, until at least the 1940s consumers were not completely familiar with synthetic dyes and their uses. Her informant explained:

> The merchants who brought the dye here were good salesmen. They would take white cloth and spit on it, apply the red dye and rub the cloth. They'd show this to the people and say "see how easy this is to make". Then everybody would buy it up, and that's how they all started wearing dyed clothes. But few of these people actually knew how to apply these dyes and not only would the cloth become red, but also their body!
>
> (Ahmed 2002:108)

The role of cultural innovators in introducing synthetic dyes in Ladakh places the trading community at the center of local processes of global cultural change. The introduction of synthetic dyes had a profound cultural effect in many countries, as the development of synthetic dyes exploded social concepts of color around the world. The 1870s were called the "mauve decade" in Britain (Wingate 1982:12) as society popularly embraced Perkin's new dyes. Before synthetic dyes, there were a variety of natural dyes choices such as those used in Ladakh, including madder, wild rose leaves, nettle, apple tree bark, soot and walnut (Ahmed 2002). These choices were costly, time consuming, and not always effective. Wingate describes:

> Before Perkin made his great discovery in 1856 even kings had trouble finding enough dye to color their royal raiment. A monarch in those days, unless he was a truly mighty one, usually had the collar of his royal robe dyed with cochineal crimson or tyrian purple but the rest of his cloak was likely to be a faded indigo blue, a streaky alizarin red, or some muddy-looking mixture of these two dyes obtained from plant sources. In fact, the king's coat, except for its collar, might be an undyed [*sic*] dirty white. It was just too costly to obtain enough cochineal insects for the crimson or enough shellfish (*murex brandaris*) for the purple, to color an entire robe.
>
> (Wingate 1982:22)

In most cultures the color of clothing had a great deal more social significance than today, when anyone can afford a red or purple cloth, if they can afford the cloth at all; cultural signifiers of cost are in materials, design, cut, etc. Ahmed writes of such change in Ladakh, explaining that before widespread use of synthetic dyes, color was a "marker of a person's social status" in many of the more remote areas of Ladakh and wearing white was considered low status (Ahmed 2002:108). She explains that synthetic dyes had widespread social impact as it gave "ordinary people" the opportunity to also dye their clothing, which caused elites to then start distinguishing themselves through the purchase and use of more expensive foreign cloths "such as brocade, velvet, and later machine-woven cloths," as symbolic statements of their elite status (Ahmed 2002:108). Thus as the purveyors of synthetic dyes, these Arghun traders were agents of broad cultural changes in Ladakh that fueled other market shifts in the area's trade.

Clothing was not the only source of interest in synthetic dyes in early twentieth-century Ladakh. As astute businessmen, the Ladakhi Arghun traders would have quickly seen the importance of synthetic dyes in the production of their own regional products such as woolen and *pashmina* products. Traders and wool producers would have been interested in their ability to produce a higher quality of finished textile product that would be competitive in world markets.

As traders in synthetic dyes, the Ladakhi Arghun community had material connections to economic forces shaping early twentieth-century India, and contemporary discourses about science, technology, and power in the global arena. The trade in synthetic dyes prompted a significant change in Indian economic history, due to its role as a competitor on the market for indigo, a natural dye and high income yielding product. Indian indigo was exported to Europe in small amounts until the sixteenth-century establishment of a maritime route between Europe and Asia. The maritime linkage formed by indigo trade furthered other types of global commerce and although the trade fluctuated in response to several historical economic trends, Indian indigo strengthened the East India Company presence in India. The introduction of synthetic dyes in the late nineteenth century, however, reversed the roles of importers and exporters in the world dye market.

In response to market pressures from synthetic dyes natural indigo exports, prices, and indigo plantation acreage quickly fell within a ten year period at the end of the nineteenth century and beginning of the twentieth century. This shift from indigo dye production to the consumption of synthetic dyes in India was an economic change with social significance in India. Many Indian indigo planters engaged in economic decision making left the industry to pursue other trades, while the British investors claimed that a "native" distrust of science failed to allow the planters to investigate ways to make indigo more competitive in the market (Kumar 2002). Indian nationalist interests were expressed within the dye arena, as the declining plantations faced increased financial pressures, and the dissatisfaction of the workers for the decaying system resulted in a resistance movement called the Champaran resistance, or rebellion. The Champaran movement of 1907–08 has been called "the emergence of nationalist elements on the scene of peasant resistance" (Pouchepadass 1999:156). Indigo workers, increasingly disenfranchised by the popularity of synthetic dyes on the market, gradually formed a coherent movement, in which Gandhi played an important role, the Champaran Movement of Bihar. Thus the transition from indigo to synthetic dyes incorporated segments of colonial discourse about "native knowledge," and played a role in the nationalist movement.

The role of synthetic dyes on the global market also was fraught with cultural and political symbolism, as a representation of scientific advancement that formed the basis for national pride in countries such as Britain, Germany, and the USA. The development of synthetic dyes in the late nineteenth century represented the "expanding frontiers of organic chemistry" as "leading chemists of the day [made] significant strides towards an understanding of the structure of matter" (Fox 1987:10). From all accounts, the making of synthetic dyes was the beginning of the industrial application of chemistry, which funded and encouraged a variety of chemical research in the twentieth century.

The process of creating aniline dyes thus played a crucial role in the creation of new substances, devices, and processes, which have shaped technological advances. British chemists developing dyes produced a variety of improvements for life in the later part of the nineteenth century, signified by their patents on articles such as "lamps using the vapour of naphtha or other hydrocarbons without the use of a wick" in 1848, acetylene lamps (1898), and acetone solvent for paints and varnishes (1892) (Fox 1987:234–248). Throughout the development of chemical dyes in the late nineteenth and early twentieth century chemists associated with dye manufacture pioneered and perfected a variety of chemical methods, including the basic distillation of tar and pitch (1846), the utilization of hydrocarbons to recover solvents from organic materials (1867), the fabrication of nitro and amino derivatives (1911), and the general manufacturing of chemical compounds for industrial use (Fox 1987:235–248). Perkin's original goal when he produced mauve had been to make quinine in the laboratory, and although he never succeeded, the dye industry supplied organic chemistry with knowledge that would make quinine a laboratory product nearly a century later (Wingate 1982:15). Friedrick August Kekule's conceptualization of the benzene ring, which proved to be a keystone concept in organic chemistry, was developed in the midst of chemical knowledge associated with synthetic dye development (Wingate 1982:24). British citizens were proud of the scientific advances that occurred in their country and saw them as signifiers of their nation. So much so that King Edward awarded Perkin with a knighthood for his discovery in 1906.[4] While Perkin, an Englishman, started the synthetic dye business, all accounts concur that German chemists soon had the lead. In part this can be attributed to the research institution education system prevalent in Germany, through which such key chemists as Kekule and Wilhem Von Hoffman were mentoring students on their own projects. Kekule and Von Hoffman were temporarily in England during Perkin's discovery, and are attributed with bringing the idea quickly back to Germany, where other chemists continued research work. German dye manufacturers subsequently appeared, and there were thirteen major dye firms in Germany at the beginning of the Second World War (Wingate 1982:37).

The First and Second World Wars reorganized the pre-existing patterns of the global dye industry. Fox describes how the American dye industry was forced into an existence, in response to World War One market fluctuations (Fox 1987:168). While Germany maintained its stronghold of the dye industry through World War One, the dye manufacturing world changed after World War Two. When Germany was divided by the occupying forces of USA, Russia, France, and Great Britain, the occupying forces set up post-war legislation that disassembled industrial units related to the German war industry, redistributing the assets of Germans who had participated in the Nazi government, and controlling industrial research and production units (Fox 1987:204). The German dye-making conglomerate I.G. Farben was broken down into Bayer, Hoechst and Badische by 1952, and other countries surged ahead in dye production. American companies such as DuPont began to have a greater toehold in world dye markets, and fund their own further industrial chemistry revolutions.

The presence of synthetic dyes in Ladakhi markets thus plays a role in defining the Arghun trading community as a cosmopolitan elite and, as in the case of the cotton piece goods, these Arghun traders were agents in broader historical narratives. Arghun traders made decisions about the purchase of aniline dyes in the context of building relationships with representatives of global dye firms in British India, such as the Punjabi trading houses mentioned earlier. The purchase and purveyance of synthetic dyes linked these traders to the scientific revolution in Europe, shifting colonial economies in India, fashion trends in Europe and the USA, and the difficulties of post-World War settlements in Germany.

Charas

Another good that represented a significant portion of the trade coming through Ladakh is the drug *charas*.[5] Unlike cotton piece goods and synthetic dyes, brought from British India, this good came from Chinese Turkistan to British India. *Charas*, according to most authors, is a highly potent product of *Cannabis indica*. There is some confusion in literature on *charas*, as there are a number of terms for products of *Cannabis* plants, which have slightly different meanings in different parts of the world. Most authors agree that the three main types of *Cannabis* preparations used in India, which serve as a folk standard of potency, are known as *bhang*, *ganja*, and *charas* (Grinspoon 1993). *Bhang* is considered the least potent of the drug preparations, made from the dried broken leaves, stems, and some flowers of the *Cannabis* plant. In India *bhang* is sometimes used in a beverage. Some authors have claimed that the creation of *bhang* depends upon tending the *Cannabis* plants in a particular way while they are grown; that the cannabis plants from which *bhang* is made "receive relatively little attention during the growing season in contrast to plants used to make *charas* and *ganja*" (Abel 1982:114). *Ganja*, in contrast, is a higher potency drug, although the standards of its composition are unclear (see for example Abel 1982:117, Lingeman 1969:37, and Johnston 1878:91). The general composition is thought to be plant pieces with resin fashioned into a more solid form. Most sources agree that *ganja* is smoked or eaten when used in India.

Charas is the pure resin of the *Cannabis* plant, which most authors agree is also known as hashish in the Middle East (e.g. Grinspoon 1993 and Lingeman 1969:37). If indeed hashish is synonymous with *charas* as these authors have suggested, then it may also include some *Cannabis* flower parts in the resin (Abel 1982:118). In South Asia *charas* is smoked, often mixed with tobacco, in cigarettes, a *chilam* pipe, or a water pipe (*hookah*); *charas* can also be eaten baked in confections. Ingested *charas* can equal in hallucinogenic effects a small amount of LSD and when smoked it is approximately eight times as potent as most of the marijuana smoked in the USA (Lingeman 1969:39). Its market advantage is that the sticky resin can be pressed together to make hard blocks that are sold in market (Khan, et al. 1975:352).

The *charas* trade in Ladakh depended in part on the nature of the Cannabis plant that produces *charas*. Long distance trade of *charas* occurred due to the specific conditions in Chinese Turkistan, which yielded a reportedly higher quality crop. Potency in *Cannabis* plants has been a matter of some recent controversy.[6] In the late nineteenth and early twentieth century, however, the distinctly resinous quality of *Cannabis indica* was yet to be disputed, and the composition of *charas* as coming from the *Cannabis indica* plant was emphasized by colonial writers. While the *Cannabis* species was certainly emphasized historically for *charas* production, producers also realized that the climate of Chinese Central Asia was particularly good for high quality *charas*. The materials transported from Yarkend were sometimes referred to as "Indian Hemp" as this was a generally used term for *Cannabis indica* in the late nineteenth and early twentieth centuries, regardless of its country of production.

Early twentieth-century *charas* trade was legal, and there were many established merchants, commission agents, and bankers in South Asia who earned their livelihood through *charas* and other similar goods. The Khan Archives thus contain a number of documents written on company stationary headings that include mention of *charas* as a chief commodity of trade. The trade of *charas* between Chinese Central Asia and British South Asia through Ladakh was regulated by multiple governments including those of China, Jammu and Kashmir, and British India. In order to transport *charas* from Ladakh to Srinagar for eventual transport to British India, traders needed to get permission for specific loads, with the numbers of bundles, invoice numbers, amount of duty deposited and destination port stated. These permits were issued by the British Joint Commissioner in Ladakh, working in conjunction with the Kashmir Customs and Excise Office, customs officers stationed in *serais*, a Special *Charas* Officer stationed in Ladakh, and the British Customs officer in Srinagar. *Charas* had high excise duties attached that reached into sums of thousands of rupees for each shipment, and those who traded in *charas* also had to pay for their licensing from the government. Ladakh's storage facilities, *charas godowns*, were sites of the production of high profit for traders and at the center of the political economy. At the same time, they were only a small part of the state duty revenue of Jammu and Kashmir (Jammu and Kashmir 1939–40).

Defining the social role of *charas* in Ladakh is a difficult task. Oral accounts of *charas* use are absent from all ethnographic interview discussions of the trade, and few people admit to knowing of anyone in Ladakh who was a *charas* user in the early twentieth century. At the same time, informal discussions acknowledged the possible existence of some use of *charas* on the part of traders, although no one trading group or person has been identified as a user. In the material culture, there is possible evidence for the use of *charas* in the Ladakh region, with the presence of multiple "hubble-bubbles" – a *hookah* or water pipe for smoking marijuana, hashish, or tobacco – in the goods at the Kargil *serai*.

In spite of the presence of these hubble-bubbles, and some general local perceptions that wealthy traders may have indulged in such consumption, I heard no tales of wealthy Arghun or other traders in Ladakh being regular consumers of *charas*. Furthermore, there is no record of local sales to be found in any of the Khan Archives documents. This is unlike transport and consumption patterns found in other parts of Central Asia, where authors have claimed that *charas* was an accepted substance (Trocki 1999:19) or reported that trade laborers were commonly paid in the drug they transported, such as the payment of Wakhi valley laborers of Afghanistan with opium (Shahrani 1979). Consumption patterns in Ladakh were different due to the aforementioned government control, a system of strict set of regulations that limited access. The political economy of Jammu and Kashmir, as well as British India, thus shaped social interactions with consumer products in the Ladakh trading networks. The outcome was a local population with limited access to the good they were transporting and a cosmopolitan elite that had increased access to these goods, but a limited power on their dispersal.

Charas trade was featured in the political maneuvering between British and Chinese officials and represented a powerful political tool for the Chinese. In 1898 when the Chinese leader considered stopping *charas* cultivation in the region, British officials in North India saw it as an attempt to destabilize the basis of British trade as it was "the chief export from Kasgaria [*sic*] to India and without it trade would be crippled" (Skrine and Nightingale 1973:96). *Charas* was a significant good in British India that played a role in European discourse about health and the body in the nineteenth and early twentieth century, discourse that changed dramatically over time. From approximately 1840 to 1900 *Cannabis* was considered to be a new resource for European doctors (for an example of the medical uses of *Cannabis*, see Mikuriya 1973), and over one hundred scholarly papers were published during this time in European and American medical literature recommending cannabis for treatments with patients (Grinspoon 1993). By the end of the nineteenth century, however, attitudes towards cannabis were rapidly changing. The variability of the potency of *Cannabis*, along with variations in individual responses, made doctors reluctant to rely on cannabis for patient treatment. The invention of the hypodermic syringe in the 1850s allowed other drugs to be injected, which increased the use of opiates in the medical profession. The late nineteenth-century development of more chemically stable synthetic drugs like aspirin and barbiturates had all but made *Cannabis* preparations obsolete in European and American medical circles (Grinspoon 1993). These changes in European and American needs for *Cannabis* caused subtle changes in their perceptions of the drug.

While these changes were occurring in European and American arenas, the use of cannabis preparations changed little at the end of the nineteenth century in British India. Unlike alcohol, cannabis preparations had a place for use in upper caste Hindu communities, and all three types of preparations were used in various Hindu religious ceremonies (Hasan 1975). Some Hindu sects maintained a belief that the deity Shiva was fond of hemp, and on Shivaratri day (the fourteenth day in the month of Phalgun in the Vikram Samvat calendar) in Shiva temples, hemp products were commonly given as offerings (Hasan 1975). The usage patterns of modern communities suggest that regular *Cannabis* use was rare; in one relatively recent consumer study of an Indian village researchers found that while most of the village will use *Cannabis* preparations in festivals, only four individuals of a population of 1,190 were regular users (Hasan 1975:245). European travelers in Asia in the late nineteenth century, however, frequently remarked on the use of *Cannabis* preparations (e.g. Johnston 1878:94).

Studies of Indian *Cannabis* use in British literature can be read as expressions of the changes in attitudes towards the colonial subjects of British India, perceptions of interactions between social habits and physical embodiments. The "effects of *churrus* or natural resin", studied in India by a Dr. O'Shaughnessy in the mid-nineteenth century were described in positive terms as an increased appetite and cheerfulness, with excess causing delirium and the curious ability to move a man's limbs into any position and have them stay there, like a "waxen figure" (Johnston 1878:95–96). This study thus supports the general colonial conceptualization of Indian habits that create a pliant and cheerful native, perhaps given to delusional excesses. Dr. O'Shaughnessy also mentioned in the course of this study that he considered a large dose of *charas* for users in India to be one and a half grains, but for those using it in England to be ten or twelve grains (Johnston 1878:99), making the measurement of excess a culturally variable one.

When the Indian Hemp Drugs Commission, a British Indian government sponsored study of the physical effects of *Cannabis* from 1893 to 1894 was undertaken, varying perceptions of the interaction between colonial subjects and their social habit were expressed. The examiners appointed by the British viceroy in India eventually concluded that "moderate" use by Indian subjects was harmless and users harmed themselves only when exceeding that moderation, although they failed to define moderation (Abel 1982:56). Thus the use of *Cannabis* preparations became more negative. Problems with *Cannabis* were not thought of as a characteristic of the substance, but rather attributed to Indian users who lacked the ability to control their desires, habits, or actions. This viewpoint of Indian *charas* users supported colonial arguments of the "white man's burden" during this time period, or British paternalism in the colonial setting that justified colonial rule as necessary for the good of the subjects unable to rule themselves.

By 1942, colonial studies of *Cannabis* product use claimed that *Cannabis* was a criminally dangerous drug (see for example Chopra, et al. 1942:244–245). These studies emphasized a much darker picture of perceived lack of social moderation in European terms, speaking of *ganja* or *charas* users as those responsible for "heinous" crimes and requiring institutionalization or even incarceration (Hasan 1975). These representations of the social habits of Indian colonial subjects in British medical literature reflect the widespread fears of violence and resistance from the colonial population.

The trade of *charas* represented two opportunities for Arghun and other traders to claim elite status in Ladakh. The traders involved in *charas* buying and selling and transport would have earned a large amount of money, creating economic positions that would support an elite lifestyle. Unlike the previous two commodities, the trade of *charas* products has, at first glance, less apparent evidence of being associated with a cosmopolitan status in the Ladakhi community. The changing global attitudes about *charas*, while culturally significant, seem to be located firmly within cultural spheres that were inaccessible to Ladakhi traders. With control on the commodity tightly restricted, Ladakhi Arghun traders as trade middlemen had limited decision making beyond the initial decision to engage in *charas* trade. In fact, we may ask why Ladakhi traders participated in the trade of *charas* at all.

Charas from Chinese Turkistan was a valuable commodity in the Ladakh trade networks of the early twentieth century. The good lends itself to easy trade and transport, as drug crops do not "perish quickly or easily", are simple to process (Stares 1996:52), and would yield high prices in the South Asian markets. In the late nineteenth century, Punjabi traders from British India would come to Leh and meet with merchants from Chinese Turkistan who would offer valuable goods such as "their gold, silver, and *charas*" for the cotton goods and tea of the Indian traders (Godfrey 1899:256). At the same time the licensing system of the *charas* trade meant that those trading in *charas* had to have certain political connections to maintain their standing within the system; here we can begin to see the cosmopolitan nature of this interaction

for Ladakhi traders. Obtaining a license meant control over a part
of the market, as well as a guarantee of continuing business interactions with the Jammu and Kashmir and British Indian governments.
Charas traders were thus, through the nature of the political control
of the trade, intimately linked to the colonial government of British
India. The *charas* trade was of such high value in British India that
regulation of this trade was one of the primary tasks of the British Joint
Commissioner stationed in Leh during the trading season. Business
relationships between Ladakhi elites and British colonial officials,
and subsequent social relationships, most often began as part of the
charas trade. The most successful *charas* traders were those who
could maintain the most varied social networks with British, Indian,
Kashmiri, and Chinese communities.

The cosmopolitan revisited

While earlier chapters have looked at more traditionally anthropological ways of defining social identity or social status, this chapter has
shown how attention to the role of material culture, specifically commercial goods, can facilitate a more detailed understanding of the social
networks embedded in Ladakh's regional trade system. The consumer
trade goods helped to define the Arghun community as a cosmopolitan elite by offering material connections to other commercial and
cultural systems only available to a limited section of trade participants.
Cosmopolitans are formed through the movement of goods in historical trade, as commodities offer material connections to multiple
cultural viewpoints and create new social movements in the public sphere.
Commodities are linkages between people in these cultural arenas; they
can be vehicles for communication, as well as agents of change in society.

The trading system of Ladakh necessitated cosmopolitanism; as
shown in this chapter traders need to constantly be in contact with and
concerned about events in other regions. This de-localization of community identity is furthered by the way the Arghun community was
formed, as mentioned in earlier chapters, as international kinship
networks. Kinship helped Arghun traders enter into, and maintain,
their economic and political status within multiple cultural settings.
Therefore Arghun kinship networks, like those of historical Hadrami
Arab communities, employed ". . . interethnic unions, creoles, cross-
cultural alliances, multilingual families, and transregional networks of
kinsfolk [that] became integral to the social substance of such politics"
(Ho 2006:158). Additionally, through their goods and correspondence
the Arghun traders were located within transregional systems such as

national economies, global markets, colonial empires, and global cultural movements. As discussion of each of the commodities featured in this chapter has shown, however, Arghuns formulated selective multi-local perceptions of the significance of these varying cultural systems. The connection between cosmopolitan elites and commodities continues to be represented in many Ladakhi Arghun homes today, in displays of historical goods from around the world that have been treasured since the early twentieth century. This connection persists in spite of the severance of trading networks in the mid-twentieth century, as discussed in the next chapter. In the introduction of this book I asked the question, can cosmopolitanism be "lost"; that is, is cosmopolitanism intimately related to particular economic and political contexts. The significance and social roles of commodities central to this discussion of cosmopolitanism have drastically changed in Ladakh over the past few decades due to the cessation of trade through Ladakh. Thus we must return to this question in the final chapters, when examining the memory and legacy of trade in Ladakh, after discussing the severance of Ladakhi trading networks in the mid-twentieth century.

6 The demise of trade
Coping with borders

Ethnographic present: The Amritsar trader and the missing voices

In Amritsar, we began hunting for historical connections to Ladakh with confidence, being armed with many business names, addresses, and market locations from our documents. Our search was initially not fruitful. For a few days Nasir and I walked through the bazaar streets, stopping and asking older businessmen whether they had heard of any of these merchants, and receiving only negative replies.

One day, after many people gave us a series of directions, some correct, some too complicated to ascertain whether they were correct or not, we made our way to a small alley. The way was barely wide enough for one car, and crowded with pedestrian traffic and cycle rickshaws. We stood to the side, trying to dodge people, and looking around at the cloth stores. Suddenly, a signboard between two shops caught our eye. There was a familiar store name, an almost exact replica of the sixty-six year old letterhead on the document we were holding.

We passed back and forth in front of the sign, trying to figure out how to get into the place, until a roadside vendor pointed to a small doorway between the two shops. The door led to a dark passageway to the back of the building. We walked through uncertainly, to find ourselves in a large and busy room. On one end were stacks of plastic wrapped cloth goods, while three low accounting desks were lined up against the wall on the other side. At one desk a man dressed in a suit sat on cushions, eating his lunch and surveying a stack of papers an assistant was showing him. "Yes, can I help you?" he said.

We explained what we were doing in our usual fashion . . . "trade in Ladakh . . .", "some old papers . . .", "an address from here . . . ," and showed the businessman the document we had brought. He paused and adjusted his glasses to read. Then, he motioned us to sit, and told his assistant to bring us tea from a nearby shop. "This paper is from our office," he exclaimed, "and is signed by my father." We smiled, having bridged the spatial and chronological gaps, and leaned forward. "May we ask you a few questions?"

After a cordial discussion about the types of trade his father's firm had done in Ladakh and related subjects, we prepared to leave the shop. Before doing so, however, we asked the Amritsar trader whether he recognized any of the other names we had of traders in Amritsar. He looked at our list of names and answered, "Now they are . . . these parties don't exist in Amritsar". He paused and said sadly, "None of these. They don't exist. You see, these are from pre-Partition, when Hindus and Muslims used to live together. These," and here he pointed at some papers, "are dated, 1934. I don't think many of these people exist here."

After a few more days, I found that most of the historical documents I had used successfully as a guide in other areas had indeed become almost useless in Amritsar. The market areas of Amritsar most commonly used by traders coming through Ladakh had become a modern Indian market with few traces of the past traders that had once occupied commercial and residential quarters there.

Walking along Hall *Bazaar* today, it is easy to miss the signs that this market road has historical significance. Only if one looks up, above

Figure 6.1 Hall Bazaar in Amritsar, 2001. Photograph by Abdul Nasir Khan.

the stationary shops and bicycle salesrooms, do the intricate second floor building facades hint at what the market might have been like in the 1920s and 1930s, as a flourishing business center that connected Central Asia with South Asia and other parts of the world.

Searching for further signs of the past, we found another – literally. On one road we noticed a hotel sign written in Urdu – the only one in the market, in marked contrast to the numerous Urdu language documents from the same road in the 1930s.

This hotel was run by the family of an elderly Muslim man, Abdullah, who claimed to be the only Muslim left in the market who had been a resident of Amritsar before the partition of India and Pakistan. He explained that he escaped much of the violence and upheaval of Partition because, as a trader in shawls, he had been temporarily stationed in Calcutta in 1947. The elderly man remembered many of the traders named in the documents we carried. Some of those traders had been important politicians before Partition, while some had been small traders. Some of those traders had survived, and had sons and daughters still living, while others had perished without any descendents. The Muslim traders listed in the documents we carried around were no longer in Amritsar. Most were now, according to Mr. Abdullah, resettled in Lahore. He thought that a number of those trader's families now owned industrial complexes or businesses in Lahore, although he was not sure as he did not have a great deal of communication with those across the border.

Later that week we visited Wagah border, a crossing point between India and Pakistan that lies approximately 17 miles from Amritsar. There one can walk along garden pathways to look across at Pakistan, and this is apparently a popular tourist activity.

The main event, a flag-lowering ritual, occurs every evening at the Wagah border station as personnel on each side of the border attempts to lower their flag before sundown, but not before the flag of the rival nation across the way. As the flags are lowered in time together the border guards perform for a huge crowd seated on bleachers on both sides of the border gates. Indian and Pakistani spectators cheer as their guards face off to stamp emphatically and gesture insultingly towards each other. The Wagah spectacle is like a cheering display at an athletic event, but the game is between nations rather than national teams.

As we watched this spectacle, I could not help but wonder whether perhaps any of the traders or their descendents sat in the bleachers on the other side of the border. Unfortunately, I have not yet been able to visit Pakistan to meet them and find out. The twentieth-century formation of borders has dramatically altered social life in all the regions

Figure 6.2 Looking across the barbed wire fence from the Indian side of Wagah border to see a Pakistani tourist and guard staring back from their side. Wagah Border Checkpoint, 2000. Photograph by Abdul Nasir Khan.

associated with trade through Ladakh, as the partition of India and Pakistan shaped social relations in the Punjab. The many missing traders of Amritsar were a poignant reminder that the legacy of trade, while experienced by all participants of the former trade networks, is not experienced in the same way by all those members. While making sense of the relationship between the past and present was a central interest for all the traders and their descendents I spoke with, their memories of the past were informed and shaped by varied regional, familial, and personal experiences.

The few descendents of Amritsari traders with Ladakh that remained in Amritsar remembered their families' trading experiences through the lens of Partition experiences, as their memories of traders in the past were linked to other memories about helping the traders and their families prepare to leave Amritsar. As in Ladakh, although the border with Pakistan is close, the gulf between what is now India and Pakistan occupies vast conceptual spaces. In conversation about the trading past one Amritsari man reflected on how the borders have, over time, expanded spaces and redefined local geographies. He mused with wonder, recalling going to college in Lahore before Partition, "We used to go every evening to Lahore because that was only a thirty-five, forty-five minutes ride . . . very calm. I used to be able to drive there from Amritsar . . ."

If taken, those evening drives now end at Wagah border and the performance of national identity.

Shifting borders

The closing of Ladakh's borders with Pakistan and China during the mid-twentieth century, which led to the end of the regional role in trade with Central Asia, represents only one historical example of a type of border. Numerous other political boundaries had shaped social networks in earlier times. Historian Alistair Lamb, who has written a number of works on borders in the Ladakh region, provides a useful distinction between use of the terms "boundary" and "frontier" when discussing geopolitical issues in the region. Lamb writes that a boundary refers to "a clear divide between sovereignties which can be marked as a line on a map", with "length but not area" (Lamb 1968:4). In contrast, use of the term frontier refers to "a zone rather than a line", being a "tract of territory separating the centres of two sovereignties" (Lamb 1968:6). Thus I discuss Ladakh as both as a region that contains boundaries and a frontier region. Another useful distinction to recognize is the difference between a demarcated boundary, one that has been physically marked and usually enforced *in situ*, and a delimited boundary, one which is set on a map and "explicitly accepted by the states which it divides" (Lamb 1968:4–5). The political struggles expressed in this chapter are in relation to successive delimitations of boundaries that were eventually demarcated. While Ladakh remained a frontier zone through the nineteenth and twentieth centuries, Ladakhi traders have coped with varying degrees of trade restrictions in relation to the delimitation, and eventual partial demarcation, of political borders. The geographic fluctuation of Ladakh's borders can be charted clearly through political treaties and maps over the course of the mid-nineteenth century.

The British colonial government mapped the boundaries of the Ladakh territory in 1846 after establishment of the Treaty of Amritsar with the government of Jammu and Kashmir. As Lamb notes, however, "within 20 years in the 1868 Kashmir Atlas this had changed, and the border had moved approximately 60 miles to the east to include more territory" (Lamb 1973:107). By the late nineteenth century the British government included even more areas north and east of Leh town in maps of India.[1] Border fluctuations defined many nineteenth-century social and economic structures in the region. While main needs for border delimitation between Ladakh and Chinese Central Asia arose within the British colonial political context of South Asia, regional boundary demarcation was necessitated by the trade communities and arose in the form of trade regulating institutions such as customs posts and stations for state revenue officers.

In my discussion of borders in the Ladakh region I am not only concerned with the ways in which demarcation of boundaries occurred, but also the historical contexts in which the methods of demarcation were formulated and maintained. There were two boundary fronts in Ladakh at which this occurred: the borders to the north-west with Pakistan within the partition of South Asia after the end of British colonialism, and the border to the east with China, which became of great importance to the newly independent nation of India in the 1950s and 1960s.

South Asian borders in Ladakh

The border formation processes with Pakistan are perhaps the first borders that come to mind when we think of North India. As accounts of the instability and violence of the Partition era in South Asia remind us, the division of the sub-continent into the two countries of India and Pakistan became a political, cultural, and social minefield. Political structures developed under British colonialism made the task even more difficult. During the late British colonial regime in the sub-continent there were over five hundred semi-independent princely states similar to Jammu and Kashmir. Political agents of the British colonial government hurriedly attempted to solidify the plan for independent Pakistan and India and convince the rulers of these areas to join the envisioned new countries, sometimes trying to apply pressure to persuade, and other times enticing them with political concessions. The kingdom of Jammu and Kashmir, under the rule of Maharaja Hari Singh, became a focal point of tension with its key geographic position on the border of what would become India and Pakistan.

The uncertain position of Jammu and Kashmir, including Ladakh, resulted in armed insurgency, political instability in the region, and conflict between Pakistan and India. This instability reportedly forced the hand of Maharaja of Jammu and Kashmir, who decided to sign a treaty of accession to India (Varshney 1991). The political coupe of bringing Jammu and Kashmir into India was achieved, by large, through the formulation of several important political concessions by the Indian federal government. Jammu and Kashmir's distinct legal status was specifically protected by a special provision, Article 370, in the Indian constitution and through a series of political agreements in 1952. One of the political privileges of these agreements gave more power to the state constitution of Jammu and Kashmir which was presented to the public on November 17, 1956. The state constitution sanctioned several important legal points for the new state, including Section 6 that defined the status of a permanent resident of the state. The permanent resident status made residency in Jammu and Kashmir State a separate legal category from citizenship in India, thus limiting access to property ownership in the state by excluding residents of other Indian states. The Ladakh region was subject to all these governmental decisions as a part of the new state of Jammu and Kashmir. Thus the division of India and Pakistan would create a unique political atmosphere in the region, one that had broad socio-political implications that continue to be articulated in the Ladakhi political arena and public sphere.

Close to the towns of Kargil and Leh, the pains of Indian–Pakistani Partition just before the independence of India were felt most keenly in the Skardo–Gilgit area to the north-west. One Ladakhi man, posted in Skardo as an assistant to the W*azir-i-wazarat* (state minister) of Jammu and Kashmir in 1946, remembered that feelings of tension and unease caused him to request a transfer back to Leh just before militant forces attacked the area. He would listen to the news of Pakistani force movements in 1947, and think, "Now they will come sooner or later to Skardo."

He requested leave from his superiors to visit his home in Leh, and was granted a five month leave. The assistant *Wazir-i-wazarat* left immediately with a friend, and the two men traveled for seven days on horseback. Shortly after, fighting began in Skardo. He remembered,

These Leh people were very unhappy; [they asked,] "What is happening in Skardo?" Now ultimately those raiders, those raiders were coming to Skardo also. From Gilgit and from Kashmir side, Kashmir side, there is a route, still . . . So, they started coming to Skardo. Then, the Indian government sent troops to Skardo. In battalions, so many troops, and there was a battle, they fought in Skardo for about a month. Then, they were defeated, Indian army were defeated due to the terrain. . . . Yes. There was a fort in Skardo. They surrendered that fort; it was on a hilltop just like this Leh fort . . . So ultimately the enemy forces started, they advanced towards Kargil. Then you know Zoji-la? That was the only route for coming to Leh. . . . [The forces] captured this Zoji-la pass. Now, this is the pass between Srinagar and Kargil, Dras. Which was also important during these days also, the Zoji-la pass. So, they came from that pass, and ultimately Leh was cut off from Srinagar. We were cut off from Srinagar. During winter, that was during winter, we were cut off. Ultimately, they came to Kargil; after one or two months, they came right up to this Basgo.

The places this man mentioned, Zoji-la, a mountain pass near Kargil, and Basgo, a town approximately 24 miles from Leh town, drive home the message of how startlingly far into Ladakh, and close to Leh, Pakistani forces came during this time period. Furthermore, although the winter timing of this border conflict meant most traders were not actively engaged in travel, the conflict destabilized the regional economy. The traders in Leh had heard a number of Indian traders from the Punjab were killed in Skardo during the fighting, and enemy control of the main route to the rest of Jammu and Kashmir meant traders residing in Leh would not be able to easily bring goods to and from South Asia.

The isolation of Ladakh through the closure of the border with Pakistan near Kargil, and movement of Pakistan based forces into the region around Leh, emphasized the vulnerability of the area. The Ladakh region was targeted for transportation development by the Indian government, and the Ladakhi engineer Sonam Norbu began designing and supervising construction of an airport in Leh, with government support. This airport was the key factor in India's defense of Ladakh, as one elderly Ladakhi recalled, saying, "Sonam Norbu came here and he started construction, planning this airport. Ultimately, the Indian air force in their plane, in the quarter plane, landed here, and so many troops landed here. So, Leh was of course saved."

Sonam Norbu's work can still be seen in Ladakh today, and his contributions to Ladakh's public works are widely recognized. In a survey I conducted with Leh town residents in 2001, Sonam Norbu was one of the four most often mentioned individuals in answer to the question, "Who are the most important people in Ladakhi history?" Reasons given in support of this answer included lists of his accomplishments, as well as a simple but common claim that he "did good for Ladakh."

The building of the airport and subsequent airlifting of army vehicles into the Ladakh region signified military securement of the area, and a new era in transport and migration patterns. The development of multiple forms of transport facilities was central to the Indian government's effort to secure the Ladakh region. The political status of Ladakh as a borderland, while closing trade routes and severing trade networks, also served to open new routes and transform the significance of the connections between Ladakh and other parts of South Asia. Thus the closing of the borders with Pakistan was not simply a severance of networks and end to migration in Ladakh, but a re-direction of the flow of people.

Central Asian borders in Ladakh

In contrast, the political formation of a demarcated Chinese–Indian border at Ladakh's eastern boundaries was a gradual process. Military action was not the central feature in disrupting Central Asia trade networks on the China side; instead, a series of political maneuvers in British India and Chinese Central Asia slowly strangled networks from the late nineteenth century until approximately 1958. The eventual full scale border dispute between India and China then sealed Ladakh's role in the twentieth century as a heavily militarized border zone.

The seeds of dispute between India and China had been sown before the independence of India from the British colonial government. In 1914 Chinese, Tibetan and British Indian authorities had participated in the Simla convention and produced the McMahon Line, a boundary between China and India with weakly subscribed powers of delimitation. The Chinese government refused to ratify parts of the treaty concerning the McMahon line (Steiner 1959:172),[2] although it was used as a *de facto* boundary for many years. During this time period traders from British South Asia carried passports in Central Asia, which were used to prove that the traders were subjects of the British Empire.

The information recorded in these passports suggests the documents were not initially required for regional border crossing, as the passports were issued in Chinese Central Asia before the South Asian traders had traveled across the borders. Border demarcation in the form of check-posts for human traffic, as opposed to goods, were not in evidence in the early twentieth-century Ladakh region. Within the trading community, however, these documents had a great deal of significance. Rather than being travel documents, the passports of British Indian traders were identification documents used to signify their rights to certain goods, responsibilities for customs taxes, and place within the British trading community headed by the British Indian *aqsaquals* in Central Asian cities.

The British government and Ladakhi traders alike had to re-adjust their policies for Chinese Central Asia multiple times to accommodate

Figure 6.3 Passports of Punjabi traders (Lajpat Rai, top, and Sansar Chand, bottom) stationed in Chinese Central Asia. These passports are still owned by the descendents of the traders, living in Hoshiarpur, India. Photograph by Abdul Nasir Khan.

changes due to regional political upheaval. For example, nineteenth century Uighur and Kazakh rebellions against the Chinese government in Central Asia gave the Russian government an opportunity to establish an official presence in the region. The presence of Russians in the region then became a political pretext for the establishment of the British Treaty Road to Chinese Central Asia, and this event in turn necessitated new taxation practices in Ladakh (Lamb 1968:197).

This gradual growth of political constraints on trading networks continued in the early twentieth century. In the 1940s local rebellions in Chinese Central Asia caused numerous legal problems in Leh; traders on both sides of the boundaries could not travel to claim their goods or communicate to their trading partners on the other side of the border how to dispose of those goods. Correspondence from this time period shows a trading community caught in between the contesting needs of the localized politics of regional revolutionary governments and the international concerns of powers such as the Chinese and British governments. A series of letters between Shamsuddin Khan, the son of Bahauddin Khan, and the British Joint Commissioner of Ladakh in 1944 documents one such legal tangle. In one letter Shamsuddin Khan writes:

> Due to some unfavorable circumstances that arose in Central Asia, the road from Leh to Yarkend was closed and is still closed. The closing of the road resulted in the withholding of some of the articles that were held with me by those merchants of Khotan and Yarkend with whom I had commercial relations as the merchants could not be allowed under orders to come to Leh. These articles were kept with me as trust. Some of the articles, as time suited, were disposed of and the rest of them were preserved.

While Shamsuddin attempted to safeguard the inventory and interests of his trading partner in Central Asia, in the absence of communication the goods were confiscated by Jammu and Kashmir state government representatives with a claim for wrongful management of properties. Such a breakdown in communications, mobility, and general reliability of the trade networks in the 1940s signified the beginning of less profitable circumstances for trade relations between many of the Ladakhi and Central Asian traders.

Trade with Chinese Central Asia declined further with the 1949 march of Chinese forces into Yarkend to fight against regional rebel forces. These political events directed the course of regional trade and Ladakhi traders kept informed about the events through letters. In one such letter a Ladakhi trader wrote to another in Kashmir:

> I am glad to know the news received from Kashmir through your letter. And the news received here, we have come to know that the Tungans never came from inside but they are busy fighting [with] Yunis Beg and Urumchi and Mao Young are helping them.

The political turbulence in Chinese Central Asia also caused the large scale political exodus of approximately five hundred Turkic Muslim refugees, who were fleeing from the Chinese government (Kak 1978:37). Many these refugees had been a part of the trading networks in Ladakh, and thus came to Ladakh. Older Ladakhis clearly remember the arrival of these Central Asian refugees, although some of those interviewed were unsure of the specific political struggle behind the fleeing. One informant explained, when asked when they ran, repeated the question in surprise, saying:

> When did they run? When I went there at that time, they were governing in Kargilik. Then some forces came from there and killed them, and half of them ran to Ladakh, half of them were killed. *Whose forces?*
> The Chinese . . . or Russian. They brought tanks and bombarded them, at that time...

The journey to Ladakh was arduous; one descendent of these refugees mentioned that his father had told him the original number who emigrated from Chinese Central Asia was 5000, but only 500 survived the journey.

These refugees arrived in Ladakh in October 1949, and their numbers included such important political figures of Central Asia as Isa Yusul Alptekin, the former Secretary General of Sinkiang, and Mohammed Amin Bogra, the former Deputy Governor of Sinkiang (Kak 1978:37). In Ladakh the so-called "Sinkiang refugees" are remembered clearly as many of them settled briefly in the region. The Sinkiang refugees spoke Uighur and reportedly did not know Ladakhi. They would communicate in Uighur with Ladakhis who had traded in Chinese Central Asia and knew the language, and with other local residents in English, which they had learned from British sources in Sinkiang. The needs of the Sinkiang refugees benefited many in Leh, who bought horses and sheep cheaply from those refugees who had brought livestock.

As the Chinese government re-secured the Central Asian region they also reasserted their international borders, and in 1949 the Chinese authorities stated in an official message to the Indian government that the McMahon based border was invalid as it had not been universally ratified (Maxwell 1970:47). Chinese denials of the political validity of the McMahon line continued in the 1950s. In 1959 Chinese premier Chou En-lai stated, "The so-called McMahon Line . . . was a product of the British policy of aggression against the Tibet region of China and has never been recognized by any Chinese Central Government and therefore is decidedly illegal" (as quoted in Steiner 1959:169).

Chinese governmental rhetoric frequently utilized the language of international law to dispute the frontier territories.[3] In contrast, Indian Prime minister Jawaharlal Nehru stated in 1959 the McMahon line was a "firm frontier – firm by treaty, firm by right, firm by usage and firm by geography",[4] claiming that "[n]o discussions can be fruitful unless the posts on the Indian side of the *traditional frontier* now held by the Chinese forces are first evacuated by them and further threats and intimidations immediately cease" (quoted in Steiner 1959:168, emphasis added here).

Inter-government discussions, border encroachments, and finally the construction of a segment of the Chinese Tibet–Sinkiang Highway within the Aksai Chin plateau slowly escalated conflicting Sino-Indian relations, which culminated in the 1962 border war between India and China. Trade between Ladakh and Tibet, which had continued to decline throughout the 1950s, now ceased altogether in 1962. Ladakhis who had continued to trade in Chinese Central Asia, and sometimes lived there for generations, were forced to leave their homes. In Tibet at least 350 Ladakhis, including monks, religious students and traders, were marooned across the border (Kak 1978:33–34). Many of their families in Ladakh had to wait to hear news of their fate until the 1980s. This number included several members of international families from Kashmir, who are reportedly still living in Lhasa (Gaborieau 2000:193–196).

Yet, Leh residents who lived during the time period remember the cessation of trade with Chinese regions as a gradual occurrence, commenting that it was hard to pinpoint any particular time where trade ended. As one former trader related,

> [s]o after that [Chinese aggression at borders] I have not seen any caravans coming to Leh. That was in 1942, or 43 or 4, no, 53 or 54 . . . That was the last caravan that came to Leh, and the state government, the ruler, asked them to go back immediately, because they are not allowed to stay here.

In this case, a last caravan is particularly remembered as it became a political issue. The spectacle was more significant than the time period, as the informant did not remember in what decade this occurred, and whether the incident was under the Maharaja's government or the state government of Jammu and Kashmir. These events most probably occurred within independent India in the late 1950s.

Regardless of the ambiguity of the time, the end of trade was certain. As another former trader summarized:

And after that nobody came. Because the route was cut. That region had gone to Chinese, Chinese had occupied that region. And they wouldn't allow any of these to come via caravan or by road. That route was closed. . . .

Leh becomes a new market

After the trade between Chinese Central Asia and South Asia was ceased, the most lucrative forms of trade in Ladakh ended. One type of trade did remain – trade that focused on Leh and surrounding areas such as Kargil and Zanskar as markets rather than entrepôs. Thus the formation of borders in the region re-defined Ladakh politically, as a part of the Indian nation, and as a new commercial zone. Interviewed traders from Amritsar and Hoshiarpur who still trade today in Ladakh repeatedly pointed out that Ladakh became a market as it became a border region. One merchant explained that a new type of trade reappeared after the Indian army had secured Ladakh and industries began developing in the region, saying:

> Pakistan took far flung Indian territories and the Chinese were under military rule, up to Pakistan. Then, after that, we started this business with Ladakh. It used to be that there was only one [shop], but there was really development, after the army went and settled Kargil, and all that. So, in that region, I think the new industry grows there. . . . Ladakhis and Kargilis used to come [to our shop in the Punjab] because we had links earlier with the old *Hajis* [groups of traders through Ladakh]. They used to come to us for all their purchasing. Then we thought [of] the area, and Ladakh . . . the area and the region, like that . . . Ladakh trade, you know, developed because of the requirements [for goods within the market] there, you know. So ever since [the times of] my father and his family, [there has been] all this business. When he died, you know, then we have taken over, my brother and [I] . . . so both of us are supplying their requirements of Ladakh and Kargil. And it is still going on . . . mainly they buy from here tea, cloth, and utensils, and these rations, the grocer's requirements.

These business choices, to establish markets in relation to the new needs and consumer populations in Ladakh, were made by many of the former traders in India who had previously traveled through Ladakh on their way elsewhere. Thus in spite of the dramatic demise of many of the long distance trading networks in Ladakh during the 1940s and

1950s, some trade networks were reformulated to fit new market circumstances. In this particular case, Ladakhi and Kargili consumers looking for wholesalers revived their older trade associations in the Punjab after approximately ten to twenty years, even though other regional Indian markets were geographically closer.

Part III
The modern context

7   The memory and legacy of trade

Ethnographic present: The Yarkendi woman in Ladakh

Yarkendi traders are often remembered in Ladakh in highly idealized terms such as those in the *kiraiyakash's* account in Chapter 4 – healthy, wealthy, and generous, etc. Yarkendis were also frequently recalled by Ladakhis in relation to the items they owned and goods they carried. For example, when asked about who the Hors were, one older man replied not with a description of the people, but rather with a list of their goods, listing ". . . carpets, rugs, gold, pearls . . ." He went on to explain with delight that Yarkendis were so rich that if you gave one two pieces of bread, they would give you a whole sheep in return.

Thus when I was invited to visit the house of a Yarkendi woman who had been married to a trader from the same place, I set out with expectations of stories of great wealth and abundance. The elderly woman greeted me with warmth, and we began talking about her children, two young women I knew. As the conversation continued, I looked around the small and sparsely decorated apartment with some surprise, having expected to see many lavish artifacts of the legendary goods from Yarkend. She began talking about trade with Central Asia with a modest disclaimer, saying, "I stayed at home, I didn't go to anywhere, I don't know anything."

After some discussion, however, I discovered that she knew many stories about the trading past. Like others, she spoke about wealth in Yarkend – but as she explained how the family fared after regional trade ended, the narrative changed drastically. Her father had lost a lucrative business in Yarkend during the Central Asia government changes, and after receiving a cash settlement from the local government he purchased some goods with a portion of the devalued currency and left with his family for Leh. On the journey the group met with heavy snowfall and most of the goods had to be jettisoned on a mountain pass. Later her father tried to return to collect them but he was not allowed to go near the border area, and thus lost everything. He had to sell his personal horse and clothes in order to survive, but for years he would show visitors the now worthless paper money he had received as a settlement, to show that he was once very rich in Yarkend. She went on to explain that Yarkendis who settled in Ladakh after the end of trade faced discrimination and legal difficulties, saying, ". . . at that time Yarkendis who were in Srinagar, in Kargil, or in Leh wanted to go . . . here our children couldn't get jobs because we didn't have the state subject [certificate]."

As she continued to detail some of the difficulties faced by her community after the end of trade, I was surprised to hear that the Yarkendi community in Ladakh was so small today because of a mass migration that happened approximately in the 1970s. This migration was not a return to Yarkend, however, but to a new country – Turkey. She explained,

> Their government, the Turkish government, funded the trips – airfare, visa, everything . . . and took them there. The father of my children was also ready to go . . . he told me, 'We will also go'. He even took pictures of our children at that time . . . and made passports for every one. At that time my father and mother both were alive and we told all our relatives that we were going with the children. [But then we thought], how far Turkey is. Can we visit here or not? [We decided] that it was better to stay here with our relatives and everyone, than going there – so we didn't go. Almost everyone else went . . . everyone from Srinagar went . . . now their children got jobs and became rich. They got an education and some are working in factories, now they are comfortable.

After this she paused, shrugged, and summarized, simply saying, "We didn't go."

The Turkish invitation, political sponsorship, and funding of the Yarkendi migration from Ladakh is linked with concepts of pan-Turkic identity. This identity category is not documented within the historical trading communities of Ladakh – there is no mention in the Khan Archives documents or interviews with older traders. The traders conceptualized, and defined themselves, in relation to their place of origin as Yarkendi, or in ethnic terms as Hors.

This identification of the Yarkendi community developed in relation to the formation of borders between India and China, and to the problems that Yarkendi traders faced once finding themselves stranded on the wrong side of the border. Unable to either place themselves or be placed into the necessary political categories of state subject in Jammu and Kashmir, these traders embraced the concept of Turkic identity. Turkic identity was offered to them by the Turkish government, whose interest in the development of an ethnic identity independent of religious or tribal affiliations was related to the Turkish movement towards European style nationalism since the late nineteenth century (Kushner 1997:219), when contact with "Turkic" peoples from Central Asia inspired redefinition of Turks as a modern interest group (Kushner 1997:220).

Not all the Yarkendi community in India chose to move to Turkey. Some, like the families of Yarkendi woman featured in this conversation, felt that they had too many ties in India to migrate to a new country. A man of Yarkendi descent echoed these sentiments, saying,

> My father told us that we will also go [to Turkey]. But we thought that we were born in this country, all of my mother's relatives are here, we knew everyone here . . . so we didn't agree because at that time we were mature, especially me because I was the eldest. I told him that I can't leave from here, so he told me, 'If you were not going, then why will I go there, who is there of mine?' Then he cancelled [the trip] and stayed here.

In these cases where families remained in Ladakh, the concept of a Turkic identity was not a strong motivator in the decision-making process. Instead, these two families focused on their local kinship ties and perceived themselves as Ladakhis of Yarkendi heritage. As the Yarkendi woman's story shows us, the social impact of the bordering of Ladakh did not end with the severance of trading networks.

Thus in the rest of this chapter I will continue to address the modern ethnographic context of Ladakh. Here we will see how Ladakh's trade history and the existence of a cosmopolitan identity group have complicated discourse about social identity in the region. Ladakh's trading cosmopolitan elite plays a central part in Ladakhi identity struggles today through the intersubjectivity of memories and legacies.

Memory and legacy

The effects of historical trade connections are felt in diverse ways in present day Ladakh, which I divide into the categories of "memories" and "legacies". Memories are the ways in which narratives about historical trade connections have been reshaped by individuals and groups to have lasting significance. In memory narratives past trade connections take on new meanings to descendents of the traders, such as the idealized notions of goods carried by traders, or of Yarkendi visitors to the region. The legacies of trade are the ways in which social relations formulated within trading networks continue to provide patterns for interactions within, and discourse about, contemporary Ladakh. In structuring discourses, then, legacies shape memory narratives as well.

Upon initial consideration, popular discussions of Ladakhi identity in recent years seem to employ a standardized political vocabulary, one that conforms to Indian national discourses about ethnicity, such as the debates over becoming a Scheduled Tribe. As a diverse young nation with an established policy for the political categorization of ethnic groups in the form of Scheduled Caste and Tribe status, India has utilized social signifiers such as religion, caste, and ethnicity to mobilize national interests, Ladakh is no exception to this general trend; thus existing scholarly works that discuss the roles of ethnicity and cultural difference in the nation building programs of India are relevant to consider (see for example Brass 1994, van der Veer 1994, Brown 1994).

Yet discussions about identity within the public sphere of Ladakh do not conform to a national standard or type; ideas about Ladakhiness are also articulated in relation to social contexts shaped by the legacy of trade in the region. As we will see in the case of the Scheduled Tribe status debate, the historical roles of Ladakh's Arghun cosmopolitan elite play a significant role in the community discourse on being Ladakhi. The tensions of this identity are articulated through other channels as well, as Ladakhis define themselves in relation to regional and global processes, such as international movements for sustainable development, and critiques of what are commonly viewed as "western"[1] influences.

Legacies in the political arena: Arghuns and the struggle for Scheduled Tribe status

While past definitions of an Arghun individual, and the Arghun community as a whole, emphasized cultural hybridity and cosmopolitan identities (as discussed in Chapter 3), contemporary usages may suggest that Arghun identity is conceptualized differently in Ladakh today. While people in Ladakh still discuss Central Asian, and sometimes Kashmiri, heritage as descent criteria for Arghuns, most Ladakhis use the term popularly to specifically discuss the Ladakhi Sunni Muslim community. In literature Sunni Muslims are sometimes even referred to by the same criteria as Arghuns, such as in this informational pamphlet excerpt, where the author writes:

A significant number of traders from Central Asia, Kashmir, and other parts of India settled down in Ladakh permanently, they married with Ladakhi women. Thousands of Sunni Muslims of Leh town and other parts of Ladakh are their offspring.

(Sheikh 2000)

This definition of the Sunni Muslim community is nearly synonymous with that of Arghuns. Most modern authors, when establishing the criteria of descent, also establish the religious criteria of Arghun identity, either as a sub-section of the Muslim community of Ladakh, such as "Argon group of Muslims" (Sheikh and Aggarwal 2001), or with a distinction between "pure Kashmiris" and "hybrid Arghuns" (Chohan 1994:28), thus specifically as the Sunni Muslims of Ladakh.

The actual use of the term Arghun in everyday Ladakhi conversation is specific and complex. A first common pattern of use indicates that being Arghun is an all or nothing proposition. An individual in Ladakh who had a Central Asian ancestor and who is Muslim is called an Arghun, not part Arghun or even descended from Arghuns. This is in contrast to use of the term Yarkendi – when discussing the ethnicity of a descendent of a Yarkendi, Ladakhis will usually explain that the person is part Yarkendi or descended from a Yarkendi. Yet a Sunni Muslim descendent of a Yarkendi, who lives in Ladakh, is usually called both an Arghun and "part" Yarkendi. The term Arghun, therefore, is not used as other ethnic terms.

The second common discursive pattern is that use of the term Arghun is linked to two types of social practices – those of religion and kinship. A Ladakhi Buddhist woman who in her youth married a Muslim trader of Central Asian descent, and converted to Islam, is called Arghun. Other communities in Ladakh are discussed in similarly conflated terms; for example the Shia community of Ladakh is often called Balti, even if particular individuals are not definitively of Balti descent.[2] A Christian would not be called Arghun, even if they are descended from Central Asian traders and "local" Ladakhis. Muslims descended from Ladakhi Christians and Central Asia traders are, however, considered fully Arghun. This means that being Arghun involves both religious practice, and certain social networks.

The final general rule of use for the term Arghun excludes large segments of the Muslim community, particularly Shia (as mentioned earlier), and Kashmiri Muslims. One Muslim girl I knew who was born and raised in Ladakh is called "Kashmiri" in conversation, because her parents are from Kashmir, but I have never heard her called Arghun by anyone speaking of her family. Kashmiri merchants living in

Ladakh, even for generations, are not called Arghuns unless married into a family designated as Arghun. This means that Arghun cannot simply be a synonym for Muslim.

An Arghun, under this system of classification, is anyone with Ladakhi heritage who is Sunni Muslim, defined at least in part in opposition to Sunni Muslims from other areas, or without local descent groups. Thus these definitions of Arghuns as the Ladakhi Sunni Muslims emphasize a distinct identity that depends as much on some concept of ties to the local area, "Ladakhi-ness," as Islamic identity and/or Muslim community practices.

This conceptualization of Arghun identity is relevant when discussing the Scheduled Tribe status in Ladakh, offering a more nuanced way of understanding social violence in Ladakh during the 1980s. For, although many authors writing about the time period seem to imply that this was a religious communal struggle, we can see that the hostility was not focused simply in religious communal terms. Instead, multiple Ladakhi communities were involved as targets. Thus during this time period, van Beek writes that, "several Christian houses and other properties were damaged by explosions, while the community as a whole was put under social boycott" (van Beek 1998a:304). The Kargili Shia Muslim community was not as much the focal point of violence as was the Leh Sunni Muslim community – and a few authors have mentioned that Sunni Muslims were particularly targeted because of their supposed ties to the Kashmiri Muslims. Additionally, during the *bazaar* riots between local Muslims and local Buddhists property destroyed specifically included shops owned by the Kashmiri Muslim population (van Beek 1998a:309). Thus this communalization of politics in Ladakh could be conceptualized as a movement against those that were perceived as fundamentally non-Ladakhi, for reasons of difference, rather than specifically targeted at the religious Muslim community. The Arghun community, as a large non-Buddhist minority, was an evident target for aggression. This hostility over perceptions of who is fundamentally Ladakhi plays a large role in the modern perceptions of the Arghun community in Ladakh today, as well as the outcome of the autonomy struggle.

Today many Arghuns feel excluded from definitions of the Scheduled Tribe in Ladakh. Some Arghun community members reported being denied Scheduled Tribe status with an explanation that they were not "native" Ladakhis. Other Arghuns managed to get Scheduled Tribe status by proving their descendence from Buddhist relatives as part of a tribe called *Bhot*/*Bhoto*; this classification seems to exclude Muslim participants, although the actual meaning of the term does not necessarily do so.[3] Curiously not all Arghun were able to achieve Scheduled Tribe status through descent, although most classic definitions of Arghuns all definitively state that Arghuns are descended from both Central Asian/Kashmiri and Ladakhi progenitors. Considering that the Arghun community as a whole has a history of at least approximately two hundred years of settlement in Ladakh, many are led to question how "Ladakhi" an individual would have to be to claim Scheduled Tribe status.

At the heart of this debate is a public consciousness, a memory, of the cosmopolitan nature of the Arghun community during the trading period in Ladakhi history. What makes the Arghun community suspect as locals from this point of view is their long historical participation in larger socio-economic system. This concern about what is local, and what is not, is mirrored and expressed in new terms today, such as in terms of international Islamic identity in relation to local Ladakhi identity. Issues of the Islamic communities of Ladakh's relationships to the rest of the Islamic world community, in the form of *Haj* participation, Islamic schooling, and international funding thus play an important role in discussions of Arghun identity in Ladakh. Repeatedly in the course of my interviews with members of the Arghun community and Muslim community association leaders, informants expressed frustration that they should be so cut off from the world Muslim community in many ways, such as lack of international monetary support for the Sunni community, and yet perceived as not being a part of the local community in other forums. Thus the centrality of Ladakhi identity in a group's identity, rather than the mere presence, is one of the social issues in question within the modern political arena. This social struggle is even further complicated by the ways in which Ladakh's trading past is considered to be a quintessential part of local history, and the cosmopolitan Arghun traders are a part of local concepts of what it means to be Ladakhi.

This juxtaposition, the inclusion of a cosmopolitan past in defining a precisely local identity, was most clearly articulated in one political speech by Mr. P. Namgyal, who represented Ladakh in the Indian House of the People (the lower house of the Parliament of India) to argue for tax exempt status for Ladakhi Scheduled Tribe members. While arguing that Ladakhis should be exempt from income tax as a Scheduled Tribe, Mr. Namgyal also cited Ladakh's trading history, and the demise of said trade, as a reason that residents of Ladakh deserved this tax status. He argued:

The residents of Ladakh region of Jammu and Kashmir were exempted from payment of Income Tax under Clause (26) Section 10 of Income Tax Act of 1961 with effect from the assessment year 1962 to 1988–89 on the ground of Chinese aggression on Ladakh in 1962 which resulted in stoppage of border trades between Ladakh and Tibet and Ladakh with Shinjiang (China). With the result, the business of hundreds of Ladakhi traders was totally ruined overnight and the economy of Ladakh was badly affected. Consequent to this, the Central Government had given exemption of Income Tax to Ladakh till 1989.[4]

Here we can see that Ladakh's trading history plays a role in defining the region even in conversations about defining the rights associated with residents' Scheduled Tribe status, and the trading history can be used to define what it means to be Ladakhi in the political arena.

Legacies in the global market: Tourism

There are a number of similarities between the ways in which people in Ladakh characterize interactions with foreign traders in past historical trading networks, and contemporary tourists in the present-day hospitality industry. Just as many villagers in Ladakh would marvel at the health and wealth of Hors traders without engaging in in-depth cultural exchanges, today they will often have limited cultural understanding of the tourists who stay in their guesthouses and eat in their restaurants. Many residents of Leh distinguish in general terms between the national origins of tourists (e.g. "French tourists," "British tourists," and "Israeli tourists"), but features of these categories are informed more by perceived patterns of the tourist's consumption habits and material wealth, than particular cultural characteristics.

However, not all of the interactions with tourists are characterized by Ladakhis in similar ways to the memories of interactions between traders and locals in Ladakh's recent past. Historical trade interactions are generally remembered as having opened Ladakh to extra-regional markets, while tourism is often discussed as having trapped Ladakhi in the same. Residents of Leh point out that "Tourism has made people too dependent on imports," as the demand for goods to consume increased. People worry that if the road is cut off from Srinagar then they are in trouble. In 1997, one Ladakhi from Leh gave an example of salt, which used to be produced in the surrounding areas of Ladakh. He explained that salt is no longer produced in Ladakh because it is easier to get salt commercially. In the mid-

1990s there was a supply transport problem that caused a winter salt shortage and people had a great deal of trouble meeting their own household needs. Winter is not the main tourist season in Ladakh, yet the speaker linked the demands of tourism with private household shortages in another season. The economic impact of tourism is emphasized by social fears that Ladakh is losing something in this particular transaction.

Much of the infrastructure of the initial tourist industry in Ladakh in the 1970s, however, was related directly to the trading history of the region. One of the first hotels to cater to tourists in Leh was, according to informants, one that had initially catered to the visiting merchants that had discovered Ladakh as a market after the closure of trading routes. Many of the former *serai* areas have now been converted into tourist facilities, either as hotels or shopping plazas.

Most significantly, the enduring social legacy of Ladakh's historical trade networks is expressed in the participation of many of the traders' descendents in the contemporary tourist industry. When the international tourist markets opened, many of the individuals with the linguistic skills and inter-cultural communication experience to interact with tourists were the descendents of the trade middlemen. One of Bahauddin Khan's grandsons, for example, owned a travel advisory office when tourism first began in 1975. A former trader living in Leh found, when he could no longer trade *pashmina*, that his previous hobby could be useful; he opened a photography shop, with postcards as well as supplies, for visitors. The entire family of one trader from present-day Pakistan switched business models after the severance of trade networks to include both local oriented business, such as wholesale foods, and tourist restaurants. In such ways, tourist agents, tour guides, and hotel operators all employ many of the same skills that their fathers and grandfathers employed as trade middlemen, *kiraiyakash*, and even *patawari*.

Legacies within the "global village": NGOs and development discourse

In the post-1980s period Ladakhi identity discourse has been positioned in relation to global debates about the meaning of culturally appropriate local development. Development workers in Ladakh participate in many international forums for discussion about sustainable development through membership in locally-run internationally-supported organizations such as Ladakh Ecological Development Organization (LEDeG), the Ladakh Nutritional Project (LNP), the Students'

Educational and Cultural Movement of Ladakh (SECMOL), and the Women's Alliance of Ladakh. International organizations such as the Save the Children Fund (SC-UK) and the International Centre for Integrated Mountain Development (ICIMOD) also have local offices, and/or partnerships with organizations, in Ladakh.

These organizations deal with a variety of development issues. In education Ladakhi groups have challenged the efficacy of curriculums that do not reflect local lifestyles and realities, in either the content of teaching materials[5] or overall educational goals. In agriculture, local groups have addressed the need to continue using traditional organic farming methods, and critically examining the percentage of cash crops being grown in the region (Angeles, 2001:100). The global energy crisis has been discussed in Ladakh, and a variety of solar and hydro-electric energy producing schemes have been introduced in the region (see for example the LEDeG publication "Energy Supply and Demand in the Himalayan Region of Ladakh in Jammu and Cashmere of India" 1997). The issues surrounding culturally appropriate and sustainable development, which became a focal point for debate in the Ladakhi public sphere in the late 1990s, continue to be part of regional discussion today.

Within many of the discussions about cultural change and sustainable development in some of the NGO forums runs a vein of commentary about a perceived insular Ladakh and the threats that it faces from the outside world. Much of this discussion is centered on the dramatic cultural changes that Ladakh has undergone within one generation, with a critical eye towards future change. One particular strand of this development debate in Ladakhi focuses on the consumption of foreign goods in relation to "Ladakhi-ness," a relationship that many view as one of opposition. A clear articulation of this opposition is presented to international tourists and Ladakhi guests alike in a LEDeG art display. This public gallery contains small exhibits with life-sized figures, pictures and text. The text and tableaux represent idealized views of "traditional Ladakhi life." There is a focus on the positive aspects of traditional Ladakhi culture, such as respect for elders, the high status of women in households, and the co-operative work in agricultural communities. There is no mention of regional trade, international influences, or diverse ethnic communities in this version of traditional Ladakh. Instead, the visitor is presented with a startling juxtaposition between the idealized past, and a vilified possible future if "foreign" influences continue to pervade the region. If we examine two particular scenes in the gallery, we can understand representations of Ladakhi-ness in relation to ideas about modernity in this setting.

Figure 7.1 "Traditional" Ladakh picture, photographed 2000.

The first scene of traditional Ladakh, Figure 7.1, is presented in the gallery as the ideal or utopia. This representation of Ladakh may at first be read as a statement of religious communal identity, as the image emphasizes Ladakh's Buddhist identity with elements such as prayer flags and *stupas*. Every building in this picture is either a Buddhist temple/monastery or a Buddhist home, marked as such with prayer flags on their roofs. However, this emphasis on a Buddhist Ladakh does not necessarily have to be viewed as a religious statement. Instead, we can see it as a statement of what is perceived as being primarily Ladakhi, albeit using the unchallenged version of religiously based identity politics. In this representation of Ladakh's resistance to the negative aspects of development, the utopia is "locally" oriented – in direct contrast with the dystopia pictured next.

The visitor is lead by a sign ominously titled "Ladakh's Future?" to this second section of the public gallery, pictured in Figure 7.2. In this display, the negative aspects of technological development are portrayed

Figure 7.2 "Future" Ladakh picture, photographed 2000.

in lurid colors to show what the NGO workers fear that Ladakh could become without judicious participation in global markets. Notice that this second picture of Ladakh's perceived negative future (Figure 7.2), or image as a dystopia, does not feature any other supplanting religion. Instead, the negative representations of development are all commodities linked to the "modern" and "Western" world. A few of these commodities are in production, in factories that litter the landscape and pollute the air. But most of the commodities alluded to here are in some stage of consumption, either in the advertisements for cigarettes, with a blue-jeans clad model, the selling of sex or the heaps of trash that are significantly filled with pieces of cars, motorcycles, and televisions. Ironically, literature adjacent to the gallery invites visitors to join the "international anti-globalisation" campaign of a sister organization.

The legacy of trade in Ladakh has thus shaped discourses of the global in the public sphere into discussions on the ways in which the local place, Ladakh, interacts with foreign goods. Participants in this debate do not perceive of the legacy of Ladakh's position in trade routes, perched on two roads between major trading areas of the world, as discordant with this conceptual framework. Instead, many discussants work within the paradigm of the historical background of Ladakh, emphasizing regional participation from a particularly passive point of view, as a stopping point between other hubs and an area shaped by political and economic forces beyond the control of the average Ladakhi. Trade networks are used by some Ladakhis as the basis for perceptions of commodities as coming from other places, as being foreign to Ladakh. The memories of Ladakh's trading history therefore inform Ladakhi participation in global discussions about whether increased participation in global markets is a necessary feature of modernity or not, and what it means to be "modern."

Conclusion

In this book I have brought together ethnographic, archival, and material culture evidence to outline Ladakh's trading history as social system, and show the relationship between the past and the present. We have seen that some of the most pressing debates currently circulating in Ladakhi discourse, about identity and relations to global networks of commodities, have a link to Ladakh's historical role as a trading entrepôt between South and Central Asia and in relation to the historical British, Russian, and Chinese empires.

Within the late nineteenth- and early twentieth-century trading networks, a variety of social/cultural groups worked together. These groups, comprised of members from diverse cultural and religious backgrounds, were bound together through both economic interactions and social practices such as intermarriage. The economic features of this trade system created social niches, as particular roles were created to maximize strategies for profit within the existing political and geographic features of the system. The Arghun community, in particular, occupied a unique position within trade networks. This community formed a cosmopolitan elite, through both intermarriage and relationships to commercial goods, both as consumers and purveyors of elite materials that provided connections to other commercial and cultural systems.

While the formation of modern political borders severed Ladakhi trade connections and social structures, the closing of national borders around Ladakh was only one facet of the border formation experience of the region. Over the course of boundary demarcation, regional trade networks were adapted to new contexts of trade relations, political systems, and global interests.

Thus in the contemporary ethnographic context of Ladakh, the legacies of the regional trade history continue to shape local discourse.

While the existence of the Arghun community as a cosmopolitan elite identity group has complicated discourse about social identity, the fluidity of cultural boundaries in the cosmopolitan world has also enabled Ladakhis to reconcile notions of the past and present through the intersubjectivity of memories and legacies.

The intersubjectivity of memory and legacy

Repeatedly during the course of interviews my informants discussed features of the past in idealized terms. For example, one man said wistfully,

> Now we say that everything here is developed . . . But people in those times were joyful . . . they were comfortable and had peace. Now, people don't have satisfaction or peace. Those times people had no religious tension . . . No bad things . . . there was very good cooperation. Everyone was living with unity. Even in joy and sorrows, if anything happened to anyone, everyone was together like it had happened in their own house.

This idealized past seemed to directly contradict other memories of Ladakh's past – ones of general poverty and scarcity of goods, such the following featured in another man's account. This informant told a story about how, in his childhood, they needed to steal sticks from neighboring land in order to have a stick with which to guide their plow animals. He explained,

> In my village there were only two forest areas, small forest areas belonging to one or two families. We used to go, to steal that stick, from that farmer. I mean, what I mean to say is, can you imagine the plantation, what was [the farmland like] in our area, when people had no stick of their own to cut?

When prompted, my informants confronted the contrasts in these narratives by recounting both scarcity and a more joyful past, but contrasting notions of quality and quantity. For example, one older man remembered that most families could not afford to buy rice regularly, but exclaimed how wonderful it was, because if you were given even one cup of rice on a special event like Eid, you were counted as lucky and wealthy. As another man explained that although today there is more food, "there is not the food of those times . . . whatever the food we were eating then was very good, simple food". He then went on to discuss how the foods now readily available in the market in Ladakh are made with unhealthy ingredients.

All of these comments would not make sense together unless the past and present were understood as informing each other in dialogue. Contemporary experiences, such as access to subsidized rice and social boycotts in Ladakh, inform how Ladakhis remember issues such as food scarcity and conflict in the past, which in turn play a role in how people understand the present. Thus both scarcity and abundance are made part of the same memories in reference to contemporary and historical knowledge, i.e. a dialogue between past and present.

In parallel narratives, many Ladakhi memories were used to emphasize the notion that Ladakh was a part of a complex transregional trading network, yet simplify and idealize the business dealings of that past. Informants remembered trade as occurring solely on the word of honest traders, who dealt fairly with each other without the complex legalities of business today. There were common references to anecdotes about past methods of trade where goods and payment alike were left under a rock to be picked up by other traders at another time.[1] These same informants, however, were also able to explain why the historical documents we brought contained a number of references to court cases for property disputes and receipts for goods. Few casual discussions about historical trade referred to the detailed business accounting or political regulation of trade that was commonly represented in the documents of the Khan Archives, yet many discussants recognized features of this system. Like narratives of simultaneous abundance and scarcity, popular idealized versions of a simple trading past can be reconciled with an understanding of the past as a legally complex and economically competitive time period only as part of a dialogue. In this case the dialogue is between the memories and the legacies of trade in Ladakhi social life.

The legacies of Ladakh's trade history are the historical phenomena that people in local areas continue to experience, as the roots of contemporary social, political, and economic contexts. The close examination of the political and economic processes that severed trade networks in the Ladakh region has revealed how these events provide a base for many economic and political issues in Ladakh today. Ladakh's current political and economic status is defined in part by the new patterns of trade that emerged in the late nineteenth and early twentieth century as a part of Anglo-Russian rivalry in Central Asia, and the mid-twentieth century emphasis on border control. The roads and borders at the heart of so many debates concerning the future of

Ladakh are products of the new role of Ladakh in India since the 1940s and 1950s. This legacy provides a context for modern issues as varied as the 1980 communal conflict in Ladakh, interactions with tourists, and attitudes towards consumption of foreign commodities. Thus modern Ladakhi discourse about global connections reflects the legacy of trading networks as participants struggle to articulate the concept of "Ladakhi-ness" as a relationship between people and commodities. The participation of the region in global flows of capital and ideas continues to be expressed as one made of contrasting, yet overlapping, sets of interests; perceived interests are simultaneously expressed as particularly local and non-local. This engagement, within multiple spheres of cultural influences, suggests that the descendents of Ladakhi traders are involved in cosmopolitan identity negotiations.

Ladakhi traders engaged in a cosmopolitan process[2]

The cosmopolitan experience is often viewed as one that brings together multiple cultural backgrounds (e.g. Gutmann 1993), and ascribed to this type of cosmopolitan is a cultural universalism that leaves no room for regionalism or local ethnic identities (e.g. Walzer 1987). This is only one dimension of the word, however, as the term also carries with it a sense of separateness. Cosmopolitans are people experiencing cultural diversity in a particularly identifiable manner. For example, a community is often identified as cosmopolitan in contrast to others within a cultural sphere – for example, the same time period, social networks, city, region, or even global community. Thus cosmopolitanism is recognized in contrast to cultural particularism and cosmopolitans are most often identified as such in spaces, either geographic or social, or at times when others are not participating. This idea of the cosmopolitan may then seem problematic – how can cosmopolitans simultaneously be universalists, by opposition to particularists, and yet identifiable as a separate cultural or social group?

A universalist approach to the world, one that is unbound by particular cultural perspectives, is impossible if cultural perspectives are understood as conceptual frameworks. Conceptual boundaries are necessary for making sense of the world – we require a conceptual framework within which to understand our experience, as noted most famously by Immanuel Kant (see Kant 1887). Concepts must selectively emphasize particular features of that which they represent in order to organize information, and therefore conceptualizing the world is inherently distorting. Since we cannot assess our information outside of our conceptualization of the world, there is no way to may sure that our concepts of the world are in any way "correct", or at least represent the world adequately for our purposes. If we want our conceptions of the world to be true in some sense, the best we can do is take a somewhat pragmatic approach: construct our conceptions in such a way that they emphasize those features that we take to be important, neglect only aspects that seem irrelevant, and do so in such a way that allows for a degree of flexibility.[3] Most of us frequently operate this way already, as in social contexts we often allow flexibility to enable conversation, such as interpreting terms in conversation less rigidly than we might if asked to provide definitions. Keeping our conceptions fluid and allowing them to be flexible is precisely what enables us to come to new understandings about the world.

In the socio-cultural realm, such a readiness to interact with new understandings translates to the attitude of the cosmopolitan. Cosmopolitans are those who have taken the opportunity to recognize limitations of their conceptions, and found cause to take into consideration some set of expectations other than their own. The conceptual boundaries that cosmopolitans traverse are cultural boundaries, overcome by cultural exchange. Cosmopolitans practice a fluidity of conceptual boundaries in the cultural sphere without relinquishing such boundaries altogether.

Using such a definition of cosmopolitanism, I would argue that the late nineteenth- and early twentieth-century Ladakhi traders were indeed cosmopolitans. Historical Ladakhis may not seem to be cosmopolitan consumers because of the relatively small size of the market for goods during that time period, and the small percentage of Ladakhis who are thought to have participated in consumer markets in the region. We can understand Ladakhi trading communities as cosmopolitan, however, through recognition of their roles both as consumers and, most significantly, as cultural brokers in the Central/South Asian trade system.

Each trading decision by Ladakhi traders was made in response to a variety of perspectives of the significance of the individual commodities. Regional trade participants could therefore have negotiated a sense of belonging to larger social networks within their own cultural frameworks, creating their own symbolic system of commercial goods. Earlier discussion of the particular commodities that Ladakhi traders dealt with – cotton piece goods, synthetic dyes, and *charas* – emphasized that they had to be able to navigate between the differing views of socio-cultural significance attributed to these goods' contexts of production, distribution and production in the global arena. Cotton piece goods helped Ladakhi traders participate in global discourse on colonial economies and independence struggles in India. Through the brokerage of synthetic dyes Ladakhi traders were agents in the industrial application of the scientific revolution in Europe, shifting colonial economies in India, and changing fashion in the USA and Europe. While we do not have written documents where Ladakhi traders explicitly articulated negotiating their own cultural understanding of the commodities within the contesting meanings in the global arena, I have argued that it is reasonable to consider their interactions with commodities as evidence of such negotiations. Ladakhi traders had to be aware of the shifting meanings of the traded goods in order to make reasonable choices for their businesses. Through such work they would have been prompted to recognize how cultural contexts played a role in organizing relevant features of an experience. As seen in the examples of particular commodities, the historical trade networks in South and Central Asia provided the opportunity for exposure to diverse cultural spheres, linking the lives of Ladakhi traders to those of others throughout Asia, as well as in Europe and the United States, and to significant global debates of the period. It is also reasonable to assume that these traders had exposure to the differing viewpoints associated with the commodities, as the historical documents provide evidence that they had access to newspapers, magazines, and books from around the world.

As seen in the *charas* example, participants who cultivated a cosmopolitan outlook were rewarded in this business environment. The most successful *charas* traders were those who could maintain the most varied social networks with British, Indian, Kashmiri, Chinese, and Central Asian communities. Substantial economic gain was more likely if traders participated in trans-regional trade networks where their understanding of multiple local perspectives, and associated material contexts, translated into economic success. Hence the more cosmopolitan traders of the region were most likely to be successful.

We have also seen a variety of evidence suggesting that cosmopolitans in trading situations were engaged in the process of negotiating between multiple cultural perspectives and contexts for profit. This includes the systems of languages, currencies, and calendrics outlined earlier in this book. All of these systems had to be understood, and negotiated, by individuals involved in trade – for example, crossing linguistic boundaries allowed villagers to sell provisions to foreign travelers who came through their area, negotiating between currencies allowed traders to participate in economically diverse marketplaces, and traders who were not able to traverse calendric boundaries could violate business or governmental dictates. Cosmopolitans in all of these cases were those learned to accommodate various sets of boundaries, and could fluidly jump from one set to the other when necessary. In the case of the Ladakh traders, we can see that being cosmopolitan meant being successful.

The philosophical considerations discussed earlier in this section, and the ways in which the data about Ladakhi traders fits into this conceptual framework, both suggest that cosmopolitans are not simply cultural universalists, relying on common cultural grounds, or merely open to other cultural perspectives. Cosmopolitans were those engaged in an active process of negotiating cultural differences, and of testing newly encountered cultural perspectives in new social situations and/or contexts. This last idea of methods for adapting to new contexts becomes significant when addressing the legacy of trade in Ladakh.

The implications of this model of cosmopolitanism are significant, and require further consideration. If we recognize that people are cosmopolitan in the ways that they treat concepts, rather than by mere exposure to concepts and the social and/or material forms associated with them, than we can separate privilege from cosmopolitanism. The ability to own a particular item, an ability based on factors such as economic status, is then distinct from being cosmopolitan. Those who cannot afford – or choose not to – access certain technologies (e.g. computers or cell phones) or spaces (e.g. a city or internet chatrooms) can still be a part of cosmopolitanism. For these items and spaces are only part of the process of becoming cosmopolitan for some individuals, they are not cosmopolitan themselves.

While particular economic, political, or social contexts may be part of the settings in which individuals/communities are engaged in cosmopolitan processes, engagement in that process actually defines the cosmopolitan. More specifically, the cosmopolitan is defined by engagement with diverse cultural viewpoints, a process that can continue even after particular contexts have changed. Thus while Ladakhi trading networks were severed in the mid-twentieth century, cosmopolitanism was definitively not "lost" in the region. Instead, negotiation of the memories and legacies of trade continue to involve the descendents of Ladakhi traders in the cosmopolitan process.

The dialogue between past and present

Through the intersubjectivity of the memories and legacies of trade in Ladakh, the traders' kinship networks have shaped how their descendents conceptualize their identity. Individuals are constantly engaged in negotiating their identities in social context. One small incident I once overheard illustrates this contextual nature of identity. A young boy, upon being lectured that a "Ladakhi" boy should not act the way he was acting, retaliated with the statement, "But I'm not Ladakhi, I'm. . . . my grandfather was from . . ." The boy then paused, and turning to his mother, asked, "Where was he from?"

The exact points of community origin may be forgotten by the younger generations of traders' descendents, but there is still a sense of belonging to something larger, and being able to contest one's belonging to specific, limited, group identities. This is a flexible system of group identification – the same boy on another day was quick to explain something in terms of ". . . we Ladakhis . . ."

Consider also the following story of a trader explaining his family's origins in Ladakh. The trader said,

> [my father's] ancestors came from Switzerland. Yes, they were two brothers. The elder brother stayed there and the younger brother came to Kashmir. In Kashmir he married with a Kashmiri woman. Then they became parents of my grandfather's grandfather . . . his name was . . . something.
> *Why did he come from Switzerland to Kashmir?*
> Maybe for business. I don't know exactly, I only know [he came from] Switzerland. Then in Kashmir [his wife] gave birth to two children, one was the father of . . . my grandfather's grandfather. What was his father's name? I don't know. I didn't hear his name. And his children came to Leh for business. And after that the business continued . . . [That was approximately] six hundred years ago.

In this statement of family origins the trader expresses multiple points of group identity formation processes. Within the context of a family history, his identity is linked to Europe and Kashmir, though he is identified by many in Ladakh simply as a Kashmiri. The depth of historical time embraced in his family history shows the ways in which narratives of otherness and ethnic origins in the Ladakh community can extend far back into history. These accounts of identity, which weave together communities of ethnic identification, extend further than the descent groups of the past two centuries outlined in this book. Later in our discussion the trader in the above passage associated his ancestor's move to Ladakh with the coming of the historical figure Sayyid Ali Hamadani, who is popularly attributed with bringing Islam to Ladakh, as mentioned in Chapter 2. Thus in his narrative the trader contextualized his kin group identity variously within larger identity groups based on both ethnic and religious criteria.

As cosmopolitan elites many of the traders based in Ladakh had multiple cultural identities that they actively negotiated between, forming at times overlapping categories. One trader like Bahauddin Khan could be considered Arghun, Muslim, and of the Khan family, as each of those terms carried its own social significance, and offered particular political and economic opportunities. Individual negotiation between these identities offered the opportunity to strategically negotiate political and economic opportunities as well.

The continued significance of this flexibility of identification is contrary to common expectations about cross-cultural trading societies. In *Cross Cultural Trade in World History*, Phillip Curtin wrote:

> People of a trade diaspora were not only member of an urban society; they were also members of a plural society, where two or more cultures existed side by side. In most instances, this was a source of stress – alongside the other tension between merchants and other occupations. With the passage of time, cultural differences in a single society would be expected to disappear. Indeed, this was part of the process by which a trade diaspora worked itself out of existence. But the actual course of cultural integration was extremely variable.
>
> (Curtin 1984:11)

While the first part of this quote is true in the Ladakhi case – Ladakhi traders were members of a plural society, often in urban (although urban sometimes only in a regional context) settings – the second part of this quote can be drawn into question in the Ladakhi trading context. The Ladakhi historical data shows how merchants and other occupations fit together in complementary roles, and notions of cultural difference have remained even after the trade system has disappeared. This is more than a difference in "the actual course of cultural integration"; Curtin's claim crucially depends on his concept of events as occurring "with the passage of time" and within socially discrete communities. In the Ladakh case flexible identity groups were conceptualized without opposition to specific communities of "others", and, crucially, cosmopolitan negotiation of cultural difference did not progress in a linear fashion over time. History cannot be thought of as belonging entirely to the past.

While in the introduction I wrote that this study was undertaken as an ethnohistorical project so as to understand the past in as detailed terms as we understand the present, we find now that this statement is incomplete. This research was undertaken as ethnohistorical work simply because there was no other way through which to understand the topic. "Ladakhi-ness", as an identity constructed through the interpenetration of past and present, must be understood through a study of both.[4] Only through the intersubjectivity of memory and legacy can we understand how members of the Ladakhi community continue to produce new possibilities for the concept of "Ladakhi-ness". Furthermore, as this process continues to be informed by multiple cultural viewpoints, through both interpersonal interactions and relationships to commodities, the Ladakhi community continues to engage in the cosmopolitan process.

Glossary

Anna A unit of British Indian currency worth one sixteenth of a rupee.

Aqsaqual Literally "white beard" in Persian, this term was used to refer to trade officials posted in towns by governments in other areas. Each town on the trading route could then potentially have multiple aqsaqual who acted as representatives for various regional governments.

Bazaar A marketplace.

Bo A measure commonly used for grains in historical Ladakh that is equivalent to a little over two pounds (see Rizvi 1999, 301); the measure is usually mentioned in Ladakhi narratives as an addition to larger amounts.

Bodyig The written version of the Ladakhi language derived from the Tibetan script.

Challan A receipt used to provide the details for a shipment, usually written in triplicate so *that* the owner, transporter and/or middleman, and recipient could all receive copies.

Charas A *cannabis* product that was commonly brought from Chinese Turkistan into British India.

Charkha A small spinning wheel used as a symbol of South Asian self-sufficiency in Gandhi's movement for independence from the British colonial rule.

Dak bungalow Government guesthouses that were constructed and maintained at regular intervals on heavily travelled routes throughout colonial South Asia.

Dzo A yak/cow hybrid.

Gaddi A term commonly used in the Ladakhi trading networks to refer to traders from Amritsar or Hoshiarpur in the Punjab region of northern Indian, usually used as a synonym for Lala. While some informants suggested that this term was synonymous with Hindu, not all informants agreed.

Godown A storage facility.

Gos/Goncha The thick woolen robe worn by Ladakhi men that is sewn straight and gathered with a belt.

Gos-sulma The thick woolen robe worn by Ladakhi women that has gathers sewn in at the waist.

Gyathuk A type of Ladakhi noodle soup.

Haj The Islamic pilgrimage to Mecca.

Hor A term commonly used in the Ladakhi trading networks to refer to traders from Chinese Central Asia, considered an identity group name rather than a label of geographic origin.

Hubble-bubble A water pipe used to smoke tobacco or *cannabis* products.

Khadi Hand-spun cloth.

Khal A unit of measurement for grains, usually about twenty-two pounds (see Rizvi 1999 302).

Khambir Homemade Ladakhi bread.

Khatags White scarves that are presented with gifts, on celebrations, or to revered figures in the Ladakh culture.

Khura A fried dough delicacy in Ladakhi cooking.

Kiraiyakash Transporters for the goods who would lead livestock along the route.

Kocha Quarters, or a neighborhood.

Lakh A unit in the South Asian numbering system equal to one hundred thousand.

Lala A term commonly used in the Ladakhi trading networks to refer to traders from Amritsar or Hoshiarpur in the Punjab region of northern Indian, usually used as a synonym for Gaddi. While some informants suggested that this term was synonymous with Hindu, not all informants agreed.

Munim A clerk or agent for a trading firm.

Munshi Secretaries, hired by traders and trading firms, responsible for tasks such as accounting, bookkeeping, legal documentation, and correspondence.

Nikkha An Islamic marriage agreement.

Paisa A unit of British Indian currency worth one quarter of an *anna*.

Pashmina Wool from goats in the Himalayas that has a high value when traded on the world market. Commonly used as a synonym for cashmere.

Patawari A land settlement officer or a lower ranked revenue officer of local governments in India and other parts of South Asia in charge of land rights documentation and other official writing tasks.

Phating High quality apricots grown in Ladakh that are often dried or used for juice.

Piece goods A term commonly used in the early twentieth century to refer to fabrics that were sold by length from larger bolts. Also referred to as "yard goods".

Rupees A unit of Indian currency that was also used during the British colonial period in South Asia. The rupees was broken down into unites of *anna* and *paisa* during the colonial period, and is comprised only of *paisa* during the contemporary period.

Seer A unit of measurement for weight, approximately two pounds (see Rizvi 1999 304).

Serai An inn where traders would stay while visiting towns. These building were more than hotels, however, and could be used to conduct business, store goods, and house livestock.

State Subject A legal status in the state of Jammu and Kashmir that allows an individual to own land and access other state privileges.

Stupas Buddhist monuments that frequently serve as reliquaries.

Swadeshi movement The Indian independence movement.

Thammadar A government official.

Wazir-i-wazarat A government official for the Maharaja's government of Jammu and Kashmir.

Notes

Introduction: Global memories, local accounts

1 As noted earlier, I have named these papers the "The Khan Archives", although they do not currently reside in any formal archival collection.
2 Originally I began with the intent to preserve all of the trade documents found; after a year of cleaning and archiving documents the discovery of several other boxes made me realize that this project would, out of necessity, have to be more selective. Thus after the year 2000 I began going through remaining boxes to select particular documents. The Khan Archives documents are in general randomly sampled and representative of larger patterns of trade with two exceptions. Preferential selection for longer letters and those dated in the 1930s decade inhibits comparative statements between decades or concerning correspondence length.
3 Common Era, equivalent to Gregorian AD; BCE or Before Common Era is used in this manuscript as an equivalent for BC.
4 The Hijri calendar is sometimes noted with the abbreviation AH after the year, reportedly a later European convention as abbreviations of the Latin phrase "Anno Hegirae", or "in the year of the Hijri". Many European authors who mark the years before Hijra thus use the abbreviation BH.
5 The Ladakhi language written in Tibetan script.
6 For this work I am indebted to volunteers from the Save the Children Leh branch and the Kargil Development Project.
7 With slight wording changes to make local references specific to Kargil, and translated into vernacular Kargili for the research team.
8 The family of Munshi Habibullah has since opened a museum to showcase the variety of trade goods that came through Kargil in the early twentieth century, called the Munshi Aziz Bhat Museum. This museum is one of the first regionally planned and established historical institutions that display Ladakh's contribution to, and participation in, trade between South and Central Asia.

1 Beyond the roof of the world

1 Authors referred to in this chapter spell this, and many other geographic terms, in a variety of ways depending on the popular transcriptions of their own time periods.

2 The Leh district is the significantly larger of the two, with the largest urban areas.
3 XuanZang in Pinyin.
4 Emphasis added.
5 Many of these linkages are due to the multiple positions held in Ladakh by LBA leadership. For example, the 1998 president of LBA, Mr. Tsering Samphel, also acted as the Executive Director of Leh Nutrition Project, a non-profit development agency.
6 The social boycott may also have been used in Leh earlier, perhaps in the late 1970s or early 1980s. This information was offered by some informants, but has not been verified.

2 Recognizing the terrain: An historical background

1 German geographer Ferdinand Von Richthofen (1833–1905) coined the term "Silk Road" to describe the network of travel routes stretching between China and Eastern Europe, with branches that extended in north–south directions.
2 They are also referred to as "Hunas" in South Asian literature and Huns in some European and American literature. Author E.V. Zeimal has proposed that the term "Hunas" was used in South Asia to refer to Hephthalites and the Kidaras, groups from areas in modern Pakistan and Afghanistan (Zeimal 1996 123).
3 This text published by the Leh Nutrition Project, an NGO in Ladakh, is of particular importance because it represents an amalgamation of local views of history, and has been used as a teaching aid by Ladakhi schools for their students studying local history.
4 Controversy exists over whether this palace was that constructed in Sabu or Shey (see Jina 1994 23 and Leh Nutrition Project 1989 6B).
5 *Rasalah Mastürät*, MS. India Office Library, p. 72.
6 While most authors provide the year of 1834 for invasion (e.g. Snellgrove 1977, Jina 1994, Rizvi 1999), Michaud focuses on the colonization of Ladakh, which he dates at 1841 (1996:289). Jina provides an alternative for this date, stating that Ladakhi revolts were not finally quelled until 1840, and in September 1842 "Ladakh came permanently under the Maharaja of Jammu and Kashmir" (Jina 1994:24).
7 The conversion rates from the Indian system of *lakhs* and *crores* to the American system of thousands and millions is as follows one *lakh* equals one hundred thousand and one *crore* equals ten million. This is a system commonly used in India when referring to monetary values in rupees.
8 Prakrit is a South Asian language group often associated with the spread of Buddhism in Central Asia.
9 Sinkiang Province became a part of China at the same time as the regions of Inner Mongolia, Tibet and Ningsia.
10 Singey (or Sengge) Namgyal's reign has been written as variously as 1590–1620 (Leh Nutrition Project 1989:12B), 1590–1640 (Huttenback 1961), and 1570–1642 (Snellgrove and Skorupski 1977:xii).
11 This area is also called Sinkiang in some of these sections.
12 *Pashmina* is referred to in the Rizvi 1999 text as *pashm*.
13 This information was communicated by the mosque's caretaker in a 1998 tour of the premises. There was also apparently a third carpet that did not

reach Leh because it was washed away in a flood near the Shayok River along the treacherous trade route from Chinese Central Asia.

3 The family business: Community, kinship and identity

1 Arghun has been transliterated a variety of ways by different authors, including Argoon, Argon, and Arghon; I use the first spelling out of personal preference.
2 More specifically, authors of critiques of the term "Mohammedanism" or "Mohammedan" point out that the terms incorrectly imply that the Prophet Mohammed is a central focus of worship in Islam.
3 Some of the words used in historical Ladakhi trading vocabularies appear as common usage in Central and South Asia languages. These include terms for goods such as *charas* (found in Ladakhi, Urdu, Uyghur and Punjabi) for the cannabis preparation, and common objects used by traders such as *chapan* (a term used in Kirghiz for a long quilted robe), thick woolen socks called *jurab* (in Wakhi and Dari), and thin soled, heel-less Central Asian boots called *maseh* (Wakhi, Kirghiz and Dari). Alternating terms for the same item made Ladakhi traders' vocabularies more broadly accessible, such as their use of either *hati* or *dukan* for a shop, terms that would have been recognizable to speakers Urdu, Hindi, Farsi, Uyghur, Wakhi, Kirghiz, Dari, Punjabi, and Pashto, and *tsong/piaz* for onion (found in Hindi, Urdu, Ladakhi, Farsi, Uighur, Tibetan, and Pashto). Language sources Urdu (Hamid 1998 and Badakhshani 2000), Ladakhi (Hamid 1998), Farsi (Lambton 1954), Hindi (Raker 1995), Uyghur (Hahn 1991), Wakhi (Shahrani 1979), Kirghiz (Sharani 1979), Dari (Sharani 1979), Punjabi (Hamid 1998), Kashmiri (Hamid 1998), Tibetan (Gupta 1992), and Pashto (Bellew 1982).

4 Social strategies for profit

1 See Rizvi 1999:275–278 for information about weights and measures.
2 Most information in this section on post offices, telegraph offices, and telephones is derived from Chohan 1994, a source that offers a very complete summary of communications facilities in Jammu and Kashmir during the late nineteenth and early twentieth century. Specific information, unless otherwise noted, is from this source.

5 Living in a material world: Cosmopolitan elites

1 I am indebted to Dr. Amy McLaughlin, of the Wilkes Honors College of Florida Atlantic University for her aid in my understanding philosophical pragmatism and its relevance for defining abstract concepts such as cosmopolitanism.
2 A store where men's clothes, and cloth for clothes, are sold.
3 The Ashoka Chakra is modeled after the symbol of a wheel inscribed on artifacts associated with the Mauryan Emperor Ashoka (273–232) including the Ashoka Pillar, which is also featured on some Indian coins.
4 Wingate makes a point that Queen Victoria pointedly did not knight Perkin in her day, although she favored other scientists, and speculates "[p]erhaps Victoria was offended by what she probably regarded as the loose morals

of the 'mauve decade' and thought that the somewhat lurid shade of mauve had contributed to the laxity" (Wingate 1982:18), a fascinating suggestion in its consideration of the cultural role of color.

5 *Charas* is also known as *chira* and *churus* (see, for example, Abel 1982:24–25).

6 *Cannabis indica* was identified in 1783 by a French naturalist and considered distinct from the European *Cannabis sativa*, the former being more resinous with greater psychoactive properties and the latter more fibrous (Abel 1982:22–23). Although some authors discussing *Cannabis* species still adhere to this distinction, later researchers have contradicted the typology claiming that variation is purely dependent on regional growing conditions, a concept supported by USA Federal Bureau of Narcotics guidelines (Lingeman 1969:37). Experiments with the growth of *Cannabis* plants from different areas have yielded results that only partially support this view; while seeds from Afghanistan grown in the USA yielded plants with THC (the active drug ingredient) of the same potency as those grown in Afghanistan, the plants contained a lesser amount of the active ingredient, leading to the conclusion that the overall effects of *Cannabis* are determined by both plant genetics and growing climates (Abel 1982:22).

6 The demise of trade: Coping with borders

1 This area would eventually include the Aksai Chin in the post-independence maps of India, and the boundary remains an issue of dispute between China and India today.

2 Yet, the Chinese government would uncharacteristically refer to this treaty in the late 1940s, protesting British annexation of an area by pointing out that it was, by McMahon line standards, a part of China (Maxwell 1970:47).

3 See, for example, Halpern 1962 and Stahnke 1970.

4 This was a slightly enlarged statement from his earlier 1950s claim that the "frontier from Ladakh to Nepal is defined chiefly by long usage and custom" (Maxwell 1970:48). These statements for boundary delimitation by "usage" patterns are curious upon consideration of the history of movement between Chinese Sinkiang, Tibet, and Jammu and Kashmir regions (including Ladakh). Traders who had traversed these borders during the past few centuries had certainly not used fixed notions of demarcated national boundaries. While the geography of the region offered some cartographically represented boundaries they were, as seen, porous boundaries that often acted much more as political guides than limits. The political rhetoric of Indian leaders invoked boundaries of usage, custom, and geography in Ladakh as part of a larger state project to re-center the region, to stabilize the area as a border and more clearly define the nation of India. Through discussion of the region as a customary, used, and geographically defined border, Indian leaders sought to naturalize the role that they wanted Ladakh to play within the national agenda, that of a frontier zone. For further reading, see the article "Tibet in Sino-Indian Relations: The Centrality of Marginality" (Norbu 1997), in which the author discusses a similar set of circumstances as they occurred across the border in Tibet.

7 The memory and legacy of trade

1 While I use this term cautiously, believing that it has little use for social scientists without specific contextualization, in this case the context is a well established discourse in Ladakh.

2 I have only heard people make a distinction between ethnic Baltis and the Shia religious community of Ladakh in the scholarly setting, particularly at the Institute of Balti Studies in Kargil.

3 This misunderstanding of the term *Bhot/Bhoto* is furthered in part by some writing on the subject, e.g. a text that claims that "the average Kashmiri disdainfully calls the Ladakhi *bhoto*, which perhaps means non-Muslim" (Stobdan 1995:7). This claim rests on an assumption that the underlying issues in the confrontations between Ladakhis and others in Kashmir were based on religious communalism. The name *bhoto* more likely is an ethnic label meaning "Tibetan", as the local name of Tibet is "*Bhod*" (spelled phonetically), which is often pronounced "*Bhot*" in India and Nepal. Historically, the term has been used to refer to a number of Himalayan communities. The term appears in literature in the form of "*Bot-pa*", as early as 1854, to signify Ladakhis in general (Cunningham 1854:18), or in other regions to signify Tibetans in 1856 (see, for example, "Nepal-Tibet Treaty of 1856" in Uprety 1980). In Rasool Galwan's 1923 publication there are several references to individuals described simply as a "*Bhot*" man" (Galwan 1923:8), although according to the glossary in Rassul Galwan's book, "*Bhot*" is a native of "Bhutan" (Galwan 1923:280). Additionally, in the historical case of Richen discussed in an earlier chapter, another author cites historic use of the word *bhoti* to simply mean "Tibetan" (Rizvi 1983:43). Today "*Bhotia*" is a term used for various Himalayan ethnic groups of Tibetan or Mongol ethnic origins (see Ives and Messerli 1989) and "*bhoti*" is used to refer to the Ladakhi language. In interviews descendents of traders based in Kargil, originally from Srinagar, also used a similar term to describe Ladakhis as being related to Tibet. They explained that their ancestors were often identified in Srinagar as "Tibet traders", or "Bhatwani". Thus, the central issues of such debates over who is a "*Bhot*" are not religious, but rather about ethnic identity.

4 Excerpt from a speech by Shri P. Namgyal in the *Xi lok sabha debates, Session V (Monsoon)*. Thursday, August 07/Shravana 16, 1919 (Saka); Title: "Need to exempt residents of Ladakh region of J & K from the payment of Income Tax". Website accessed online at the government website http//parliamentofindia. nic.in/lsdeb/ls11/ses5/50070897.htm; last accessed March 18, 2008.

5 Some groups, such as SECMOL, have thus produced alternative teaching materials; see for example the Operation New Hope textbook series from SECMOL, published by the Jammu and Kashmir Board of School Education.

Conclusion

1 The description of this process is remarkably like Herodotus' description of a silent trade system in Africa (see Curtin 1984:12–13) and therefore raises the possibility that some Ladakhi memory dialogues are informed by further cultural and scholarly contexts of knowledge about trade.

2 The argument summarized in this section was developed in collaboration with Amy McLaughlin (Philosophy, Wilkes Honors College at Florida Atlantic

University) for the conference paper "Negotiating Cultural/Conceptual Boundaries: Cosmopolitanism as Process" (see McLaughlin and Fewkes 2007), and is currently under review as a co-authored article titled "Cosmopolitanism as Process: Conceptual Fluidity and Cultural Boundary Jumping".

3 For a complete version of this argument see McLaughlin 2004.

4 As such, my research supports John Comaroff's statement that "there ought to be no 'relationship' between history and anthropology, since there should be no division to begin with. A theory of society which is not also a theory of history, or *vice versa*, is hardly a theory at all" (Comaroff 1982:144). The impact of this research on our understanding of the disciplinary relationship between history and anthropology, however, would require further investigation.

Bibliography

Abel, E. L. (1982) *A Marihuana Dictionary: Words, Terms, Events, and Persons Relating to Cannabis*, Westport CT, Greenwood Press.

Abercrombie, T. J. (1978) Ladakh – the last Shangri-la. *National Geographic Magazine*, 153, 332–359.

Adair, F. E. S. and Godfrey, S. H. (1899) *The Big Game of Baltistan and Ladakh. A Summer in High Asia, Being a Record of Sport and Travel in Baltistan and Ladakh*, London, W. Thacker & Co.

Aggarwal, R. (1995) Shadow Work Women in the Workplace in Ladakh, India. *Anthropology of Work Review*, 16, 33–38.

—— (2001) At the Margins of Death: Ritual Space and the Politics of Location in an Indo-Himalayan Border Village. *American Ethnologist*, 28, 549–573.

Ahluwalia, M. S. (1988) *History of Himachel Pradesh*, New Delhi, Intellectual Publishing House.

Ahmed, M. (2002) *Living Fabric Weaving among the Nomads of Ladakh Himalaya*, Trumbull CT, Weatherhill.

Allan, N. J. R. (1998) *Karakorum Himalaya A Bibliography*, Bangkok, Orchid Press.

Allen, G. C. (1972) *A Short Economic History of Modern Japan 1867–1937*, London, George Allen & Unwin Ltd.

Anderson, B. (1983) *Imagined Communities: Reflections on the Origins and Spread of Nationalism*, London, Verso.

Angeles, L. C. and Tarbotton, R. (2001) Local Transformation through Global Connection Women's Assets and Environmental Activism for Sustainable Agriculture in Ladakh, India. *Women's Studies Quarterly*, 29, 99–115.

Asboe, W. (1951) Farmers and Farming in Ladakh. *Human Relations Area Files*, AJ4, www.yale.edu/hraf/. 186–192.

Badakshani, M. R. (2000) *Gem Pocket Twentieth Century Dictionary: Urdu Into English*, New Delhi, India, Educational Publishing House.

Banerjee, D. (1999) *Colonialism in Action: Trade, Development and Dependence in Late Colonial India*, Hyderabad, Orient Longman.

Bauer, K. M. (2003) *High Frontiers: Himalayan Pastoralists in a Changing World*, New York NY, Columbia University Press.

Behera, N. C. (2000a) "Autonomy" in J&K: The Forgotten Identities of Ladakh. *Faultlines*, 6, 35–60.

—— (2000b) *State, Identity, and Violence: Jammu, Kashmir, and Ladakh*, Delhi, Manohar.

Bellew, H. W. (1982) *A Dictionary of the Pukkhto or Pukshto Language*, Karachi, Pakistan Publishing House.

Bertelsen, K. B. (1997) Protestant Buddhism and Social Identification in Ladakh. *Archives de Sciences Sociales des Religions*, 99, 129–151.

Bestaggini, A. (1998) Travel The Last Shangri-La. *Geographical*, 70, 24.

Biddulph, J. (1874) Spec. Pamirs. 1874. London, Royal Geographical Society.

Birdwood, L. (1952) The Asian Frontiers of Kashmir. *Journal of the Royal Central Asian Society*, 39, 241–245.

Bishop, P. (1989) *The Myth of Shangri-La*, Los Angeles, CA, University of California Press.

Bohman, J. (1999) Citizenship and Norms of Publicity: Wide Public Reason in Cosmopolitan Societies. *Political Theory*, 27, 176–202.

Bower, H. (1894) *Diary of a Journey Across Tibet*, London, Rivington Percival & Co.

Brass, P. R. (1994) *The Politics of India Since Independence*, London, Oxford University Press.

Bray, J. (1983) The Moravian church in Ladakh: The first forty years 1885–1925. In Kantowsky, D. and Reinhard, S. (eds) *Recent Research on Ladakh. History, Culture, Sociology, Ecology. Proceedings of a Conference held at the Universitaet Konstanz, 23–26 November 1981.* Muechen, Koeln, Schriftenreihe Internationales Asienforum.

—— (1985) Christianity in Ladakh: The Moravian Church from 1920–1956. In Dendaletche, C. (ed.) *Ladakh, Himalaya Occidental. Ethnologie, Ecologie.* Montana, Acta Biologica.

—— (1997) The Roman Catholic Mission in Ladakh, 1888–1898. In Osmaston, H., and Nawang Tsering (ed.) *Recent Research on Ladakh 6. Proceedings of the Sixth International Colloquium on Ladakh.* Bristol, University of Bristol.

Brenner, S. (1998) *The Domestication of Desire: Women, Wealth, and Modernity in Java*, Princeton NJ, Princeton University Press.

Brinckman, A. (1862) *The Rifle in Cashmere: A Narrative of Shooting Expeditions in Ladak, Cashmere, Punjaub, etc., with Advice on Travelling, Shooting, and Stalking: To Which are Added Notes on Army Reform and Indian Politics*, London, Smith, Elder.

Brown, B. A. (1994) Political Developments in Soviet Central Asia: Some Aspects of the Restructuring Process in Turkmenistan, Kirgizia, and Kazakhstan in the late 1980s. In Akiner, S. (ed.) *Political and Economic Trends in Central Asia.* London, British Academic Press.

Burton, J. W. (1981) Ethnicity on the Hoof: On the Economics of Nuer Identity. *Ethnology*, 20, 157–162.

Census of India (1981) Jammu and Kashmir, Series 8. Parts 1 and 2 compiled by A.H. Khan. Srinagar, State Government Press.

Census of India (2001) Final Population Totals: Jammu and Kashmir. Series 2. Srinagar, Directorate of Census Operations.

Chohan, A. S. (1994) *Economic Conditions in the Frontier Territories of Jammu and Kashmir Under the Dogras*, New Delhi, Atlantic Publishers and Distributors.

Chopra, R. N., Chopra, G. S. and Chopra, I. C. (1942) Cannabis Sativa in Relation to Mental Diseases and Crime in India. *Indian Journal of Medical Research*, 30, 155–171.

Clauson, G. (1944) British Colonial Currency System. *Economic Journal* 54, 1–25.

Cohen, A. (1969) *Custom and Politics in Urban Africa A Study of Hausa Migrants in a Yoruba Town*, Berkeley CA, University of California Press.

—— (1974a) Introduction: The Lesson of Ethnicity. In Cohen, A. (ed.) *Urban Ethnicity*. London, Tavistock.

—— (1974b) *Two-Dimensional Man*, Berkeley CA, University of California Press.

Cohn, B. (1980) History and Anthropology: The State of Play. *Comparative Studies in Society and History*, 22, 198–221.

Comaroff, J. and Comaroff, J. L. (1992) *Ethnography and the Historical Imagination*, Boulder CO, Westview Press.

Comaroff, J. (1982) Dialectical Systems, History and Anthropology: Units of Study and Questions of Theory. *Journal of Southern African Studies*, 8, 143–172.

—— (1985) *Body of Power, Spirit of Resistance: The Culture and History of a South African People*, Chicago IL, University of Chicago Press.

Cunningham, A. (1854) *Ladak, Physical, Statistical, and Historical; with Notices of the Surrounding Countries*, London, W.H. Allen & Co.

Curtin, P. (1984) *Cross-Cultural Trade in World History*, Cambridge, Cambridge University Press.

Curzon, G. N. (1896) The Pamirs and the Source of the Oxus. *The Geographical Journal*, 8, 239–260.

Day, S. (1989) *Embodying spirits village oracles and possession ritual in Ladakh, North India*, Boston Spa, UK, British Library Document Supply Centre.

De Bourbel, R. (1897) *Routes in Jammu and Kashmir Arranged Topographically with Descriptions of Routes, Distances by Stages, and Information as to Supplies and Transport*, Calcutta, Thacker Spink.

Drege, J. P. and Buhrer, E. (1989) *The Silk Road Saga*, New York, Facts on File.

East, P., Inmann, K. and Luger, K. (1998) *Sustainability in mountain tourism: Perspectives for the Himalayan countries*, Delhi/Kathmandu, Book Faith.

Etherton, P. G. (1911) *Across the Roof of the World*, London, Constable & Co.

Fisher, M. W., Rose, L. E. and Huttenback, R. A. (1963) *Himalayan Battleground: Sino-Indian Rivalry in Ladakh*, New York NY, Fredrick A. Praeger.

Foltz, R. C. (1999) *Religions of the Silk Road*, New York, St. Martin's Griffin.

Fox, M. R. (1987) *Dye Makers of Great Britain 1856–1976: A History of Chemists, Companies, Products and Changes*, Manchester, Imperial Chemical Industries PLC.

Franck, I. M. (1986) *The Silk Road: A History*, New York NY, Facts on File Publications.

Francke, A. H. (1914) *Antiquities of Indian Tibet*, Calcutta, Archaeological Survey of India.

Frye, R. N. (1998) *The Heritage of Central Asia: From Antiquity to the Turkish Expansion*, Princeton NJ, Markus Wiener Publishers.

Gaborieau, M. (2000) Kashmiri Muslim Merchants in Tibet, Nepal, and Northern India. In Lombard, D. and Aubin, J. (eds) *Asian Merchants and Businessmen in the Indian Ocean and the China Sea*. New Delhi, Oxford University Press.

Gadru, S. N. (ed.) (1973) *Kashmir Papers: British Intervention in Kashmir*, Srinagar, Freethought Literature Company.

Galwan, G. R. (1923) *Servant of Sahibs*, Cambridge, W. Heffer & Sons Ltd.

Geertz, C. (1980) *Negara: Theatre State in Nineteenth-Century Bali*, New Jersey, Princeton University Press.

Genoud, C. and Inoue, T. (1982) *Buddhist wall-painting of Ladakh*, Geneva, Switzerland, Edition Olizane.

Gewertz, D. B. and Schieffelin, E. (eds) (1985) *History and Ethnohistory in Papua New Guinea*, Sidney, University of Sidney.

Godfrey, S. H. (1899) The Trade of Ladakh with China and Thibet. In Adair, F. E. S. and Godfrey, S. H. (eds) *The Big Game of Baltistan and Ladakh. A Summer in High Asia, Being a Record of Sport and Travel in Baltistan and Ladakh*. London, W. Thacker & Co.

Gompertz, M. L. A. (1926) *The Road to Lamaland: Impressions of a journey to western Thibet*, London, Hodder & Stoughton.

—— (1928) *Magic Ladakh: An intimate picture of a land of topsy-turvy customs and great natural beauty*, London, Seeley, Service & Co.

Goswami, O. (1989) Sahibs, Babus, and Banias: Changes in Industrial Control in Eastern India, 1918–50. *The Journal of Asian Studies*, 48, 289–309.

Grinspoon, L. (1993) *The History of Cannabis*, New Haven CT, Yale University Press.

Grotzbach, E. (1984) Mobility of Labour in High Mountains and the Socio-economic Integration of Peripheral Areas. *Mountain Research and Development*, 4, 229–235.

Gupta, A. (1992) *Conversational English–Tibetan Dictionary*, Delhi, Indian Books Centre.

Gutmann, A. (1993) The Challenge of Multiculturalism in Political Ethics. *Philosophy and Public Affairs*, 22, 171–206.

Haellquist, K. R. (ed.) (1991) *Asian Trade Routes: Continental and Maritime*, London, Curzon.

Hahn, R. F. (1991) *Spoken Uyghur*, Seattle and London, University of Washington Press.

Halpern, A. M. (1962) Communist China's Foreign Policy: The Recent Phase (in Recent Developments; The National People's Congress). *The China Quarterly*, 11, 89–104.

Hamadani, A. H. (1984) *The Life and Works of Sayyid Ali Hamadani, (A.D. 1314–1385)*, Islamabad, National Institute of Historical and Cultural Research.

Hambly, G. (ed.) (1966) *Central Asia*, New York, Delacorte Press.

Hamid, A. (1998) *Ladakhi–English–Urdu Dictionary*, Leh, Melongs Publications.

Harvey, A. (1983) *A Journey in Ladakh*, Boston MA, Houghton Mifflin.

Hasan, K. A. (1975) Social Aspects of the Use of Cannabis in India. In Rubin, V. (ed.) *Cannabis and Culture*. The Hague, Paris, Mouton Publishers.

Haskett, R. S. (1988) Living in Two Worlds: Cultural Continuity and Change Among Cuernavaca's Colonial Indigenous Ruling Elite. *Ethnohistory*, 35.1, 34–59.

Hedin, S. (1940) *The Wandering Lake*, New York NY, E. P. Dutton & Co., Inc.

Henderson, G. and Hume, A. O. (1981) *Lahore to Yârkend. Incidents of the Route and Natural History of the Countries Traversed by the Expedition of 1870 Under T. D. Forsyth, Esq., C.B.*, Lahore, Sang-E-Meel Publications.

Ho, E. (2006) *The Graves of Tarim*, Berkeley CA, University of California Press.

Hopkirk, P. (1980) *Foreign Devils on the Silk Road*, Amherst MA, University of Massachusetts Press.

—— (1995) *Trespassers on the Roof of the World*, London, Oxford University Press.

Horsman, S. (2006) The Politics of Toponyms in the Pamir Mountains. *Area*, 38, 279–291.

Huttenback, R. A. (1961) Gulab Singh and the Creation of the Dogra State of Jammu, Kashmir and Ladakh. *Journal of Asian Studies*, XX.

Inden, R. (1986) Orientalist Constructions of India. *Modern Asian Studies*, 20, 401–446.

Indianvisit.Com (2006) Ladakh Holidays. Indianvisit.com Pvt. Ltd.

Ives, J. D., and B. Messerli (1989) *The Himalayan Dilemma: Reconciling development and conservation*, London, Routledge.

Jacob, S. M. (1913) *An Administrative Calendar for Use in Delhi and the Punjab*, Delhi, I.M.H. Press.

Jaeschke, H. H. (1965) *A Tibetan–English Dictionary*, London, Routledge & Kegan Paul.

Jalalzai, M. K. (ed.) (1992) *Road From Afghanistan to Central Asia*, Lahore, Institute of Current Affairs.

Jammu and Kashmir (1939–40) *General Summary of the Administration Report for S. 1996–97*, Jammu, Ranbir Government Press.

Jammu and Kashmir, G. P. (1941a) List of Castes and Tribes, Their Locality. *Code of Census Procedure*. Jammu, Ranbir Government Press.

Jammu and Kashmir, S. G. (1941b) Code of Census Procedure. Jammu, Ranbir Government Press.

Jayetilleke, R. L. (2005) Ladakh – the land of Vajrayana Buddhism. *Lanka Daily News*.

Jina, P. S. (1994) *Tourism in Ladakh Himalaya*, Delhi, Indus Publishing Co.
—— (1996) *Ladakh: The land and the people*, New Delhi, Indus Publishing Co.
—— (1998) *Tibetan manuscripts and inscriptions of Ladakh Himalaya*, Delhi, Sri Satguru Publications.
—— (1999) *Changing face of Ladakh Himalaya*, Faridabad, India, Om Publications.
—— (2001) *Religious History of Ladakh*, Delhi, Sri Satguru Publications.
Johnson, W. H. (1868) Leh to Khotan. *Royal Geographic Society*, 11.
Johnston, J. F. (1878) *The Chemistry of Common Life*, New York NY, D.Appleton and Company.
Johri, S. (1969) *Chinese Invasion of Ladakh*, Lucknow, Himalaya Publications.
Joldan, E. (1985) *Harvest Festival of Buddhist Dards of Ladakh and Other Essays*, Srinagar, Kashmir, Kapoor Bros.
Kak, B. L. (1978) *Chasing Shadows in Ladakh*, New Delhi, Light and Life Publishers.
Kant, I. (1887) *Critique of Pure Reason*, London, George Bell & Sons.
Kapur, M. L. (1992) *Social and Economic History of Jammu and Kashmir State (1885 to 1925 AD)*, Delhi, Anmol Publications.
Kapur, T. B. (1987) *Ladakh, the Wonderland: A Geographical, Historical and Sociological Study*, Delhi, India, Mittal Publications.
Kaul, M. K. (1997) *Medicinal plants of Kashmir and Ladakh: Temperate and Cold Arid Himalaya*, New Delhi, Indus Publishing Co.
Kaul, S. and Kaul, H. N. (1992) *Ladakh Through the Ages: Towards a New Identity*, New Delhi, Indus Publishing Company.
Kaumudi, M. A. (1952) *Kashmir: Its Cultural Heritage*, Bombay, Asia Publishing House.
Khan, M. A., Abbas, A. and Jensen, K. (1975) Cannabis Usage in Pakistan: A Pilot Study of Long Term Effects on Social Status and Physical Health. In Rubin, V. (ed.) *Cannabis and Culture.* The Hague, Paris, Mouton Publishers.
Khosa, S. (1984) *Art History of Kashmir and Ladakh, Medieval Period*, New Delhi, Sagar Publications.
Klimburg-Salter, D. E. (1982) *The Silk Route and the Diamond Path: Esoteric Buddhist Art on the Trans-Himalayan Trade Routes*, Los Angeles CA., Published under the sponsorship of the UCLA Art Council.
Knight, E. F. (1905) *Where Three Empires Meet: A Narrative of Recent Travel in Kashmir, Western Tibet, Gilgit and the Adjoining Countries*, London, Longmans, Green & Co.
Kreutzmann, H. (1991) The Karakoram Highway: The Impact of Road Construction on Mountain Societies. *Modern Asian Studies*, 25, 711–736.
Kumar, P. (2002) Scientific Experiments in British India: Scientists, Indigo Planters and the State. San Francisco. American Historical Association.
Kushner, D. (1997) Self Perception and Identity in Contemporary Turkey. *Journal of Contemporary History*, 32, 219–33.
Lamb, A. (1960) *Britain and Chinese Central Asia*, London, Routledge & Kegan Paul.

—— (1968) *Asian Frontiers: Studies in a Continuing Problem*, New York NY, Fredrick A. Praeger.

—— (1973) *The Sino-Indian Border in Ladakh*, Columbia SC, University of South Carolina Press.

Lambton, A. (1954) *Persian Vocabulary*, Cambridge, Cambridge University Press.

Lattimore, E. H. (1935) *Turkestan Reunion*, New York NY, The John Day Company.

Ledeg, Zeri and Borda (1997) *Energy Supply and Demand in the Himalayan Region of Ladakh in Jammu and Cashmere of India*, Bremen, Germany, Bremen Overseas Research and Development Association.

Leh Nutrition Project (1989) *History of Ladakh Supplementary Curriculum for Teachers*, Leh, Training Section, Save the Children Fund.

Lingeman, R. R. (1969) *Drugs from A to Z: A Dictionary*, New York NY, McGraw Hill.

Lopez, D. S. J. (ed.) (1997) *Religions of Tibet in Practice*, Princeton NJ, Princeton University Press.

—— (1998) *Prisoners of Shangri-la: Tibetan Buddhism and the West*, Chicago IL, University of Chicago Press.

McLaughlin, A. (2004) Scientific Progress and Its Metaphysical Foundations (Ph.D. Thesis). *Department of Philosophy*. Austin TX, University of Texas.

McLaughlin, A. and Fewkes, J. H. (2007) Negotiating Cultural/Conceptual Boundaries Cosmopolitanism as Process. *Cosmopolitanism Past and Present Conference*. University of Dundee, Scotland (UK).

Major, J. S. (1995) *The Silk Route: 7,000 Miles of History*, New York NY, Harper Collins.

Markovits, C. (2000a) Major Indian Capitalists. In Lombard, D. and Aubin, J. (eds) *Asian Merchants and Businessmen in the Indian Ocean and the China Sea*. New Delhi, Oxford University Press.

—— (2000b) *The Global World of Indian Merchants 1750–1947: Traders of Sind from Bukhara to Panama*, Cambridge, Cambridge University Press.

Mason, K. (1935) The Study of Threatening Glaciers. *Geography Journal*, 85, 24–41.

—— (1938) Karakoram Nomenclature. *Geographical Journal*, 91, 123–128.

Maxwell, N. (1970) China and India: The Un-Negotiated Dispute. *The China Quarterly*, 43, 47–80.

Mehta, V. (1975) *Folk Tales of Ladakh*, Bombay, India Book House Education Trust.

Michaud, J. (1996) A Historical Account of Modern Social Change in Ladakh (Indian Kashmir) With Special Attention Paid to Tourism. *International Journal of Comparative Sociology*, 37, 286–304.

Mikuriya, T. H. (ed.) (1973) *Marijuana: Medical Papers, 1839–1972*, Oakland CA, MediComp Press.

Miller, D. (1995a) *Acknowledging Consumption: A Review of New Studies*, London; New York, Routledge.

—— (1995b) Consumption and Commodities. *Annual Review of Anthropology*, 24, 141–161.

—— (1995c) *Worlds Apart: Modernity through the Prism of the Local*, London; New York, Routledge.

—— (1998) *Material Cultures: Why Some Things Matter*, Chicago IL, University of Chicago Press.

Minorsky, V. (1937) A Persian Geographer of A. D. 982 on the Orography of Central Asia. *The Geographical Journal*, 90, 259–264.

Mintz, S. (1987) *Sweetness and Power: The Place of Sugar in Modern History*, New York NY, Penguin Books.

Mohi-Ud-Din-Dar, G. (1992) *Social and religious conditions on the eve of spread of Islam in Kashmir*, Srinagar, Gulshan Publishers.

Moorcroft, W. and Trebeck, G. (1841) *Travels in the Himalayan provinces of Hindustan & the Panjab, in Ladakh & Kashmir, in Peshawar, Kabul, Kunduz, & Bokhara, 1819–25; prepared for the press, from original journals & correspondence*, London, John Murray.

Murdoch, P. (1981) Vernacular House Form in Ladakh. *Homme et la maison en Himalaya*. Paris, Centre national de la recherche scientifique.

Myer, K. E. and Brysac, S. B. (1999) *Tournament of Shadows: The Great Game and the Race for Empire in Central Asia*, Washington DC, Counterpoint.

Neve, A. (1913) *Tourist's Guide to Kashmir, Ladakh, and Skardo*, Lahore, Superintendent of Government Printing.

—— (1918) *The Tourist's Guide to Kashmir, Ladakh and Skardo*, Lahore, Civil and Military Gazette Press.

—— (1923) *The Tourist's Guide to Kashmir, Ladakh and Skardo*, Lahore, Civil and Military Gazette Press.

Norbu, D. (1997) Tibet in Sino-Indian Relations: The Centrality of Marginality. *Asian Survey*, 37, 1078–1095.

Pal, P. (1983) Realm of Splendor: The Alchi monastery of Ladakh. *Archaeology*, 36, 46–53.

Pallis, M. (1997) Preface. In Henry, G. (ed.) *Islam in Tibet.* Louisville KY, Fons Vitae.

Pandit, M. A. (1997) *Ladakh: Land of Possessive Powers and Charm*, Srinagar, Gulshan Publishers.

Petech, L. (1977) *The Kingdom of Ladakh: c. 950–1842 A.D.*, Rome, Istituto Italiano per il Medio ed Estremo Oriente.

Phylactou, M. C. (1989) Household Organisation and Marriage in Ladakh, Indian Himalaya. *Anthropology*. London, London School of Economics.

Postnikov, A. V. (2001) *Схватка на «Крыше Мире» – Политики, разведчики и географы в борьбе за Памир в XIX веке ("Struggle on the 'Roof of the World': Politicians, Spies and Geographers in the Contest for the Pamir in the XIX Century")*, Moskow, Pamiatniki istoricheskoi mysli.

Pouchepadass, J. (1999) *Champaran and Gandhi: Planters, Peasants and Gandhian Politics*, Delhi, Oxford University Press.

Powell, A. (1992) *Heirs to Tibet: Travels Among the Exiles in India*, London, Heinemann.

Radhu, A. W. (1997) Tibetan Caravans: The Illustrated Narrative. In Henry, G. (ed.) *Islam in Tibet.* Louisville KY, Fons Vitae.

Raether, H. (2000) The Mouths of People, the Voice of God. Buddhists and Muslims in a Frontier Community of Ladakh by Smriti Srinivas. *Tibet Journal*, 25, 99.

Raker, J. W. and Shukla, R. S. (1995) *English–Hindi, Hindi–English Standard Dictionary*, New York NY, Hippocrene Books.

Rizvi, J. (1983) *Ladakh, Crossroads of High Asia*, Delhi, Oxford.

—— (1999) *Trans-Himalayan Caravans*, New Delhi, Oxford University Press.

Roerich, G. N. (1931) *Trails to Inmost Asia: Five Years of Exploration with the Roerich Central Asian Expedition*, New Haven CT, Yale University Press.

Roy, T. (1995) Price Movements in Early Twentieth-Century India. *The Economic History Review*, 48, 118–133.

Sagwal, S. S. (1991) *Ladakh, Ecology and Environment*, New Delhi, Ashish Publishing House.

Sahlins, M. (1985) *Islands of History*, Chicago, University of Chicago Press.

Shahrani, M. N. M. (1979) *The Kirghiz and Wakhi of Afghanistan: Adaptation to Closed Frontiers*, Seattle WA, University of Washington Press.

Sharma, K. L. (1999) Ladakh: Where Serenity Prevails. *India Perspectives*, 12, 9.

Sheikh, A. G. and Aggarwal, R. (2001) *Forsaking Paradise: Stories from Ladakh*, New Delhi, Katha.

Sheikh, A. G. (1995) A Brief History of Muslims in Ladakh. In Osmaston, H. and Denwood, P. (eds) *Recent Research on Ladakh 4 and 5*. London, SOAS.

Sheikh, A. G. (2000) At A Glance: Islam in Ladakh. Leh, Ladakh, Imam Jama Masjid Leh.

Sherring, C. A. (1906) *Western Tibet and the British Borderland: The Sacred Country of Hindus and Buddhists, with an Account of the Government, Religion, and Customs of Its Peoples*, London, Arnold.

Singh, H. (1977) Territorial organisation of gompas in ladakh. Himalaya: écologie-ethnologie. *Colloques internationaux du Centre National de la Recherche Scientifique*, 351–369.

Skrine, C. P. (1926) *Chinese Central Asia*, London, Methuen.

Skrine, C. P. and Nightingale, P. (1973) *Macartney at Kashgar: New Light on British, Chinese and Russian Activities in Sinkiang, 1890–1918*, London, Methuen.

Snellgrove, D. L. and Skorupski, T. (1977) *The Cultural Heritage of Ladakh*, Warminster, UK, Forest Grove, OR., Aris & Phillips.

Soucek, S. (2001) *A History of Inner Asia*, Cambridge, Cambridge University Press.

Spooner, B. (1986) Weavers and Dealers: The Authenticity of a Persian Carpet. In Appadurai, A. (ed.) *The Social Life of Things*. Cambridge, Cambridge University Press.

Spyer, P. (2000) *The Memory of Trade: Modernity's Entanglements on an Eastern Indonesian Island*, Durham NC, Duke University Press.

Stahnke, A. A. (1970) The Place of International Law in Chinese Strategy and Tactics: The Case of the Sino-Indian Boundary Dispute. *The Journal of Asian Studies*, 30, 95–119.

Stares, P. B. (1996) *Global Habit: The Drug Problem in a Borderless World*, Washington, DC, Brookings Institute.

Steiner, H. A. (1959) India Looks to Her Northern Frontiers. *Far Eastern Survey*, 28, 167–173.

Steinsholt, H., Wisborg, P., Raza, M. A. and Sevatdal, H. (1998) *High Altitude Integrated Natural Resource Management*, Lahore, Aga Khan Rural Support Programme.

Stellrecht, I., Beitr. V., Janjua, Z. J., Hewitt, K., Kuhle, M. and Itturizaga, L. (eds) (1998) *Karakorum–Hindukush–Himalaya: Dynamics of Change*.

Stobdan, P. (1995) Mishandling Ladakh May Prove Costly. *Ladags Melong: SECMOL*.

Sumi, T., Oki, M. and Hassnain, F. M. (1975) *Ladakh, the Moonland*, New Delhi, Light and Life Publishers.

Tomlinson, B. R. (1982) The Political Economy of the Raj: The Decline of Colonialism. *The Journal of Economic History*, 42, 133–137.

Travis, A. (1993) *The Rainbow Makers: The Origins of the Synthetic Dyestuffs Industry in Western Europe*, London, Lehigh University Press.

Trocki, C. A. (1999) *Opium, Empire, and the Global Political Economy*, London, Routledge.

Trotter, H. (1877) On the Geographical Results of the Mission to Kashgar, under Sir T. Dougals Forsyth, in 1873–4. *Proceedings of the Royal Geographical Society of London*, 22, 287–291.

Upadhyay, R., Ram-Awatar, Kar, R. K. and Sinha, A. K. (2005) First Record of Middle–Late Jurassic Palynomorphs from the Lamayuru Complex, Indus Suture Zone, Ladakh, India. *Current Science*, 88, 980–986.

Uprety, P. (1980) *Nepal–Tibet Relations, 1850–1930*, Kathmandu.

van Beek, M. (1998a) True Patriots: Justifying Autonomy for Ladakh. *Himalayan Research Bulletin*, 18, 35.

—— (1998b) Worlds Apart: Autobiographies of Two Ladakhi Caravaneers Compared. *Focaal*, 32, 51–69.

—— (1999) Hill Councils, Development, and Democracy: Assumptions and Experiences from Ladakh. *Alternatives*, 24, 435.

—— (2000a) Beyond Identity Fetishism: "Communal" Conflict in Ladakh and the Limits of Autonomy. *Cultural Anthropology*, 15, 525–569.

—— (2000b) Lessons from Ladakh? Local Responses to Globalization and Social Change. *Routledge Advances in International Political Economy*, 6, 250–266.

—— (2000c) Dissimulations: Representing Ladakhi Identity. In Driessen, Henk and Otto, Ton (eds) *Perplexities of Identification: Anthropological Studies in Cultural Differentiation and the Use of Resources*. Aarhus, Aarhus University Press, 164–188.

—— (2002) (Book review). Janet Rizvi: Trans-Himalayan Caravans: Merchant Princes and Peasant Traders in Ladakh. *Commonwealth and Comparative Politics*, 40, 118–119.

—— (2003) The Art of Representation: Domesticating Ladakhi Identity. In Dollfus, P. and Lecomte-Tilouine, M. (eds) *Ethnic Revival and Religious Turmoil*. New Delhi, Oxford University Press, 283–301.

Van Der Veer, P. (1994) *Religious Nationalism: Hindus and Muslims in India*, Berkeley CA, University of California Press.

Varshney, A. (1991) India, Pakistan, and Kashmir: Antinomies of Nationalism. *Asian Survey*, 31, 997–1019.

Vigne, G. T. (1844) *Travels in Kashmir, Ladak, Skardo: the countries adjoining the mountain-course of the Indus and the Himalaya, north of the Punjab*, London, H. Colburn.

Virmani, A. (1999) National Symbols under Colonial Domination The Nationalization of the Indian Flag, March–August 1923. *Past and Present*, August, 169–197.

Vohra, R. (1989) *An Ethnography: The Buddhist Dards of Ladakh: Mythic Lore, Household, Alliance System, Kinship*, Ettelbruck, Grand Duchy of Luxembourg, Skydie Brown International.

Wahid, S. and Storm, K. R. (1981) *Ladakh: Between Earth and Sky*, New York, Norton.

Walia, V. (2001) Revenue Officials in Cahoots with Land Mafia. *The Tribune*. Chandigarh, India.

Walzer, M. (1987) *Interpretation and Social Criticism*, Cambridge MA, Harvard University Press.

Ward, M. (1983) The Kongur Massif in Southern Sinkiang. *The Geographical Journal*, 149, 137–152.

Warikoo, K. (1989) *Central Asia and Kashmir: A Study in the Context of Anglo-Russian Rivalry*, Delhi, Gian Publishing House.

Wignall, S. (2000) *Spy on the Roof of the World*, Guilford CT, The Lyons Press.

Williams, B. (1989) A Class Act: Anthropology and the Race to Nation Across Ethnic Terrain. *Annual Review of Anthropology*, 18, 401–445.

Wingate, P. J. (1982) *The Colorful Du Pont Company*, Wilmington DE, Serendipity Press.

Younghusband, F. (1896) *The Heart of a Continent*, London, John Murray.

Zeimal, E. V. (1996) *The Kidarite Kingdom in Central Asia*, Paris, UNESCO.

Zeitler, P. K., Sutter, J. F., Williams, I. S., Zartman, R. E. and Tarkheli, R. A. K. (1989) Geochronology and Temperature History of the Nanga–Parbat–Haramosh Massif, Pakistan. In Malinconico, L. L., and Lillie, R. J. (ed.) *Tectonics of the Western Himalaya*. Geological Society of America.

Zolov, E. (2003) Arnold J. Bauer. Goods, Power, History: Latin America's Material Culture. *The American Historical Review*, 108.

Index

Afghanistan 3, 22, 41, 43, 70, 125
Aggarwal, Ravina 74
agriculture 20–1, 81–2, 105–6, 156
Ahmed, Monisha 118–20
Alimkul, Khudoyar Khan 50
America *see* United States of
    America
Amritsar 3, 49; contemporary trade
    with 143; ethnographic work in
    7–8, 130–4; kinship practices in
    77–9; as place of origin for traders
    66, 69, 72–3; travel to/from 41–3,
    46; *see also* Punjab and treaty
Anderson, Benedict 1
aqsaqual 76, 94–6, 138; *see also*
    Khotan and Yarkend
architecture: historical 8, 50, 61,
    132; as related to environmental
    conditions 20–1; as related to
    social issues 34–6, 40, 61, 156
Arghun community 2, 67–9;
    alternate spellings of 63n1, 74;
    contemporary uses of term 150–3,
    160–1, 168; as cosmopolitans
    109, 116, 128–9; as an ethnic
    community 68, 73–5; historical
    background 63–5; as an identity
    group 79–80; as a kin-based
    identity group 62, 67–8, 75–80,
    83; in relation to commodities
    105–7, 110, 113–15, 120, 122, 125,
    127
army *see* Indian army
art: analysis of public 156–8;
    historical studies of 25, 39–40;
    as a trade item 39
Assam 36

Bara-Lacha-la 42
Bauer, Kenneth 65
Beg, Yakub 50; called Yunis in a
    letter 140
Bhat, Munshi Aziz 9–10, 88, 105,
    107, 109, 114, 118; *see also*
    Munshi Aziz Bhat *serai*
Biddulph, John 3, 51
Bishop, Peter 30
Bohman, James 112
Bombay 107, 116
borders 1, 12, 160, 162–3; Central
    Asian 138–43; definition of 134;
    in conflicts and dispute 23–4, 137;
    nationalist performance at 132–4;
    passport control for 62, 138–9,
    148; in relation to economic
    development 31, 143; role in
    defining Ladakh's income tax
    status 153–4; role in defining
    Turkic identity 147–8; South
    Asian 132–8; *see also* boundaries
boundaries: of China and India
    24, 138–40; conceptual 163–5;
    definition of 134–5; formed by
    geography 38; general roles of
    12; of India and Pakistan 137;
    for land surveying 101; role of in
    forming Ladakhi regional identity
    24, 160; *see also* borders
Bower, Hamilton 64, 73
Brenner, Suzanne 104
Britain: businesses in India 107;
    historical scholarship from 21–3;
    industrial revolution in 116–17;
    production of commodities in 116,
    119, 121–2; tourists from 154

CPSIA information can be obtained at www.ICGtesting.com
Printed in the USA
BVOW040457160812

297928BV00005B/147/P